The Tears I Couldn't Cry

Behind Convent Doors

Patricia Grueninger Beasley

authorHOUSE®

AuthorHouse™
1663 Liberty Drive, Suite 200
Bloomington, IN 47403
www.authorhouse.com
Phone: 1-800-839-8640

This book is a work of non-fiction. Unless otherwise noted, the author and the publisher make no explicit guarantees as to the accuracy of the information contained in this book and in some cases, names of people and places have been altered to protect their privacy.

First published by AuthorHouse 4/14/2009

ISBN: 978-1-4389-6290-0 (sc)

Library of Congress Control Number: 2009902487

Printed in the United States of America
Bloomington, Indiana

This book is printed on acid-free paper.

Registered with Writer's Guild of America West since 2004.

Cover photo taken by Pat's Dad, M.A. Grueninger, Sr., August 1964 during Summer Visitation Day at Emmitsburg, MD.

Cover design by Mary Zentara, Pat's niece.

For Mother and Dad,
Mel, Carole, and Anne---
In my heart you were
always
my first family

*

For all the women
who gave their lives
to God
in convents
all over the world--
those who left
to choose life
as well as
those who chose
to remain

Acknowledgments

I wish to thank the many wonderful people who made this book possible:

- My family who had to sacrifice their daughter and sister and bear the pain of separation and her absence from family gatherings

- The many good Sisters with whom I lived and worked and prayed and whose example motivated me to remain a Sister for 22½ years and 25 days

- My husband Karl who brought me to the magnificent Southwest where the beauty and grandeur inspired me to write

- Mary Mank who lit a crucial spark and the late Paul N. Lazarus of Santa Barbara who fanned that spark when he wrote, "You have a great story to tell, if you can pry it loose."

- Mary and Barnaby Conrad and the staff of the Santa Barbara Writer's Conference without whom this book could not have been written

- Charles Champlin, retired arts critic for the Los Angeles Times, who provided me with a blueprint for my autobiography, critiqued it, and affirmed me as I took my first steps as an author; and Richard F.X. O'Connor, my memoir teacher.

- Ray Bradbury, whose never-ending inspiration always lifted me up and kept me believing in possibilities

- Vickie Patik, for mentoring me and believing in me as a writer

- Sue Grafton who took the time to give me feedback through Vickie

- All my relatives who encouraged me, especially my sisters Carole, Anne, and Audrey; cousin Carolyn Edwards; and my nieces and nephews

- My friends, Theresa Myers and Jean Newman, who believed in me as an author; and all who gave me wisdom and motivation: Trudi Green, Mary Ellen Hicks, Eleanor Wasson, Nelle Byrne, Elizabeth Sanders Kane, Donnie Nair, Cara Moore, Imogene Hughes, Jerry C. Iafrate, Joyce Reid, Linda Smiley, Alanna Van Winkle, Rodney L. Cron, and George Terrell.

- All who gave me technical help, especially Carole Lee Smith and Claire Hermann; Jim Fuller and the Author House staff

- The countless, nameless persons who encouraged me to keep climbing that mountain when I felt like giving up

- Betty Kelly, Paula Costa, and Toni Broaddus who finally pushed me across the finish line

- Above all, I am grateful to God for guiding me through the writing of this book; and, in the process, pouring out the marvelous gifts of new and exciting experiences, wonderful friends—and the Pacific Ocean that inundated my soul and awakened my dormant dreams and my writer's voice.

PROLOGUE

At the age of three, I was promised to God.

At the age of forty-one, I stood on a hill overlooking Bird River, letting the wind run its fingers through my hair for the first time in twenty-two and a half years. Its gentle caress rippled through my body from my head to the tips of my toes.

A small bird flying overhead caught my eye. "Be grateful you fly free," I whispered. Deep in my soul I was that bird. I had always been that bird. Now, finally, I was free, too.

Inhaling deeply, I gorged my lungs with the air that symbolized my freedom, air saturated with river smells of fish and crabs. And it was more satisfying than the rarest perfume. I thrilled to the sounds of nature bombarding my ears in a strange new way. Had I never truly heard them before? Or were my senses just waking up, because—for the first time in my adult life—I felt no guilt for loving the sensations I was feeling?

It was a spring day. I wore a sleeveless, beige blouse and the matching wraparound skirt my sister Carole made just for the occasion. Sand-colored sandals replaced my black oxfords. It felt exotic to be wearing colors other than navy blue and white. Beige, suddenly, was exhilarating! Still, it would take a while for the full impact of my decision to sink in.

Until today, I had been a woman obsessed with keeping promises. The promise my Mother made when I lay dying. The promise I made to my former teacher, a Sister, to stop fighting God's call. Years and years of promises in the form of vows made in a religious order of Catholic women that clung to its seventeenth-century identity—well into the twentieth century.

I struggled for what seemed an eternity to live a life dedicated to an ideal filled with contradictions. I turned myself into my own betrayer, intent on silencing the voice of my frustrated womanhood—before it could incite an all-out mutiny. I refused to allow my imagination the fantasy of falling in love and being cherished, marrying and giving birth to my own flesh and blood. I denied myself the pleasure and comfort of touching and being touched, by shoving beyond my reach the hugs and kisses I was starving for.

My Superiors systematically squashed my passion for art and music, assigning and reassigning work duties according to their own perceived needs, which they called "for the common good." What I wanted was never a consideration. Their will replaced my dreams, and they called it God's Will.

Obedience pervaded every aspect of my life: how I walked and talked, how I ate and slept, how I thought and related to people. The vow of obedience removed decision-making from my life. I had only to obey blindly and believe that my Superiors spoke to me in God's Name. And, in doing so, I severed blood ties and lost the family I loved.

With my vow of poverty I received no paycheck or social security. I owned nothing. I was assigned two Habits, the name for the Order's customary garb, and I shared everything else.

In fulfilling my vow to serve the poor, I strained to give every ounce of my energy. I listened. I counseled. I taught. Ignoring my own needs, I wore myself out trying to relieve humanity's ills.

Relentlessly, I fought the female drives I had boarded up within. While my virginity remained intact, it was not without agonizing struggles with chastity. I suppressed every yearning for male companionship. I repressed the attraction I felt toward the men whose paths crossed mine. And I spoke of it to no one.

I came to feel like a bird locked in a cage in the all-justifying Name of the Lord, until I felt my heart, too, would break.

As I stood on that hill above the river, a torrent of emotions surged inside me. Relief, fear, excitement, dread, loneliness, uncertainty, serenity, and last but not least, hope.

Two hours earlier, I had prayed for the last time as a Sister. Then, in secrecy, I was whisked away from my residence, the Provincial House that served as home base for the Sisters. A Superior drove me to an unoccupied building across the highway, where I took off my Habit and clothed myself as a lay woman. There were no farewells from friends, no advice or training for secular life. The Superior escorting me simply said goodbye, wished me well, and drove away. And I simply disappeared from the ranks of the Sisters, according to the custom of the day.

At the age of eighteen, I entered the convent. Now at forty-one, I was starting my life all over again. Standing on the hill above the water, I released myself from all the promises that held me captive. I was no longer the caged bird unable to fly. After being away for 8,241 days, I was finally back home.

I fluttered my new wings, ready to soar.... This is my story.

I
The Call

Swallowed Up in a Culture of Secrecy

1.

Submitting to the Unknown

I watched the valley at the foot of Maryland's Blue Ridge Mountains stretch lazily in all directions like a sleeping cat sprawled out on a rug. Seeing the mountains at a distance beneath the summer's blue sky gave me a good feeling. I loved to hike in the woods where my deep aesthetic sense made me revel in the sights I saw and nature's sounds that fell gently on my ears. Living in these majestic surroundings should be thrilling, I thought. I was right to banish the doubts that had reared up in the two weeks before I set out for Emmitsburg.

Still, the feeling of entering a foreign land welled up inside me, threatening to strangle me. I had gone away from home as a sixth grader when my sister Carole and I spent a week at camp. I was homesick the whole time. Now I was going away again. Only this time I would not be coming home, even for a visit. In fact, I had only recently found out that I would not be allowed to return to my home EVER! I cringed at the thought.

How could I give up my family and the love we shared, and forfeit my plans for the future? Would I have to kill the "Michelangelo" I was carrying inside me—that sculptor bursting to be born? How would I feel, turning my back on all that I cherished, on the things that made me who I was? Could I really give up the love of a man and extinguish all the affection my heart had to give?

Driving up the narrow paved road to the Provincial House, my new home, I noticed cast-iron hitching posts topped with horses' heads. They were remnants of the past holding rings in their mouths, flanked by trees that arched eerily over the roadway. Like the horses

3

hitched to posts in a bygone era, I was going to be tied to a life with strangers. But my new family would be composed of nuns, I argued within myself—holy Sisters who were living dedicated lives. Surely, I should find a kind of heaven on earth here.

A nineteenth-century Gothic building, nothing like my brown-shingled house, loomed before me. Centuries-old fir trees stood guard near the circular entrance that led vehicles to, then away from, the intimidating front doors of the Sisters' residence. Nothing and no one stirred the morning I arrived.

This was the day girls entering the convent started their training as postulants. If the others had come, they were already inside and their families gone. Only Mother, Audrey, and my friend Doris had accompanied me. My sisters Carole and Anne had to go to school, and my brother Mel had gone off to his job. Dad, too, had business to take care of. Although I missed them, it was probably for the best.

The night before, when I watched Dad go to his room, I had followed and knocked on his door. "Can I say goodbye?" I asked. The door opened and I reached out, pressing my high school ring in his hand. As he silently stared at it, I spoke up again.

"I can't take this with me. Will you keep it?" Looking into his eyes, I saw him fighting to hold back tears. Then he gave me a hug for which I was eternally grateful. I knew at that moment he still loved me and forgave me and would not fight my decision.

Later that night when everyone was in bed, I crept downstairs and wrote a farewell note to my family in a "thank you" card Mother would never throw away. It read:

Dear Mother, Dad, Melvin, Carole, Anne, and Audrey,

I want to tell you how much I thank you for helping me these past weeks in getting everything ready. Every one of you has helped me in some way or another, especially you, Mother and Dad!

And I want to tell you now...Thank you! I love you all so much! And, thank you too for understanding me, and not making it harder for me by opposing. I don't mean to cause any unhappiness for anyone. I only want to do God's holy will in this world. And I feel that God wants me serving His poor. And therefore that I won't be perfectly content until I do put myself aside to help others.

I shall remember all of you in my prayers—your health and your happiness! And, Mother and Dad, I hope one day in Heaven I will make you very proud of your daughter.

I'll always love you with all my heart. Thanks again for everything, my family!

We might not see each other as often as we'd like on earth, but we'll spend eternity united in Heaven!

So, pray for me always.

With all the love of my heart,
Your Patsy

I penned those words in a card that had five white rosebuds on blue satin on the front. The words "Many thanks to all of you" completed the cover. I sealed the card in an envelope and placed it where I knew they would not discover it until after I was gone. Then I went to bed.

I lay there for a long time reminiscing about my childhood. I dwelled on the faces of each of my family members, and I thanked God for them. My thoughts jumped ahead to the big step I was taking the next day. My life was about to change radically, and it was scary. In the last week I had become shaky about my decision, but I suppressed my fears and put on a good front. I didn't want anyone in my family to worry about me.

I picked up the letter of acceptance Sister Irene had sent me. The highest female Superior of the Sisters' Province, she was called their Visitatrix. In the dim light of the lamp beside my bed, I reread it to give myself reassurance. Then I turned off the light.

This morning when I got up, I forced a smile knowing I had to detach myself from all I held dear: my family, my hopes and dreams and loves. I could feel my heart break at the realization I had to sacrifice all these things in order to follow my vocation. No words could express the emotions I felt.

Now, my one-way journey was about to end.

Mother pulled up at the double doors of my new home, and we got out of the car. Audrey and Doris kissed me goodbye, then stepped back while Mother locked me in a long embrace. I let her hold me tight one last time, as I fought back tears. Did Mother remember the prayer she uttered long ago? The promise she made to God when I lay dying? "Tell me what you're thinking, Mother!" I should have screamed out. Instead, I remained frozen in her arms—speechless.

There I stood, about to fulfill her promise. Would it mean life or would it mean death? I silenced the questions, immersed in the final hug as Mother's daughter, as a member of the family God had given me—the family God was now taking away.

Two giant doors shut behind me. They shut Mother outside, and shut me inside. Only gradually would I come to realize the full impact of that moment. As of now, I was cut off from my umbilical home and the world I knew for the last eighteen years. I steeled myself to get beyond the pain and forced a smile, as Sister Mary John welcomed me.

Her lovely face with its pale waxen skin gave her a look of coldness. Large floppy wings extended from both sides of her head, starting at her cheeks that they hugged. High above her partially-hidden forehead, a stiff point protruded almost a foot. She appeared to be locked in her heavily-starched white cornette.

It was summertime and I could see beads of sweat clinging to her neck in the tiny space left open between her headdress and the stiff turtleneck collar she wore. Her navy blue wool Habit fell to the floor in layers.

I felt hot just looking at her, amazed that she could use mind over matter and put up with it. It hadn't sunk in yet that someday I would have to master that feat.

"Follow me," she beckoned. We began the trek down a long hallway that filled with the echo of my own shoes on the hardwood floor. I felt self-conscious and tried unsuccessfully to muffle my footsteps.

Large ornately-framed oil paintings lined the white walls of the first corridor—portraits of pompous-looking clerics, mostly bishops and archbishops, who had advised the Sisters for more than a century and a half. It was hard to see the humble, simply-dressed Messiah in those men.

The very arrangement of their pictures foreshadowed the formalism of my new life. I felt a lump in the pit of my stomach, as I stifled a gasp.

Taking a deep breath to calm my nerves, I found myself sniffing the air. There was no recognizable fragrance, just the antiseptic smell of meticulously-clean walls and floors. My Mother should have been here. She would have been proud of the anonymous Sisters who did the cleaning so well. Mother was a champion at housework, a talent she developed as one of the youngest of sixteen children growing up during the Depression years. At our house we never saw a speck of dust a second time.

Following Sister Mary John, I focused my eyes on the back of her cornette. At my parish school, mischievous boys used to sneak behind the Sisters and try to peek in the black hole where the headpiece came together. Some said they could see a bald head inside. I didn't think they could really see anything. But I still didn't know if the Sisters had any hair.

Here I was, a girl who grew up hating to wear hats, who took off my hat as soon as I reached the church steps after Mass on Sundays, entering the Sisterhood—a way of life that made wearing a hat mandatory all day everyday. Not just any hat, but that strange, cumbersome headdress. With a neophyte's fervor I thought that if I could make myself wear the cornette, I could make myself do anything.

The hundred-year-old building seemed devoid of air. I saw windows without screens, but most were shut, even though the heat was stifling. I felt my clothes stick to me. Still, I could not imagine how Sister Mary John felt, as I watched the hem of her heavy Habit drag along the ancient floor and the starch of her cornette wilt under her ears, making her wings flop down even more.

I was relieved when we reached the chapel and I spotted two gigantic floor fans. It was a large chapel, big enough to hold a few hundred Sisters. In some ways it resembled my parish church with its stained glass windows and its statues of angels bowing forward, directing all eyes to the tabernacle and the red light of the sanctuary lamp suspended from the ceiling. As always, I felt safe and secure in "God's House."

I followed the Sister's lead, genuflecting, entering a pew, and kneeling down to pray—when suddenly, I was distracted. Sister Mary John bent forward and kissed the pew before closing her eyes in prayer. Near the front of the church I observed another Sister genuflect and enter a pew. She too bent forward to kiss the pew.

An odd custom, I thought, as I wondered what its purpose might be. I must have been staring wide-eyed, as Sister Mary John opened her eyes, turned to me, and whispered: "Offer yourself and your vocation to God. Place your perseverance in Blessed Mother's hands."

After a short prayer, we continued to walk what seemed like miles of corridors and climb countless stairs. I found myself beginning to imitate the Sister. I lowered my eyes. Trying not to embarrass myself that first day by tripping, I focused my eyes on the large cracks in the hardwood floor beneath my feet.

Finally, she stopped at a small bedroom and spoke softly: "You may change here. This is where you'll sleep at night. It's the postulants' wing."

While the Sister stood outside the door, I started to undress. I took off my baby blue skirt and my sleeveless white blouse with its spray of colorful flowers pinned at the top button. I smoothed them out on the bed, taking a last look at the clothes I used to wear. I put on my black underclothes and attached my black stockings to my garter belt. Then I kicked aside my white sandals and put on the black shoes I had to buy in the section of the store where they sold footwear for old folks.

8

I was only eighteen, and there I was about to be clothed in black garb of a widow, signifying "death to self."

As I gazed upon my postulant dress, my mind wandered for a moment. I had watched my Mother put a lot of love into its making. Silently and dutifully, she went about that task. I should have made her speak up and say what she felt. But, long ago, I learned that, in our house, feelings were not to be revealed. What could not be dealt with had to be avoided. So I honored her silence. And I, too, hid what I really felt.

I could still see Mother, her petite frame and her blazing red hair bent over the sewing machine for hours. I clutched the dress lovingly, trying to feel my Mother's presence—when, suddenly, Sister Mary John appeared in the doorway.

"Better hurry. You live by a schedule now. Hand me the clothes you took off."

I watched her roll them up in a ball and throw the bundle in a bag labeled "For the Poor."

Quickly I put on the dress and the black postulant's cap that resembled a maid's head covering. I added the fake white collar and cuffs that felt hard against my neck and wrists. I hid my breasts under the black cape that covered my torso. I was ready, ready to begin. I looked for a mirror—and found none.

There I was, in a strange new world, mingling with other young women dressed in black. We were teenagers, most of us, a motley group that had followed God's Call to be Sisters—followed our vocation. That's what we were told, and that's what we believed. With heavy hearts we had said farewell to our natural families just minutes earlier. Now we were ready to embark on a new adventure—or so it seemed.

Blackness surrounded me, the color I usually saw at funerals and funeral parlors. But I tried not to dwell on that thought. Instead, I concentrated on the differing accents that would meld us together as a "band."

"I'm Pat," I said, as we made our introductions, then sat at a long brown conference table that spoke volumes in its starkness.

I liked blue-eyed Anna from Boston right from the start. She brought with her a bubbly personality and sophistication that her dark wavy hair and her New England accent seemed to punctuate. She regaled us with stories about her friend who was becoming an opera singer.

Jenny came from an orphanage run by our Sisters in Philadelphia. Instead of going out on her own when she turned eighteen, she decided to join the Sisters and continue the lifestyle she was familiar with. Her strong-set jaw and her big brown eyes gave her a stubborn look that belied her elfin sense of humor.

Two postulants, Mildred and Margaret, had finished nursing school, bringing to the Community a readymade skill. They were especially valuable to Superiors and it was assumed they were more mature than the rest of us. Rose's skin looked like an ad for ivory soap, and her manners were just as delicate. She and several others had graduated from my Alma Mater that June. Athletic Dottie came from my own graduating class. She and I had worked a year before joining the others to become Sisters.

Candy's face never lost its look of intenseness. She was super-conscientious and determined to make it, even if it killed her. For some reason, I found her attitude scary. Margie, on the other hand, seemed reserved and shy and had a fragile look about her.

All of the girls in our band had passed the preliminary screening. We were white, of legitimate birth, and born of parents who had married in the Catholic Church. In addition, we had documents to prove we had been baptized, made our First Communion and received Confirmation at the appropriate times. I assumed we were all virgins.

Within days we learned that our lifestyle—even our conversations—were full of restrictions. We were not allowed to talk about our families, our friends, or the life we left behind. An invisible door closed between us and our openness with each other was cut off.

Sister Angela, who took charge of our training, had frail beauty and impeccable manners. Her pure white skin that accentuated her other-worldly appearance was perfect for the convent.

Her sidekick, Sister Blanche, was a lesser Superior for us. Still, she had the authority to give us orders and monitor our behavior. Sister Angela's opposite in disposition, she gave out assignments with a twinkle in her eye that made you wonder what she was up to.

I found it hard to sleep that first night. As I stared at the narrow beam of light that crept under my closed door and darted across the room, I felt lost. I wanted to blink my eyes and be back home. I wanted to wake up in the morning, go downstairs, and join my Mother at the breakfast table. I wanted to feel her hug me.

Instead, the next morning I sat at a long table with twenty-seven other young women, eating in silence. It gave me an eerie feeling. I wanted to rush to a telephone, call home, and hear the familiar voice of a loved one. As if Sister Angela heard my thoughts, she delivered the first of many lectures about the rules.

"You will not use the telephone as Sisters. You will wait until the first scheduled visiting day in the fall. Then you will see your families again. Once a month you will gather in the community room and be given a sheet of paper on which to write a letter home. Sister Blanche will collect them when you are finished, and she will see that they get mailed. One more thing, you will submit your letters unsealed, as they will be censored. It's important that you write a pleasant letter and not say anything to disturb your loved ones."

I could not believe what I was hearing. I wanted to raise my hand like a child in class and ask, "Do you mean to say that I cannot be completely open with my own parents? That I cannot pour out my soul to my family? That I have no privacy in my communications with them?"

I looked around and saw that all the postulants were listening intently and nobody was asking questions.

Next, Sister Angela told us we could sleep late for a while, sleep until the bell would wake us up at 7 a.m. Then it would be 6 a.m. A few months later, we would start rising at 5 a.m., just like the rest of the Sisters. On Saturdays and Sundays we would sleep late; that is, sleep until the bell would awaken us at 5:50 a.m.

Another "concession" was made for us. As we learned how to meditate like the older Sisters, we would pray—not in the big chapel—but in a small oratory that was set aside just for the postulants. It looked like a mini-chapel without the tabernacle. Instead of pews, we knelt on prie-dieus—furniture that had a place for a person to kneel and another place to rest one's folded hands. Each of us was assigned her own prie-dieu.

After prayers in our oratory, we would join the other Sisters for daily Mass in Latin, with the priest's back to the congregation. On Sunday mornings, I felt rushed as we had to say vocal prayers together, meditate, go to Mass, eat breakfast, clean up afterwards, and make it back to the chapel for a mandatory second Mass.

In the course of the week, we started having lessons scheduled on how Sisters act. Everyday, thereafter, we had spiritual reading together followed by more instructions. Always we listened but never asked questions, never discussed the topic. We were products of the "be seen and not heard" generation of the 1950's, and we found that attitude transferred to the convent.

Before long, we had a lecture on keeping our hands occupied when we were not praying. As we sat and listened to readings or instructions, we were to busy our fingers with sewing. As postulants we would hem dish towels for the Sisters' dining hall which they called their refectory.

Growing up hating to sew, I found this practice especially repugnant. Still, it was justified by the familiar saying, "Idle hands are the devil's workshop." At the same time, we were also informed that sewing was one of the ways we would contribute to the stockpile of household goods used in common.

Part of me wanted to panic in those first months, and I struggled hard not to let panic take hold of me.

Both Sister Angela and Sister Blanche took our "formation," as they called it, very seriously and set about molding us into model Sisters of Charity—Sisters who lived in uniformity and obedience.

They stressed silence from the beginning to allow time for "communion with God." There were specified times of silence during the day, followed by the sacrosanct "Grand Silence" that lasted from night prayers until after breakfast the next morning. It was a serious infraction to break the Grand Silence, except for an emergency.

Lessons on detachment came next. Any kind of memento or keepsake from home, even photographs, had to be turned in to be destroyed. We were not allowed to have anything for personal satisfaction. Such things would only serve to pamper us, we were told. They would distract us from our primary goal—that of becoming Sisters who were as selfless and perfect as we could possibly be on this earth.

Furthermore, we could not be attached to anything or anybody including our own family members and the friends we had left behind. Nor could we speak of them. The Sisters were our "new family", although we were cautioned not to form "particular friendships."

Only our "Sister family" could be spoken of and always in kindness. That meant we would never discuss, even among ourselves, the rules and policies we were learning. If we were sincere in wanting to become good Sisters, we had to respect and abide by all the practices of our religious congregation.

I'll just keep my family's memory vivid, I thought. No one will ever know. But soon I found out I was wrong. "Memories too must be stamped out," came Sister Angela's voice, smashing the fragile shell of my heart. "If you are sincere in your desire to be Christ's bride one day, you must give ALL—and that includes pleasant memories that rekindle human love, even the love of parents and siblings. And it goes without saying that memories of former friends, especially boyfriends, cannot be tolerated at all. Jesus must be your only love!"

Our daily schedule left no free time, no time to think or be alone, no time to steal remembrances of the past. We had to keep busy praying, working, and learning all there was to learn about our new life.

Even recreation consisted of sitting around a table at a specified time, sewing as we conversed. Not hiking. Not swimming. Not playing the piano or pursuing hobbies. But sitting in a contrived environment in an assigned seat—SEWING! I found it excruciating to accept this notion of recreation! Still, it was part of the "package."

Although it took superhuman effort, I forced myself to accept what I was being taught, and I began what would become a lifelong battle with my feelings, struggling not to react, telling myself it was God's Will, to "offer it up" as the Sisters used to tell us in school: "Offer up the pain for the poor souls in Purgatory. Rejoice when you suffer, as pain makes you more like the Crucified Christ."

Before long, I felt like someone was ripping my heart out. The pain was intense. It was emotional torture, a pattern which would be repeated over and over throughout my convent years.

Occasionally, especially on weekends, one of our Superiors would take us in rows of threes for a walk outside. Never could we go out and amble among the trees alone or just sit and look up at the mountain. Our new lifestyle did not allow us to "waste time" in that manner.

On Sundays and special feast days we didn't have to sew, thank God! That would have been servile work—a sin for Catholics. Instead, we had extra time to pray in the chapel, read a spiritual book from the postulants' library, make the Stations of the Cross, and say the rosary.

When I first perused the books available in our library, I found a lot missing. "Where are the newspapers and magazines?" I wanted to ask. In a subsequent group instruction, I discovered the answer: All contact with the outside world was now off limits.

We were not allowed to read newspapers, magazines, novels, or any other book that was not on our library shelves. Listening to the radio and watching television were also prohibited. Furthermore, we could not inquire about the outside world during family visits or when working near the lay help in the Sisters' kitchen or anywhere else. This was a real culture shock!

Sister Angela tried to soften the "blow of adjustment" for us by scheduling occasional softball games. This was great for postulants like Dottie who thrived on athletic activities. But such games were not my idea of relaxation. Never did I care to play ball. Still, I tried to ignore my aversion and participate.

A day came when we were scheduled to walk down the hill of our vast grounds for a ballgame. We were in for a big surprise, as the chosen site was Tom's Creek. Being near water again lifted my spirits. I walked to the creek bank and sat down, enthralled by the fishy aroma and the sounds of gurgling water and birds singing.

For a moment a pleasant memory surfaced. I thought of the water—Beaver Dam—that had brought Bob and me together. And all my life, water had symbolized beauty and happiness, adventure and love. Now I could no longer bask in those wonderful sensations. But I shouldn't be thinking forbidden thoughts, especially recalling the day I met the sailor with whom I fell in love.

Still, I wanted to cherish a few moments sitting on the bank beside the water. Two other postulants joined me, and we started laughing and talking and "letting our hair down." It felt so good to have a normal conversation without a Superior breathing down our necks.

But suddenly, a Habit Sister—a Sister wearing the full dress of the Community—approached us and spoke up, "Why have you gone off alone, when you could play ball with the other postulants and contribute to the game?"

"We wanted to enjoy the water," someone answered.

"But you're members of a Community now. You do things together. Leaving the group for your own pleasure sounds selfish, doesn't it?"

Sheepishly we got up, joined the others, and began what would be a lifetime of doing everything only with each other—the group of Sisters thrown together in the same convent in obedience to an assignment.

It never dawned on me that becoming a Sister meant I would have to give up my privacy, my rendezvous' with nature, my hobbies, and my own ways of relaxing. The scope of my commitment was finally sinking in. Living the life of a Sister meant no longer being myself. My Superiors were stripping me of my personal identity, my individuality, and ultimately, my self-esteem.

15

One day I was sent for. Two people had sent me a telegram.

"May I read the telegram, Sister?" I asked.

"Now, you know I can't let you do that, Sister. You can only communicate with your immediate family, not friends or acquaintances."

"May I ask who sent it, Sister?"

"Someone named Bob and his mother," she replied.

It was all I could do to repress the emotion that welled up inside me! Bob? My sailor Bob? The Bob with whom I had fallen in love? This Bob and his mother had sent me a telegram?

"Is something wrong?" Sister Blanche blurted out.

"No, Sister, " I responded, struggling to control myself, "except that I wish I could read what they said."

"They just wanted to send you their best wishes, Sister."

I thanked her and walked away, as a thousand questions threatened to explode my brain: Did Sister Blanche tell me the whole message? What did Bob really say? That he still loved me? That we still had a chance? That he couldn't live without me? That he wanted me to leave the convent and marry him?

I couldn't stand not knowing for the rest of my life, and I could easily have pulled all my hair out at that moment. But a realization broke through my stampeding thoughts.

God called me and I answered "yes." I cannot look back. I made my sacrifice of Bob once and for all. To consider him again would only reopen wounds I'd forced myself to ignore in the hope that time would heal them. End of subject! I had to accept what happened as God's Will. After all, it was a telegram—just a piece of paper.

I had only to keep one thing in mind: I was promised to God as a child; and now as a young woman, I was intent on becoming a Sister. I had to keep myself focused on that goal—forge ahead without looking back. To falter might block whatever plan God had for me and my life.

Still, I was homesick, and no matter how hard I tried to suppress the feeling, it kept getting worse. I felt like part of me had been amputated. The emotion was so strong that I wanted to pick up a telephone and hear my Mother's voice and my Dad's, and the voice of my big tease of a brother Mel, and those of my sisters Carole and Anne NOW! I could not wait until the scheduled visiting day!

But I knew that phone calls were not permitted, and we were supposed to be mature enough not to get homesick. So I forced myself to ignore those pangs, and I threw myself into my work and prayer with all the energy I could muster.

On the next letter-writing day, I wanted to pour out my heart and soul to my family. I yearned to tell them how much I loved them and missed them.

Yes, I needed to write an uncensored letter and say exactly what I was feeling, what my life was becoming. I needed to tell them that the Pat they brought up and nurtured was being stripped away and replaced by someone I did not recognize. But, shrugging my shoulders, I accepted the inevitable—my letter would be censored. All that was left, then, was to write about the weather and the feast days coming up and how I hoped they were doing well.

One evening in October, the month of the Holy Rosary, we walked in procession outside with the Habit Sisters and the Seminary Sisters who were in the novitiate. Letting the beads slip slowly through our fingers, we prayed together. We looked down at the ground as we marched along, not up at the glorious sun setting on the mountain.

Somehow, this was supposed to lift our hearts and minds to God, as our long line snaked its way down the tree-lined avenue, then back again to the circle outside the main entrance. There we would conclude the rosary at the statue of Blessed Mother that we called "Virgo Potens".

On that particular evening, my eyes would not remain focused on the statue. Instead, they stared at the centuries-old fir tree that rose as a backdrop to the scene. As I gazed upward to the tree's highest point, I felt a sharp pain shoot through me. It was the anguish of living apart from my real family.

The tree that was a symbol of nature that I loved so dearly had become like a dagger piercing my heart. It was an experience that remained with me, although I felt restrained and unable to act on it—as if I were locked in an invisible straight jacket.

Then, tragedy struck one of us. Marsha received news that her father had died suddenly in her home state up north. From a heart attack, I guessed. Such news was dispensed in the briefest headlines. There were never enough details to satisfy our natural curiosity or assuage our anguish.

I knew, by now, that we had to give up family gatherings and rituals. This meant no celebrations of birthdays, graduations, weddings or anniversaries. Even special holidays like Father's Day, Mother's Day, and religious occasions—Christenings and First Communions— could not be shared. Still, I hoped that Marsha would be permitted to attend her father's funeral.

But that was not to be. The Sisters missioned in that region would go in her place. She could pray for her family and the repose of the soul of her Dad right where she was. That policy was a startling revelation. And cruel, I thought. How could she mourn here? She could not speak of her grief. She couldn't wander off and find a place to cry. I wanted to give her a big hug. Say how sorry I was. But I was afraid to break a rule. So I remained silent.

In those days we had intense lessons in religious decorum. We learned that Sisters could not swing their arms or look from side to side while walking, or cross their legs when sitting down. They could not cross their arms at any time, and when their hands had nothing else to do, they had to be joined and hidden beneath their long sleeves.

Sisters had to speak softly, as little as possible, and never in a familiar manner. They had to address each other as "Sister" and not by their secular names. Never, never, could they look a man directly in the eye.

Sisters were forbidden to whistle or sing songs or even hum a tune, except for the hymns they sang together in the chapel or at choir practice. At all times, they were expected to walk, not run. And they were never to touch any person, whether it be their own Sisters or an injured child who needed reassurance.

We even had lessons on how to eat like Sisters. Cut off the ends of a banana, slit it lengthwise, then open it up and fork out the fruit inside. That was peculiar, I thought.

It was comical the day I tried to eat an orange according to instructions. I watched the juice trickle down my arm before disappearing under my long sleeve. I wanted to burst out laughing, but meals were eaten in strict silence. So I had to keep a poker face at the table, let the juice stay where it was, and endure the sticky sensation.

One day my place in the refectory rotated, landing me at Sister Angela's table. After a delicious chicken dinner, she pulled me aside. I quickly examined my conscience, but believed I had done nothing wrong.

"I saw you mix together your mashed potatoes and cranberries. That's something Sisters don't do. It gives the impression that you want to enjoy your meal. Sisters eat only to become healthy instruments fit to do God's work. They never eat for pleasure. Please refrain from doing it in future."

It had not occurred to me that enjoying a meal could be wrong. Nevertheless, I accepted and obeyed what I was ordered to do.

At breakfast one morning, there were no large pitchers of milk. Sister Angela told us to start drinking coffee like the Habit Sisters did. "Drinking milk at breakfast will no longer be permitted," she said. No reason was given. The bottom line was uniformity and blind obedience, I believed. Besides, we were already learning that no Sister should ever stand out as being different from the others.

One day as I sat at the community room table studying with the other postulants, I could feel the hardness of the wooden chair under me. I could put up with the discomfort, but accepting the atmosphere around me—plain, bare, and silent—was a bigger challenge. Missing my radio and record player, I longed to hear strains of music other than church music. Soothing music was what I needed at the moment. Percy Faith or Liberace. Was that so wrong to wish for?

And I missed my piano! My fingers yearned to play Beethoven or Rachmaninoff once more, or the music of Gershwin, or Rogers and Hammerstein. I longed to play "Ebb Tide" and be whisked away in spirit to my beloved ocean. The ocean where I craved to be at this very moment. My heart was breaking over the losses.

"Pat, are you daydreaming?" My Superior's voice brought me back to reality.

"Sorry, Sister." I picked up my book knowing I was suffering from an overdose of silence. As I tried to read, I listened to a bird singing outside the window. I wanted to walk over, gaze at it, join in a duet, even fly away with it. But I remained seated where I was supposed to be, where my Superiors told me God wanted me to be, doing what they said God wanted me to do.

Music had been such a big part of my life—listening, singing, dancing, playing the piano. Previously, I would not have let anyone deprive me of it. Yet here I was, letting those in whose hands I entrusted my life tell me I no longer needed music, that it had no place in the convent, no place in the life of a woman consecrated to God. Part of the secular world, it had to be sacrificed. This was a hard saying!

As I tried to do all that was asked of me and give up all that I was told God wanted me to sacrifice, something inside me wanted to rebel. I wanted to plead for my own outlets, what I knew would work for me and refresh my spirit. I wanted to yell out that it wasn't fair. I had come to serve, but not as a slave!

I couldn't wait until visiting day, when Mother and Dad and the rest of my family would come and spend a few hours with me. I was excited, even though there were many admonitions beforehand: reminders not to eat or drink anything in their presence; reminders not to get in their car and go for a drive, even on the Sisters' property; reminders not to accept gifts from them; reminders that they were externs and we were forbidden to discuss our rules and way of life with externs.

Despite all the fervent warnings, it was great to see my dear ones at long last! I hugged them tightly, not wanting to let them go. And, for a few precious hours, we walked and talked. Being limited in places to go, I ended up giving my family a tour of the cemetery, where the remains of Mother Seton, our American foundress, were still buried. Here in the graveyard, Dad became his old self and climbed up on Saint Vincent's statue to strike a funny pose for the camera.

I laughed and recalled my dearest memories of Dad. I remembered the poignant World War II years. My six-year old heart broke the day Dad said goodbye to us, before leaving for the Army in the Pacific. I clung to two mementoes that kept me close to him in spirit during those years: a silver dollar he had given me for my birthday the year he was drafted, and the only letter he would write just to me from overseas. How I grieved when the little purse I left in my third grade desk was stolen, and I lost forever my two treasures.

Dad returned from the war a sick man in anguish, no longer his carefree self. For a long time he was silent about the war and distant from his family.

But today, my tall, handsome Dad, whose brown eyes and dimple in the chin I inherited, was the father I remembered from my youngest years. How I cherished those moments!

My former best friend Theresa and her boyfriend Harry were allowed to come that one time, too. Theresa had been away visiting relatives in Rome when I made my decision to enter the convent. Her parents had worked hard and scrimped and saved their money, until they could afford this first trip home since they had immigrated to America.

It seemed unfair that the first time Theresa had the opportunity to meet her relatives in Italy would be the very time I decided to leave home. I wondered, had she been around, would she have talked me out of leaving? I had always confided everything in my best friend and valued her opinions and advice.

In fact, the two people who had the most influence over me were Theresa and Bob. Either one might have convinced me not to become a Sister. But they were both away during my crucial moments of decision. Now it was too late, I thought. And I was not allowed to share my feelings with her or even apologize.

21

The time came to say goodbye, and I watched the family car fade in the distance. When I joined the other Sisters in the chapel for evening prayers, I felt the pain of separation cut even deeper than our initial separation. I would have to learn to numb my feelings all over again. I wanted to cry, but tears were not allowed.

A shocking event took place that week in the chapel. It was so quiet, you could hear a pin drop—when suddenly a shrill scream broke the silence. Realizing that it came from one of our number, I wanted to turn around, see what was wrong, and offer my assistance. But like the other postulants, I remained kneeling in place like a statue. I was afraid to move, afraid to break a rule, afraid to make a mistake. No longer able to think for myself or make a rational decision on my own, I did nothing.

Listening to the stage whispers of the Habit Sisters who were dealing with the situation, I was relieved when the noisy fracas stopped and the sounds of someone in pain ceased.

But what had happened? Why had someone cried out so pitifully? And who was it? The questions kept coming.

Later, I realized that one of the postulants was gone. Margie had disappeared from our ranks. Finally, Sister Angela gathered us together and spoke up with the emotion she usually hid. "All of you better thank God you are still here! Thank God for your vocation! Margie is no longer with us. She has gone home."

Was that it? Tell us more, I wanted to cry out. Why did she leave? Why couldn't we say goodbye to her? Was she all right? What happened? But none of us dared to speak up.

One of our band who was good at eavesdropping got wind of a rumor and passed it around. Margie had had an epileptic seizure. It was a condition that would have disqualified her from being accepted into the Community, had Superiors known about it.

Whether she had hidden a pre-existing condition or the stress of her new life had brought it on, she was sent home. Nothing more was said about it, and never again would a Sister's departure be explained to us.

With Anna, circumstances were different. Being invited to her friend's debut with the Boston Opera, she asked to go home for the occasion. When Superiors denied her request, she was devastated. She became sad and lost her effervescent personality.

And one day she simply disappeared with no goodbyes to us or from us. The whole process seemed so cold, and the rest of us were left to deal with the loss by ourselves and to live with more unspoken questions.

I had not foreseen the leavings. It was painful to lose Margie and Anna and the others that followed during postulatum. Despite so much repression, we were developing a sense of family. We were being taught that the Sisters were now our family, that they replaced our natural families.

So, each time a postulant left, I grieved as if a family member had died. The secrecy that shrouded such events only served to deepen the wound, and we were left with no outlet for our grief other than prayer.

At those times I withdrew more deeply into myself, while I reached out for God's Hand. Praying took on greater urgency, and I found my peace in the chapel. I relied on my faith to get me through my most difficult moments. I struggled to turn off my feelings and keep in mind what my Superiors said Jesus revealed about my vocation in the Scriptures:

"If anyone will come after me, let him take up his cross daily and come follow me…He who loves father or mother more than me is not worthy of me…He who looks back after putting his hand to the plow is not worthy of me…God loves a cheerful giver."

Otherwise, I threw myself into the tasks at hand, glad to have a schedule that kept me too busy to think.

On Christmas Eve we were sent to bed early, expecting to be awakened at 11:30 p.m. by the regular handbell. Instead, we were happily surprised to be awakened by angelic singing. The novices, called Seminary Sisters in our Community, had come caroling through the postulants' wing singing the Latin carol "Adeste Fidelis." I got dressed with a good feeling, arriving at the chapel just in time for Midnight Mass. It made my first Christmas away from home a little bit easier to bear.

Knowing I could not receive mail during Advent or Lent, my family had planned a special surprise. When our mail was passed out on Christmas Day, I discovered a gift in the form of an Advent letter. Using a long roll of paper like a scroll, my family had jotted down messages of love from mid-November until a few days before Christmas.

It was a wonderful present that put me in touch with them and renewed memories of past Christmases. A mixed blessing, it made me happy and sad. Still, I let myself enjoy reading it before tearing it up and throwing it away. That was what our regulations required: We could read our mail once, then we had to discard it.

On the next visiting day, my family excitedly asked how I liked their long letter. I told them how much I appreciated their gift and the love that went into its creation. But I felt I had to be honest when asked what I had done with it. And so, I admitted I had thrown it away.

I wanted to add that I would like to have kept it and treasured it, but I wasn't allowed to discuss Community practices with them. I believed I had to let them think I was ungrateful enough to destroy it. Burying the pain of that moment, I let them think the worst about me.

I saw a look of disbelief cross their faces, and I said nothing. Never again would they repeat that beautiful gesture.

Celebrating Christmas away from home was agonizing that year and the subsequent twenty-two years.

A high point of postulatum came with a welcome announcement: We would accompany Sister Genevieve to visit the poor on the nearby mountain in an area known as Appalachia.

I knew that, upon turning five years' vocation, I would take the traditional vows of poverty, chastity, and obedience. But in this Community we took a fourth vow, to serve the poor. I always had a special place in my heart for the needy. As a seventh-grader I had joined the Louisettes, a service organization at school, and visited the lonely old folks at the Baltimore City Home for the Aged and the nursing home run by the Little Sisters of the Poor.

I had adopted a neighborhood woman in her nineties for visits. Legally blind and living alone, she was so grateful to have a visitor that she told a Sister that an angel from heaven had come to see her. I felt honored, but humbled.

I liked the idea of being in a congregation of Sisters who vowed to serve the poor. So I looked forward to joining Sister Genevieve—Emmitsburg's "Saint of Appalachia"—on her treks up the mountain.

As I sat in the station wagon that took us up the hilly road, I wondered how such a magnificent setting could hide some of our nation's worst poverty—keeping a dark secret about the world some families were forced to live in. "Out of sight, out of mind" was a truism in these parts.

The first family we visited had ten children, no running water, no jobs and no source of income. When I asked Sister Genevieve how they could live without water, she replied that a college professor a quarter of a mile away permitted them to come and get water from him, when they "needed" it. We brought them food and clothing, and I wished there was more we could do that day.

The visits were positive experiences for me, inasmuch as they helped me regain my sense of why I was becoming a Sister. They refocused my thinking and motivated me to put up with obstacles. I was becoming a Sister hoping to be a social worker—wanting to make the world a better place for families like the poor on the mountain, for people experiencing hardship, discouragement, poverty, and the effects of prejudice and injustice.

Before deciding to enter the Sisters of Charity, I had considered two other religious congregations: a missionary order and the Little Sisters of the Poor whose work I so admired. I had chosen the Sisters of Charity, ultimately, because of the diversity of their works. They not only had teachers, but nurses and social workers as well. If I couldn't be an artist, then I wanted to be a social worker. Helping people live better lives was important to me.

After high school graduation, Mother had tried to steer me into teaching. "You'd make a good teacher, Pat!" But I had reacted with a stubborn protest: "Never will I become a teacher!" Growing up hating the rigid atmosphere of the schools I attended made the very idea of teaching repugnant to me. After that, Mother said nothing more about my future.

The visit to Appalachia confirmed for me that I was in the right Community, where I could help the poor rise out of poverty. I had to keep that conviction before me and surmount whatever stood in the way of my becoming a Sister.

One night the moon was full. It would have been a great night to walk among the trees in the valley I now called home. I could imagine how the gentle breeze would feel against my cheeks, as I ambled along delighting in every sound: the rustle of the leaves, the chirping of crickets, the yelp of a distant coyote.

I could visualize the nearby mountain with its aging hills that formed a gently-sloping horizon. I could almost feel the exhilaration of that walk, as I inhaled deeply the mountain air.

As it was, we were just crossing the walkway on the tarred roof high above the valley on our way to bed. Night prayers were finished, and the Grand Silence was in effect.

Stealing a peek at the full moon, my thoughts took me back to another moonlit night, when I walked hand-in-hand with Bob. For a fleeting moment, Bob was there with me and I could feel shivers go up my spine. I loved him so much. Yet I gave it all up. Why? Because Mother promised me to God? Because I let a Sister convince me to leave home and follow God's Call that she said I was fighting? No. I could blame no one but myself.

My thoughts continued to disconcert me. What was in that telegram? The desire to know still burned deep inside me, even though the message was long since destroyed in the incinerator down below. Would I never know what it really said?

A postulant, impatient with my dawdling, tried to pass me. Pointing to the full moon I blurted out, "Doesn't it make you sick?" She could not believe her ears. Turning toward me, she glared. I had broken silence—the unbreakable Grand Silence! Obviously appalled, she retorted with an emphatic "No!" It wasn't fair of me to disturb her quiet time to commune with God, her comfortable acceptance of the rules imposed upon us. Still, my words were saying, "I'm hurting! Really hurting! Won't somebody listen to my pain and tell me what to do?"

My words having fallen on deaf ears, I lowered my eyes and resumed a steady walking pace. I buried my pain, as I was learning to bury all pain—deep inside my soul. I had to let go of Bob and memories I wanted to hold onto. Forbidden memories.

That January I turned nineteen, not permitted to celebrate my birthday, not permitted to tell the other Sisters it was my birthday. Yet, nine months before, I was well on my way to independence—exuberant over my dream of becoming a sculptor.

A war was inevitable. Despite my best efforts to fit in the mold and emerge a model Sister, my humanness kept getting in the way. As hard as I tried to stamp out my feelings and reactions, they refused to disappear.

My formation as a postulant was drawing to a close. In order to take the next step and enter the seminary phase of my training, which would be akin to boot camp, I asked and received permission.

Why did I not simply walk out the door and go home? Did I really believe I had to stay—that leaving would mean rejecting God's Call and ultimately risking damnation?

Was I that brain-washed? Or did the answers to all of these questions lie hidden inside my brown-shingled house—the house I left behind 182 days ago?

2.

Personhood Lost

Six Months Earlier

To most people, it was just a brown-shingled house—nothing spectacular. To me, it was my safe haven, my depository of dreams, my irreplaceable home on Louise Avenue in northeast Baltimore.

That day, like a prisoner about to be yanked away, I stood before it—my heart breaking, my silent voice uttering its heart-wrenching farewell.

As if my feet were imbedded in the cement pavement, I focused my eyes on my home for the last time.

A voice from behind me called out, "Are you ready, Pat?"

Turning around, I saw my Mother standing by the open door of our family Ford, waiting to whisk me away.

Mother's red hair sparkled in the sunlight. But there was no sparkle in her eyes—no smile on the face of this petite woman who, in this very house, had given birth to me, and whose prayers had brought me back to life and to this point in time.

On that warm September day, stillness replaced any breeze—a stifling stillness that threatened to strangle me, as I fought to hold back tears.

"I'm not ready to go, Mother. I need more time," I replied.

What no one realized was that I was waging an inner war, struggling to silence voices that were tormenting me as questions emerged from deep inside my subconscious.

Will I ever by ready? Ready for what? Ready to disavow my family and all that I held dear? Ready to relinquish my aspirations and the plans I had set in motion? Ready to renounce love?

Why, Patsy, why would you do this? the voices stammered out. No one can make you do anything you don't really want to do, can they? Maybe you were too hasty in making the decision to jump into an obscure world replete with unknown consequences—a world that might swallow you up.

I reverted back to my many conversations with Sister Andrew. After all, she was the one who persuaded me to do this. When are you going to stop fighting your vocation, she had asked repeatedly, until she wore me down.

She talked as if I could land in hell someday if I did not say "yes" to God's Call. And—after 12 years in Catholic schools—I knew well that my highest goal in life had to be loving God, obeying His Will, and avoiding His wrath.

As if they could snap a picture, my eyes fixed themselves on my brown-shingled house with its memories that I would leave buried there. I loved the shutters that shielded me from storms and made me feel safe. And I loved the front porch with its swing on one side and its glider across the way. So much happened on the front porch.

My first encounter with a bee took place when, as a toddler, I reached up to pet it and got stung. Still, it would be the beginning of a life-long love affair with animals.

I thought of the zillions of hours I sat on the porch railing, sketching to my heart's content. And there was so much laughter with my brother Mel and my sisters Carole and Anne—often followed by a hike at Kratz' farm not far away. And I could still see myself sitting on a porch step, proudly holding Baby Sister Anne for a picture.

On one of those steps, dressed for high school graduation, I posed with my heart bursting with happiness. It was not so much because I was finished with school. Rather, it was because—a few days earlier—I had met Bob, and it was love at first sight.

Letting my imagination wander, I saw myself at Beaver Dam, my favorite "swimming hole," with my brother Mel whose blond hair glistened in the sun. A little taller than me, Mel, a year and a-half older, gave me a sense of security when he wasn't teasing me.

For years he had tormented me with the reminder of Mother's promise by saying, "Sister Pat will now lead us in prayer," whenever I attempted to mediate sibling arguments.

But after seeing me grow up to be a young lady in love with life— dancing, dating, and now going to art school—on the way to fulfilling my hopes and dreams, he had long since stopped pestering me.

After a good swim, I had stretched out on the sand that day in my black, one-piece bathing suit—basking in the warmth of the sun's rays.

About to graduate, I reflected on my future. "Life is good," I thought. I remembered my wonderful discovery on the beach at Ocean City, Maryland. Molding a face on a head in the wet sand was as easy as drawing someone's face on a piece of paper. That realization convinced me I had a "Michelangelo" inside me, and I yearned to become a sculptor.

What I could not have known was that my life was about to take a new and unexpected turn—beyond my wildest expectations.

I was lost in my thoughts when a foot kicked mine. I yelled, "I'm not in any mood for your jokes, Mel! Go away!"

"What mood are you in?" a voice that wasn't Mel's laughed back at me. I sat up and shielded my eyes with my hands, squinting to see who was there.

What I saw was a daydream come true. My neighbor George loomed over me, surrounded by five brawny buddies dressed only in swimming trunks and sailor hats—each one more gorgeous than the next. I could feel myself blush crimson.

As George introduced them, I smiled and greeted each one.

"These guys are stationed with me at the Chincoteague, Virginia Naval Base," he said. Then my gaze met Bob's. "This one's from Manhattan," George added. "Bob, meet Pat . . . . Patsy, meet Bob."

I was in a trance—mesmerized by Bob's smile. The sun highlighted his blond hair, and his blue eyes focused on my brown eyes. He said nothing, but he said everything. And goosebumps stampeded my body.

"My sister Charlene is getting married in two weeks, Pat. I'm sure she'd want me to invite you to her wedding," George said. "We'll all be there," he added.

The following days could not pass by fast enough. And, on the morning of my graduation, I went back to Beaver Dam to swim and think about Bob. Most of the day I spent daydreaming about the tall, handsome sailor whose path crossed mine there at the water.

I stared at the ripples, as I lay on my stomach in the sand, propped up on my elbows. I smiled and hummed along with Nat King Cole who crooned a love song on somebody's car radio.

"Unforgettable, that's what you are, Bob," I whispered.

When Charlene's wedding day finally arrived, I wanted to look fabulous. I took the time to curl my brown locks and put on red lipstick and rouge. I snuggled into my two-piece green and gold dress that a subtle sheen brought to life.

Checking myself out in a mirror, I liked the slender appearance my skirt gave me. Although I knew my full seventeen-year-old breasts did not contribute to a slim look, I was proud of my figure that made me look years older.

I put on the high heels I bought for graduation and pulled out my newest snow-white pocketbook. I was ready and bursting with anticipation! I couldn't wait to see Bob again!

In the church I let my eyes wander—searching. When I found Bob across the aisle, he too seemed to be looking for someone. Our eyes locked. He smiled at me, and I returned the smile.

At the reception we danced and talked about everything. Then we walked outside, and before long we were holding hands. I could feel the electricity between us.

We saw a lot of each other in the following months. Bob would hitchhike to Baltimore on weekends to see me. I was spellbound every moment we spent together. Although I had dated during high school, I never felt this way about anyone. I was in love, and it was a great feeling! I lived for his visits and wished I never had to let him go.

One weekend we hopped a bus to go to New York City. I was thrilled to meet Bob's mother and visit his home—a second floor apartment in the heart of Manhattan. Despite the rain, it was great to be with Bob in his own environment. By Sunday morning, the sun shone radiantly, and we walked through Central Park, hand in hand, before we hurried back to catch a bus for home.

I loved New York City and would always associate it with the special moments Bob and I spent together drinking in its exciting and romantic atmosphere.

From then on, I knew that Bob was the only one for me. I basked in the wonderful feeling of being in love. And when he was gone, I would play our theme song, "The High and Mighty", on the piano in our brown-shingled house—yearning for his return.

But Bob's Navy schedule started creating roadblocks, and his visits dwindled. The pain of missing him gnawed at me on the weekends he couldn't get away. It was as if the approaching season of Lent was thrusting upon me the biggest sacrifices that I could possibly endure: Bob's absence and the loss of the hugs and kisses I starved for.

I became grief-stricken. I knew that hitchhiking from Virginia to Maryland and back, or taking a Greyhound bus, was tedious for Bob. But was he losing interest in me? Had he found someone else to love, someone who would give him more than I could offer—someone willing to give up her virginity before marriage?

During the last week of Lent, Holy Week, I threw myself fully into the sacred rituals. I identified with the feelings of Mary who had to give up her Son and bury him. Meditating on the sufferings and death of Jesus alleviated a portion of my pain.

Then I had a unique, unexplainable experience: After fasting all day Holy Thursday and spending Good Friday at church deep in meditation on the Passion of Jesus, I found myself in a state of the deepest peace imaginable. It was as if I left the Planet Earth and was in a heavenly place that I wanted to cling to. I felt totally absorbed in

God and wished those moments would never end. But eventually—like a rainbow—they vanished.

Back in the mundane world, my thoughts reverted back to Bob. I wanted a miracle. I wanted to see Bob at my door again. But, deep down, I knew it wasn't going to happen. The phone calls had stopped. There were no more letters. Although the parish church swelled with alleluias that Easter, there were no alleluias in my heart—only sadness.

After graduation the previous June, I had gone to work at a company that printed medical journals and other treatises. When I became bored with my tasks in a building without windows, I changed jobs.

Happy to find work in the telephone company's drafting department, I found myself drawing telephone poles and cables on blueprint pages, which turned out to be another monotonous job. Still, I sat before a huge window that allowed me to peek at a sliver of sky I could see above the tops of buildings.

What kept me challenged and motivated were my night classes at the Maryland Institute of Art. I loved mingling with other artists and spending my time "creating." And so it was that Bob and my art world made my life complete.

My universe after graduation had become amazing for almost a year, when suddenly it felt like the bottom fell out of my life. Without Bob, sadness overwhelmed me. Feeling like I was in mourning, I stopped wearing makeup and stylish clothes that made me look attractive. Some of my co-workers expressed surprise at the change they witnessed in me. But I explained nothing. Without Bob, nothing else mattered.

Life was no longer joyful, and I began to ponder the meaning of human existence. I noticed that a lot of people had to live without love, without the basic necessities of life. And there were so many inequities between the "haves" and the "have-nots." This bothered me.

One day I boarded a bus heading home, down Harford Road. The bus was packed, so I accepted the fact that I would have to stand up for the trip. When I reached up to grab hold of a leather strap that hung down, I noticed something perplexing. Through the crowd of people standing, I spied an empty seat.

"That's strange," I thought. "How can so many people be standing and a seat remain vacant?" I pushed my way through, until I could see better, and I was shocked! The man sitting next to the empty seat was "colored," and the white people nearby had chosen to stand, rather than seat themselves elbow-to-elbow with him.

"How can this happen?" I almost wondered aloud. Suddenly, I knew the answer. It was the first time I was aware of prejudice.

"Shame on all of you!" I wanted to cry out, but I didn't. Instead, I shoved my way past the middle of the bus, until I reached the empty seat and sat down, ignoring the stares I was suddenly getting. I hoped my action would assuage the man's embarrassment and remove some of his pain.

That experience left an indelible imprint on me—one that would affect my dealings with others for the rest of my life.

That spring without Bob, as I dwelt on the realities of life, the newspapers flashed stories about a man soon to be executed. After I read about his tragic upbringing—without love—in a horrible neighborhood, I cried. Could I have ended up like him, had I grown up in his shoes? Was it fair that he was going to the electric chair for a crime he may not have committed, had he grown up in my shoes—with a family like mine and a neighborhood like mine?

When I could find no answers to those profound questions in the Catholic faith I had been taught, I was determined to return to the Sisters at my high school. Surely they had the answers. The philosopher and compassionate person I was becoming wanted and needed answers. Until I found them, I would not be able to find peace in the confusing secular world that I had entered after graduation.

On the spur of the moment one day after work, I stepped off the bus at my Alma Mater. I entered the school and walked down the familiar hallways that had always made me feel safe and secure. I no longer felt that sense of security out in the "real" world.

From the back, I could see a familiar figure. She walked noiselessly and looked straight ahead. It was Sister Andrew who had been the moderator of our high school orchestra. I chuckled at the flopping wings of her headdress that kept time with the steady rhythm of her gait.

Suddenly, she turned and smiled at me. "I thought I heard someone behind me. I'm so glad it's you, Pat. Let me show you around. You'll like the improvements we've made to your old orchestra room."

After showing the recent paint job and some of the new instruments, she beckoned me to sit with her. I tried to find words to express what was troubling me and the doubts I was beginning to have regarding my faith. But I never got my story out.

With raised eyebrows, she pointed to the library book I was carrying. "Lust for Life," she cried out. "Is that the sort of book you should be reading, Pat? Shame on you!"

I struggled to suppress a laugh, as I spoke up: "Sister, it's the life of Vincent Van Gogh, one of my favorite artists. I go to art school now. I plan to be an artist."

"You don't have a job yet?"

"I work during the day, Sister, and I go to the Maryland Institute of Art at night. I'm on my way to becoming a sculptor. It's a goal I've had for years. I love to kneel on the beach at Ocean City and mold a human face. I find it so easy to create. And I know I have a Michelangelo inside me. Aren't you happy for me, Sister?"

Silence.

When she finally spoke up, she redirected our conversation. "How long are you going to fight your vocation, Pat?"

"Sister, I'm doing what I always wanted to do. It makes me happy."

"Your Call comes from God. As a Child of Mary, didn't you promise to love God to the fullest, to be His obedient servant like His own Mother Mary?"

The thought of my Mother's promise flashed in my brain. Hadn't I silenced the subconscious voices that had haunted me for years?

"You've been promised to God. Don't forget that!" Through my Catholic school years, hadn't I managed to ignore the Sisters who targeted me to follow in their footsteps saying, "You have a vocation, Pat." Now Sister Andrew was back on the same subject. I could not believe it!

"Sister, I know what I want out of life. I want to get married and raise a family—a good Catholic family!"

"Isn't what God wants important to you, Pat? Don't you want to do God's Will?"

"Doesn't God want me to be happy, Sister?"

"Go home now, Pat, and take time to reflect and pray. Ask God what He is calling you to do. Then ask for the grace to respond to Him unselfishly and courageously like you've always done in the past."

Actually, Sister Andrew knew nothing about my life away from school. Still, I went home and followed her advice.

I returned to see her again a week later, as she requested.

"There's something you don't know about me, Sister. I hate to wear hats. I can't imagine wearing your headdress everyday for the rest of my life—all day long everyday!"

"Pat, do you think it's easy for me to wear it? When we answer God's Call, His grace is always sufficient for us. He will help you do what's difficult."

I left again and pondered and prayed for the Holy Spirit's guidance. A third time, I returned to talk to Sister Andrew.

"I would have to give up my plans, Sister. I could not become an artist!"

"You'd be replacing your will with God's Will, striving to live a perfect life. That's an honor, Pat, and a privilege not given to all."

"It's just too hard! I can't do it, Sister!"

"What has God promised to those who leave all to follow Him?" she asked.

"He promised a hundredfold of happiness in this life and eternal happiness in the next," I dutifully responded.

"That's everything, isn't it? How could you want for anything more, Pat? And besides, when we turn our backs on God, don't we put our souls in danger of being lost forever?"

I went home and followed her advice. I took more time to reflect and pray. I spent a long time praying in Saint Alphonsus Church downtown one day after work. I liked its atmosphere. With so many statues of the saints and the stained glass windows that allowed the sunlight to pour through, I felt like I was a short step away from Heaven.

I thought of my parents who always gave me such good example. My Catholic mother was scrupulous in her practice of religion and showed a deep sense of duty in all that she did. My Methodist Dad, too, could always be seen obeying God's laws. He was super-conscientious in every way. Even at the time of his father's death, he had quit school, unbeknown to his mother. He felt obliged to take over the responsibility of supporting her.

Both of my parents lived by the noblest of ideals. And throughout my Catholic school years, I had observed the Sisters living dedicated, self-sacrificing lives. Didn't all the people around me show by their example that there was more to life than seeking their own satisfaction?

The next time I saw Sister Andrew, I listened to her spout her most powerful argument. "Think of this, Pat: Suppose just one person's life would be better and happier, because you were there to help. Would it not be worth it to sacrifice your life for that person? Think of all the good God must want you to do as a Sister. Don't make a mistake and make the wrong decision."

I already knew well the words of Jesus in Saint John's Gospel: "There is no greater love than this, to lay down one's life for one's friends."

I believed this teaching, and I felt my idealistic side drawn to it. Was Jesus not telling me to put my happiness last?

Before giving an answer, I started inquiring about the rules of the nun's religious congregation.

"Sister, I don't know much about your life behind closed doors."

"You already know a lot about us, Pat. Our Sisters taught you for twelve years."

"I can describe individuals. I can tell you who was kind and who was not. I've watched Sisters teach in classrooms and pray in church. But I've never seen them behind convent doors. What can you tell me about that? I'd like to know."

"Pat, we live by faith. We know that God's grace will always be with us when life is difficult. I can tell you this, we use large white linen napkins to cover our collars when we eat."

"That way you won't ruin your starched linen when you spill your spaghetti down the front of you." I tried to lighten the atmosphere and relieve my nervousness. Then I continued, "But you must have rules to live by. Can't you tell me what they are?"

"Pat, put aside your fears. Just know that the God who loves you so much, who has given you the wonderful gift of a vocation, will be with you every step along the way. Trust in Divine Providence, and God will reward your trust! Now tell me. What have you decided?"

I was only eighteen, and I was on the brink of making a decision that would radically alter my life. Sister Andrew's powers of persuasion made me lean toward a "yes," but I was scared to death.

Was God really asking this total sacrifice of me? That one word, YES, would wipe out all my dreams and put a padlock on my heart. I would be shutting Bob out of my life forever and blocking the path to any human love in the future. And I would have to renounce my family.

Those considerations threatened to tear me apart, when I recalled a simple truth: My Mother offered me to God, and God evidently listened. Instead of dying I lived and grew up. I knew what my answer had to be.

"Yes, Sister," I said. "I'll become one of you."

I was too young and idealistic to realize I was being denied information about a lifestyle sealed in permanency. Convent life was going to be cloaked in secrecy, but I didn't recognize the hints hidden in our discussions at the time.

Sister Andrew hugged me with what she called a holy embrace. Then she spoke up, "Now, let's get down to business. She rattled off a long list of documents I would need to get from my pastor and said she'd have to get me an application form.

"Then, there's the dowry your father needs to submit," she added.

"What? A dowry, Sister? This is the first time I've heard that your Order required a dowry?"

"Is that a problem, Pat?"

"Yes, Sister. Most definitely! Have you forgotten that my Dad is Methodist, a good Methodist. It will be hard enough to convince him to let me go. But he will hit the ceiling if he's told he has to pay in order for the convent to accept me!"

"Don't worry about it, Pat. I'll request an exemption for you. Just concentrate on preparing to go. You only have six weeks until the next entrance day, unless you want to wait six more months."

"No, Sister. I'll be ready in September. If I put it off, I might change my mind."

I went home and, without having prepared my family for my shocking decision, I blurted out my news.

"I'm leaving home. I'm going to become a Sister of Charity."

"Sure Pat," my father responded, "and what else is new?"

"I'm serious, Dad. Here's my application form."

I handed him the long piece of paper and waited, as he read it. He looked up at the others. "She's telling the truth," he said.

His pronouncement was met with stunned silence from everyone. Dad went into his "shell," but his face clearly showed disapproval bordering on anger. Mother was strangely silent. My siblings wore looks of disappointment. Nobody was happy for me. And so I started packing up to leave for a journey to an unknown future.

As I gazed one last time at the brown-shingled house, I knew what really made my home so dear to me. It was where my life began in my Mother's womb and, nine months later, where I made my grand entrance on earth.

Three years later, when I lay dying in Union Memorial Hospital, doctors told my parents they could do nothing more for me. Either I had eaten rat poison or I had ingested lead from the paint on my bed that I liked to chew. Whatever the cause, my life was ebbing away. It was then that my Mother promised me to God—offering to give me back as a nun if only God would let me live, if only He would work that miracle. It was a pact she made with the Almighty.

Then, one day, the light of life returned to my eyes, and my parents took me home. And so I grew up in the brown-shingled house. Years later, Mother would reveal to me her secret—the promise I would inwardly fight and rebel against.

"It's time," Mother's voice—in an unfamiliar tone tinged with stoicism—called out, shaking me back to the present. I heaved a sigh and turned, knowing my act of leaving symbolized the end of my fight against "God's Will."

Walking toward Mother and the car awaiting me, I said "goodbye" to the brown-shingled house that epitomized all that I had become and all that I loved. The house that brought me to this moment forever frozen in time.

3.

Fitted into a Mold

Six Months Later

Trudging noiselessly down a long corridor with our scanty belongings, we resembled a bunch of hobos dressed in black. Earlier that day Sister Blanche had given each of us a thirty-six inch square of cotton material instructing us to wrap our trousseau garments inside by tying together opposite corners. It would have to suffice for a suitcase.

We spread out in front of the chapel's altar rail on our knees to offer our lives to God and place our vocation in Mary's hands, before continuing our quiet walk to our new quarters.

Along the way, my thoughts jumped ahead to this new step I was taking. I was going to the Seminary. Yet the Seminary Sisters were a complete mystery to me. Although I prayed with them and ate with them, I had never spoken to any of them. They kept to themselves and lived in their own private world, off limits to the rest of us. I could not imagine how it would feel to be one of them.

This phase of my formation would last a year and a-half, at the end of which I would put on what the Sisters called their "Holy Habit." That is, if Sister Directress deemed I was well enough prepared, and worthy to be and to be called a "Habit Sister."

At the entrance to the Seminary wing I looked up at the Sister who greeted us. Sister Leo stood like a statue. Her starched white collar looked bleached in its whiteness. Despite its stiffness, it was still flexible enough to bend gently over her ample bosom that her corsette could not completely flatten. Her white wings hovered over her head like a giant dove guarding the purity of the woman hidden inside the Habit.

Her beady eyes and round face disguised her sternness that bordered on callousness, but our new Superior's reputation had already preceded our first encounter with her. By now, I feared her.

Sister Directress, as she would henceforth be called, presented herself like a sergeant with a job to do. Her very demeanor communicated a clear message. She would tolerate no levity of any kind. Nor would she put up with incompetence, carelessness, or even an occasional mistake. She would expect perfection—strict adherence to every rule and policy she would teach us.

Her first official act was to assign each of us a "big sister" who would be responsible to make sure we started off right.

My big sister was a country girl from West Virginia who looked like a chubby version of the Dutch girls on the cleanser cans at home. Sister K was all business as she led me down a hallway with her eyes modestly cast down. She appeared to be gifted with an inner radar, since she knew which doorway to enter without raising her eyes.

My dormitory looked enormous with its long row of alcoves lining one wall. Across from the alcoves was a small sink I would share with the others. It had a sheet—like curtain that could be pulled around it for privacy. The room's high ceiling was what I expected in the century-old wing. Tall, narrow windows that opened with a rope, dotted the south wall. I saw no screens.

Streaks of sunlight poured through the windows, creating irregular patterns of brightness in an otherwise somber-looking room. One bolt of light hit the corpus of the large crucifix that was hung on the bare white wall.

My big sister motioned for me to enter an alcove, after she tugged on the hanging white sheets and pulled them around to enclose the space. My area, plain and spotless, contained the minimum necessities for a bedroom: a small iron bed painted white and covered with a thin white bedspread; a wooden chair up against the bed, and a simple wooden chest with one drawer and a cupboard. There was no lamp in my alcove, just the overhead light on the ceiling.

Surveying the scene, my mouth must have hung open as Sister K put on a stern face and whispered, "You can't do that!"

"Do what?" I asked.

"You'll get along better here, if you're not seen gawking or snooping around, Sister."

She proceeded to use sign language to indicate what I should take off and what I should put on. I ended up taking off and handing her everything, except my underwear, garter belt, and black stockings.

Not looking at me, she whispered, "Keep on your drawers, but take off your brassiere." Confused, I followed her orders. Then she started handing me the seminary clothing.

First, I put on a white linen chemise which had to be pinned shut at the neck with a straight pin. She showed me how to fold back the sleeves and fit them snug at my wrists before securing them with more straight pins. Next, she handed me a plain linen corset without stays that was waist-length and had three flat panels, one for the back and one for each side of the front. I had to lace up the garment of yellowed linen with a shoestring that used to be white, pulling it tight until it flattened my chest.

I put on the long bulky pockets we had made by sewing the pocket part to a narrow waistband. Then I tied them around my waist. After making sure they were secure, I put on a long blue half-slip with slits allowing me to reach deep into the pockets.

Blushing and quite modest, Sister K turned aside while I dressed. But now she seemed concerned and looked at me.

"What's holding up your stockings?"

"My garter belt."

"Sisters can't wear those things. Take it off."

Puzzled, I followed her instructions and timidly handed her her my garter belt.

"Roll your stockings down," she continued, "just below the knees. Then twist an end and tuck it under each stocking. Make it tight enough to hold."

My stockings stayed in place for a while, but it took a lot of practice to master the feat that defied gravity. Until that time, I had to live with the embarrassing sensation of stockings sliding down my legs to my ankles.

Finally, I put on the black, tight-fitting gabardine dress that reached to the floor. I pulled the two front panels together, securing them with a line of straight pins to keep the front of my dress closed.

I wasn't finished. I watched, as my big sister folded a large square of snow-white linen to make the opposite corners meet, creating a shawl-like triangle doubled over. She made several folds at the center of the crease and pinned them together using a giant straight pin.

Motioning for me to turn around, she lifted the triangle that she called a fichu and placed the pinned folds at the nape of my neck. This allowed her to pass the rest of the fichu over my shoulders, letting it hang down in front of me.

Using sign language again, she showed me how to crisscross the fichu and cover my already-flattened chest. With more straight pins, she secured the two points at my waist. I heaved a sigh of relief when she finished. Still I wondered, why not hooks or snaps instead of pins?

Now she was ready to tackle the headdress. I could see that the cap part pushed out in the back. That space would be needed, as I wouldn't be getting a haircut until Habit-taking one and a-half years from now. The forward part of the coiffe was a wide, starched band that would encircle my face like blinders on a horse, before flowing over my shoulders. I put it on, pulling it tight and secure with a drawstring that I tied in a bow before tucking it under the coiffe in back.

Fully clothed and knowing I was pinned together, I slowly relaxed my muscles, until I was sure that no pin would prick me. I tied my rosary beads to the strings hanging at my waist, and I was ready to go.

I followed my big sister to the seminary room where the others, with eyes lowered, waited on benches without a sound. Sitting down next to my big sister on the spot she pointed to, I stole a glance to see if I could recognize the Sisters of my band who were mixed in with the older band. It was hard to pick them out.

We were almost anonymous now, our faces hidden by the blinders of our coiffes, our hair concealed, and our hands covered by our long sleeves.

The room was eerily silent. To my left, I saw a small altar with a statue of Blessed Mother on it. Lines of white wooden benches with a couple of slats on which to lean back faced a middle aisle monastic-style. Three or four Sisters sat on each bench, evenly spread out.

When Sister Directress entered, we all stood and faced the doorway, looking like statues, erect and still. The Sister-in-Office followed behind her like a shadow. After welcoming us and introducing her assistant Sister Margaret James, our new Superior gave us our first lecture, setting the tone for the austere life we would find in the Seminary. She made it clear that opportunities to grow in humility and self-abnegation would not be lacking. "This is the 'meat' of your formation and will show if you have what it takes to be Sisters in this religious community of women. Here in the Seminary I will focus instructions on the rules and charism of our holy founder Saint Vincent. Your job is to listen, learn and obey."

It was obvious that expectations of me would be no different from those of our first Sisters living in seventeenth-century France.

Sister Directress laid out a detailed schedule: 5 a.m. rising at the sound of the bell; meditation, vocal prayers and Mass in the chapel, followed by the serving of breakfast to the older Sisters; refectory clean-up after the silent breakfast, then the completion of assigned duties in time for the morning instruction on the virtues of our state and the perfection God expected of us; noon prayers in the chapel before the serving of dinner in the refectory; the reading of a "holy book" during the meal, followed by clean-up duties; thirty minutes of recreation sitting in our assigned seats in the seminary room. Always we were to remember religious decorum.

She reminded us that we always had to keep our fingers busy with darning or sewing, and beware of seeking out any particular Sister to talk to or befriend. At the sound of the bell, all conversations were to cease. Additional spiritual reading would follow, then another instruction on the proper behavior of Sisters. The afternoon reading would be taken from the conferences of Saint Vincent de Paul to the Sisters in the 1600's.

Upon the completion of each Sister's assigned duty, there would be a block of time for theology study or personal reading from a spiritual book—with heavy emphasis on the thirteenth-century writings of Thomas a Kempis. Silence would prevail for that hour until the sound of the bell calling us to evening meditation, more prayers, and sometimes the ritual called Benediction.

Next, we would serve supper; then eat, clean up, have another structured half-hour of recreation in our assigned places, say night prayers together; and finally, go to bed in silence.

Baths had to be taken at night before 9:30 p.m.—never in the morning or during the day. Sister Margaret James would be responsible for checking our alcoves to make sure we were in bed going to sleep, rather than puttering around after "lights out."

It was important that we get a good night's rest and wake up alert at the sound of the 5 a.m. bell. Upon hearing that bell, we must rise immediately, kneel and kiss the floor, say our first prayers of the day, and be in the chapel ready to pray with the other Sisters at exactly 5:30 a.m., Sister Directress said.

Just hearing the schedule took my breath away. At home I did not move very fast, so I would have to focus on keeping to my new schedule and doing things faster than I normally would. Then maybe—just maybe—my overcrowded schedule would make my homesickness go away.

When Sister Leo read the list of individual duties, I learned that my first assignment would be the cleaning of the visitors' parlors at the entrance to the seminary wing. Although seldom used, they had to be kept spotless at all times. I was glad that I wouldn't have to start out cleaning the lavatories that had so many stalls. That duty would come later.

Our Seminary Directress reminded us that common work was just that—all the work we were responsible for as a group: serving meals, clean-up after meals, and any other job we would be assigned to do.

Sister Leo then instructed us to kneel down and kiss the floor in submission. We immediately got down on our knees. Before reaching the floor, I started to hesitate. This did not make sense. The Seminary Sisters shuffled back and forth so often. Even though the floor was mopped daily, dust and dirt accumulated all day long.

Weren't there other ways to practice humility? I wondered. Was this really an act God demanded of us? That we say by our behavior we're no better than dirt? It was demeaning in addition to humbling.

Observing that my big sister had already kissed the floor without hesitating, I followed her example.

That first night in the Seminary I concentrated on getting my bedtime ritual right. I undressed in my alcove and draped my seminary dress over the chair, my fichu over the dress, then my corset over the fichu and my coiffe over that. I put on my night cap, tying it under my chin like a baby's bonnet. I picked up the night fichu—the large cotton square of cloth—and folded it into a triangle. Pulling it over my shoulders, I secured it in front with a straight pin.

Wearing the night fichu over my chemise and keeping on my petticoat, I would not use a robe anymore—from spring through winter. I put on my black slippers and left my shoes under the chair before picking up my nightgown and a white towel and washcloth, and heading down the hallway to the tubroom.

I waited in place with my eyes cast down, until a bathtub became available. Then I prepared to take a bath. I was glad that the custom of wearing a bathing chemise had been discontinued in recent years, and I could wash myself without undue contortions. I could not see any logic to the former practice that made the human body seem evil and mandated that it be covered up, even during a bath. Certainly that could not be an expression of modesty.

I removed the cloth "family" scapulars we wore around our neck and kept on the miraculous medal that hung on a chain beneath the scapulars. I sat in the tub and washed my body but not my hair. I could not wash my hair without permission. That would have to wait until the monthly hair-washing day would be posted.

I knelt down and kissed the floor in my alcove before saying my final prayers and kissing the floor one last time for the day. I removed my petticoat and got into bed wearing the night fichu pinned with a straight pin on top of my long white nightgown. I kept on my night cap that was tied under my chin, and I untangled my scapulars and the miraculous medal—hoping they wouldn't choke me while I was sleeping. I wasn't used to having so much around my neck at bedtime.

I lay in my bed surrounded by hanging sheets. I lay there motionless in the dark, listening to the gradual cessation of muffled sounds from other alcoves. A bell rang at 9:30 pm followed by absolute silence.

Five minutes later I was startled to see a light flashing in my alcove. I had forgotten that Sister Directress had told us the Sister-in-Office would periodically check up on us to make sure we were in bed and quiet after the last bell. It would be one of many tests of our obedience.

A week later, as Sister Directress led us from the chapel to the Seminary wing, she stopped abruptly and walked alongside our line, as if looking for someone. Alarms went off inside me, when she stopped and called me by name. "Sister Grueninger," she bellowed.

Following Sister Leo to the visitors' parlors, I could not imagine what was wrong. Not wanting to get in any trouble, I had gone to great pains to keep the room dust-free and the furniture exactly where it was the day I started cleaning it. Why, then, was she so upset?

I could not believe what happened next! Like a crazy woman she started yanking around the sofas and chairs, pushing and pulling everything she could grab hold of.

Immediately I fell to my knees and kissed the floor, while I gawked wide-eyed in disbelief. Finally, Sister Directress spoke up, "Sister Grueninger, what in the world are you trying to do with this room? Your duty is to keep it clean and arranged tastefully, yet you've kept it looking like a morgue from day one! Can't you do better than that? This is a seminary, not a funeral parlor!"

I knew from that day forward that in order to survive the Seminary I would have to make super-human efforts to control my emotional reactions and numb my feelings. I had to be tough-skinned and fight to overcome my sensitivity when treated harshly.

Exactly two weeks after our arrival in the Seminary, we officially became members of our Catholic Religious Order, on a day that would henceforth be called our Vocation Day. We lined up outside Sister Directress' office and, one by one, we entered and signed our names in a special book. Among other things, we relinquished rights to any "remuneration" for services given, if at some future time we were to leave the Community.

Since I had already spent six months in formation and was well-instructed on the lifetime commitment to my vocation that God expected of me, the thought of working for pay never crossed my mind. I was where God wanted me to be, doing what God wanted me to do. I was offering myself—my life, my time, and my services—to God. How could I even consider payment for serving my Creator? For devoting my life to Jesus? For ministering to His people? I signed the form and kissed the floor in submission without further thought.

It did not occur to me that without a paycheck, I would have no social security—and that, perhaps in the future, I might need it. But, shouldn't my Superiors have explained this to me? Were justice and truth lacking here? I had no way of knowing that twenty-two years into the future, I would leave—step out of the convent as a pauper.

We had two Seminary dresses to wear, one for Sundays and one for the rest of the week. We brushed them and aired them out on upper porches—the cleaning method used by our Sisters for three centuries. We did this weekly, rotating our two garments.

Sister Directress made it clear that the time and place for that task was very specific, and we were not allowed to forget to do it. Not wanting to be forced to confess to my Superior that I had failed to accomplish this, I racked my brain for a solution to that dilemma.

It had been years since I had communicated with my Guardian Angel. In the lower elementary grades at Saint Dominic's School, I used to follow the Sisters' advice and leave room for my angel to sit beside me in class. But, as I grew up, I became skeptical of the existence of guardian angels. And now I was desperate, so I made a deal.

"I used to talk to you, my Guardian Angel, when I was young. Then I started doubting your existence and I stopped. If you're really here with me, I need to ask for your help. You see how tough and inflexible my Seminary Directress is. Please don't let me forget what I'm supposed to do. Help me to remember, I beg you! I don't want to get into more trouble!"

My prayer sounded ridiculous—childish even. But so much that I was required to do was childish. Instead of making mature women of us, our Superiors were treating us like children, with their childish expectations of us. How could they put "childish women" to work in a meaningful way someday? Would their plans not backfire?

By May of the following year, it dawned on me that not once did I forget to take out, then bring in on time, the two seminary dresses allocated to me. Was gratitude due to my Guardian Angel, or was there a more reasonable explanation? I chose to believe that I did indeed have an angel watching over me, and I was thankful.

From the beginning of my seminary, however, it became obvious that airing out the dresses was not enough. Manual work caused the sweat to roll down my back. And not only was it a terrible feeling to have my wet clothes stick to me, but it made me wish I had access to a washing machine to soak out the smell.

Arduous physical work was never lacking, and the job I minded most was crawling around to clean the dirt out of the cracks between the ancient floorboards. I remember the first time I did it. The day was very hot, making me conscious of every layer of clothing that clung to my skin—sopping up the perspiration that poured out of me.

I wished I could rip off my drenched garments and soak myself luxuriously in a tub filled to the top with cold water. But seeking such personal gratification was out of my life forever—like so much that I took for granted before I crossed the convent threshold.

I was realizing that walking through that doorway marked a complete break with the world I once knew. The door slammed behind me and was now padlocked in my "mind's eye."

Kneeling with twenty-three other young women that day, I kissed the floor outside the chapel—a floor made of unvarnished boards that were well-worn by the shuffle of Sisters' feet for over a century. I struggled to blot out my feelings of debasement that always accompanied our practice of kissing the floor, and I ignored the cries of my pain-racked knees while I waited, staring down at the ever-widening cracks that seemed to laugh back at me with ridicule.

I started to look down at my hands, but they were hidden in my bulky sleeves. Fixing my eyes on the cracks again, a prophecy of doom echoed in my imagination: Forget about using your hands to mold your precious sculptures. Don't even contemplate playing a piano, while you hum your favorite tune.

All that's gone—gone forever. It's for the best, after all. It's God's Will, you know, and there's nothing better than doing God's Will. That's why you were born. And never, never forget you were promised to God at the age of three.

I snapped back to reality fast, when the tips of two well-shined black shoes and the hem of a long navy-blue woolen garment blocked the floor beneath my eyes. I felt like a slave about to perform a demeaning task in obedience to my master's command.

Folding back my sleeves, I cupped my hands, lifted them and waited—not daring to look up. Then, lowering my hands, I glanced at what they held: a straight pin that was bigger and thicker than any I was wearing. Placing it between the thumb and index finger of my right hand, I bent forward—still on my knees—and proceeded to dig. So much dirt had accumulated and lodged itself in the cracks that it kept on fighting me, as I attacked it with my pin. Some of it refused to budge, despite my best efforts.

"Keep at it, Sister," I heard a voice say. "Get all the dirt out of those cracks. Do it like a good Sister. It's God's Will for you at this moment."

Her words puzzled me. I always thought God had more important things on His mind. Why would He worry about the clogged cracks in an old hardwood floor? Stopping wars, forgiving sinners and redirecting their lives, alleviating poverty and hunger, ridding the earth of evil—weren't these the things that really mattered to the God we prayed to?

After removing the debris from the cracks in front of me, I crawled forward and started cleaning out the dirt in another area I claimed for myself.

I wished I could chuckle—even laugh—to dispel the tension, as I listened to the scraping noises that made me think of chipmunks scratching away rhythmically, breaking the sounds of silence that permeated the corridor outside the chapel.

Stiff and sore from crawling around, I wanted to get up and stretch my arms and legs—run or kick for a few seconds to get my blood circulating again. But I knew such behavior would not be tolerated. Believing I had no other choice, I succumbed to passivity like the other novices crawling near me.

Struggling to use "mind over matter" and be an obedient Sister, I kept working at the feet of the Sister overseeing the job—awaiting her assessment that the floor was clean enough.

When she gave the signal, I lined up with my band and walked in a column to the seminary wing. With my eyes cast down and my lips sealed, I secretly wiggled my cramped fingers hidden in my long sleeves, and I thanked God I could exercise my legs at last.

More than once, we were assigned to clean the dirt out of the cracks between the boards that were splitting apart in the old floor outside the chapel. It was a humbling task that reinforced my sense of worthlessness. I tried to offer my degradation to God, but found it hard to believe it was really God's Will for me then and there, as I was told.

It was a happy day when I saw workmen put down linoleum and cover up the hardwood floor. I wanted to shout out, "Hurrah! No more crawling around like an insect to clean the filth out of the cracks!"

How I wanted to celebrate that occasion, as I walked past the workers with my eyes lowered and my hands buried in my sleeves on my way to the chapel. Could they not read my mind or at least hear my silent chuckle?

But in my new life I yearned for so much more than replacing old floors with linoleum. I wanted opportunities to relax after wearing myself out doing strenuous physical labor.

If only I could run down the dusty road that cut through the Sisters' old farm, inhale deeply, and savor the scent of fragrant wildflowers. If I could stop and watch the birds, and even glory in a sunrise.

After a long morning filled with non-stop chores, I longed to have the comfort of throwing myself across my bed—even for five minutes.

I would have to put up with the horrible feeling of layer upon layer of wetness sucking the very life out of me. Taking an extra bath during the day or taking off damp clothing and replacing it with dry clothes was never permitted; so I reluctantly obeyed. And somehow, I succeeded in doing just that over and over again.

One day I was in the chapel with the others meditating. We knelt for the first half, then sat back in the pew for the remainder of the time. When the Sisters knelt to conclude the prayers, I felt stuck to the back of the pew. All the layers of my clothing were already saturated with perspiration and sticking to me. But now they wanted to "glue" themselves to the varnish on the pew. I felt like I was tearing myself away, maybe leaving some of my fichu stuck to the pew.

As I followed the double column of Sisters to the refectory, I started feeling self-conscious. Some Sisters seemed to be stealing glances at me. One even had to muffle a laugh. I couldn't imagine what was wrong. Had I really left part of my fichu stuck to the pew in the chapel?

I served supper, helped clean up, then headed to the seminary room for our allotted thirty minutes of recreation time seated in our assigned places on the white benches. Leaning back, I once again felt myself sticking to the furniture.

My companions burst out laughing, but stopped abruptly when Sister Margaret James walked over to learn the reason for their boisterous behavior. "Look at her back," someone blurted out, struggling to suppress a laugh.

The Sister in charge told me to stand and turn around. Then, finding it hard to keep a straight face, she said, "Sister, tonight we'll have to find you a clean fichu to wear in the morning. Try to keep it white this time—not colored like a rainbow."

That night, when I undressed for bed, I was amazed to find my fichu soaked through from perspiration. It was heavily-stained with the colors of the cloth scapulars I wore underneath my clothes—blue, red, green, and brown. No wonder I made a spectacle of myself. Still, had I been permitted to take off my wet clothes and replace them with dry clothing, even take an extra bath, my embarrassment and discomfort could have been alleviated.

Nights were cold in the late spring. The mountain air would blow in and keep the dormitory temperature unbearably low. Often I'd end up getting a sinus headache. The stress of my new lifestyle added tension headaches. And, before long, I found myself having headaches of migraine proportions.

Another dilemma causing more stress was just what I didn't need. As much as I hated to, I approached Sister Leo to report my health problems. The coldness with which she responded served to frustrate me even more.

"I'll give you something to take for your headache this time, Sister Grueninger. But servants of the Lord can't pamper themselves. If you expect to do God's work, you can't be centered on yourself."

I took the pill she gave me, thanked her, and kissed the floor. When my headaches intensified, I tried hard to put up with them— ignore them even. When I could no longer endure the pain, I went back to her.

"I'm sorry to bother you, Sister Directress, and I don't want to pamper myself, but my headaches are so bad, I can't concentrate on my work or my prayers without taking some medication."

Her eyes pierced mine, as she glared at me in silence before speaking up. "Sister Grueninger, have you heard anything I've said in my instructions about our Sisters and their health?"

"You say that Daughters of Charity never get sick. And I've tried to obey, but my headaches are unbearable."

Sister Directress shook her head and looked at me, "That's right. Now, if our Sisters never get sick, doesn't that mean they should not have to take a lot of medicine?"

"Yes, Sister," I said. By now, I was kneeling at her feet kissing the floor.

"I'll give you something again for your headache. But, remember this, Sister, you could be jeopardizing your vocation by making requests like this."

That was the last time I approached Sister Leo to report a headache and ask for medication. From then on, I struggled to use "mind over matter." And I dragged myself through those days, even when I thought my head would explode.

I followed all of my Religious Community's policies: I did not slow down in my work assignments, and I did not sneak back to my dormitory and throw myself across my bed. I was determined not to pamper myself and risk additional humiliation or worse.

One day, as the other Seminary Sisters lined up to go to the chapel for meditation in the late afternoon, I made a quick detour. I thought that, if I hurried, I could probably get to the restroom and back, before the others finished filing out of our Seminary wing and down the corridor. I knew I couldn't make it through meditation, prayers, and supper without that stop.

So, with my eyes lowered, I rushed down a second hallway toward the restroom, when suddenly, I looked up—startled to see Sister Leo blocking my path. The look in her eyes told me she was displeased with me again.

"Sister Grueninger, aren't you supposed to be on your way to the chapel with the other Seminary Sisters?"

I fell to my knees and kissed the floor, realizing I was in trouble.

"Yes, Sister," I replied, my voice quivering.

"Then why are you here, instead of there?"

"I needed to use the restroom, Sister."

"Are you never going to learn? You are always coddling yourself. How do you expect to become a Habit Sister, behaving that way?"

"I won't let it happen in the future, Sister."

"Listen to me carefully, if you want to make progress and reach your goal of becoming a full-fledged Sister. Regarding your need to use the restroom, remember this: the more you go, the more you create the need to go. I'll grant you permission now. But, after this, go to the restroom before the study hour."

As she walked off, I kissed the floor again. I wished I had been allowed to speak up and explain what had happened—that I did go before study time, and I just needed to go again. But, according to seminary policy, I did not have the right to defend myself.

So, after that incident, I followed her orders. Even when I thought my bladder would burst, I made myself wait until after study time, prayers and meditation, meals and clean-up were over, before allowing myself to seek relief. I obeyed like a good Seminary Sister without concern for my health, ignoring my body's cries for compassion.

The Sisters ate in a huge refectory that was big enough to hold a small army of Sisters. There we sat on backless benches made of dark wood, as we nourished our bodies and our souls while eating and listening to more spiritual reading.

Each of us had her own white plate, white cup, plain glass and flatware, which consisted of a metal knife, fork, and spoon. These we kept wrapped up in a large white linen napkin.

The long tables that seated 10-12 Sisters had an aluminum pan at each end, with one in the middle. At serving time we would put pitchers of hot, soapy water in each pan. Then, as we finished eating, we would use sign language to ask for a pitcher and pan to wash our dishes, after scraping our plate into the little tin garbage bowl.

Since I was usually one of the slowest eaters, I had to get used to washing my dishes in the dirty water left in the bottom of the pan by the Sisters who had already used it.

But that's not why I came to hate mealtime.

We could leave nothing on our plate after a meal, except for bones. To scrape off anything else, we had to get permission by approaching Sister Directress and making that request kneeling at her feet.

I got to the point where I hated to cut fruit open. If there was a rotten peach in the bowl, I would somehow end up with it; and since we were required to take a serving of every food on the table, I could not ignore the fruit.

Before long, my dread of humiliating myself during meals became a self-fulfilling prophecy. My stomach would get so tied up in knots worrying, that I frequently could not finish my whole meal. I turned into the red-faced Seminary Sister who crept over the hardwood floor carrying my plate to Sister Directress' side, while a few hundred Sisters ate in silence, listening to the reading and to my footsteps on the creaky floorboards. I thought I could read their minds:

"There she goes again. The Seminary Sister who wishes the floor would swallow her up on her way to Sister Directress' table, carrying her worthless leftovers."

I would go to Sister Directress where she ate, kneel and try to kiss the floor without dropping my plate, lift it and show her what was left, while asking permission to throw it away. Then I would retrace my steps. Embarrassed in front of the whole Community, I came to feel like a groveling dog wishing I had a kinder master.

Confession was a big part of our Seminary programming. On a weekly basis Sister Margaret James would line us up and escort us to a small basement chapel that was aptly named Holy Agony Chapel. In the semi-darkness we would examine our consciences for the slightest taint of sin, as we focused our eyes on a statue of Mary holding the body of Jesus at the foot of the cross following His crucifixion.

After scraping the bottom of our soul, we would enter the dark confessional and confess through a grate to a hazy image of a priest the sins or imperfections we uncovered. Then we would say our penance, usually three Hail Marys.

After watching to see that all of us had accomplished that requirement, the Sister in charge would march us back to the Seminary wing. On Fridays we participated in a practice called the Conference of Faults. Kneeling as a group in the Seminary Room, facing the statue of Blessed Mother, we accused ourselves individually of failures against Community rules and policies.

Nothing in our lives now could escape scrutiny and the repercussion of guilt. We would have to confess aloud such things as breaking silence, laughing, glancing at our reflection in a windowpane, or raising our lowered eyes to enjoy a moment of stolen pleasure—like peeking at the sun setting over the mountain.

I never got used to this weekly spiritual exercise. Even after years and years of experience with it, my stomach would always be tied up in knots when my turn came to admit how I failed to live up to expectations. Guilt piled itself upon guilt.

While we were told over and over again that we were nothing, that we should delight in our nothingness, I felt violated and annihilated.

Only once did I find the Conference of Faults humorous. That was when a younger Sister spoke up and said, "I ask pardon for breaking the rule of silence. I talked to a cat when I took out the garbage."

It was all I could do to suppress a laugh. Her accusation highlighted the ridiculousness of some of our practices, including that very act of accusing ourselves of so-called faults.

On a daily basis after dinner, Sister Directress would make herself available for another kind of confession. In the large bare room adjacent to the Seminary Room, she would sit like a judge at a massive desk situated in the middle of the room. We would line up a short distance away and await our turn to approach her.

Then we would walk up to her desk, kneel in front of it, kiss the floor, and keeping a humble, penitential posture, confess our failures.

In response she would give us "spiritual charity." That is, she would tell us what we had to do to better ourselves and reach perfection.

I found it a real challenge whenever I had to confess breaking something, because we had to carry a piece of the broken item in one of our deep pockets, until we could get to Sister Directress after dinner. It was hard to carry a broken needle without getting stuck by it, but I managed to find a way.

On days when I interrupted her meal by asking permission to throw away my leftovers, I would have to ask pardon for this, too, in Sister Directress' after-dinner lineup.

So, over and over again, as she sat at her ominous desk, she would repeat what was becoming a recurring refrain, "Sister Grueninger, I cannot recommend you for the Holy Habit, as long as you're like this."

I had to listen in silence with my hands hidden in my sleeves, kneeling across from her. Afterwards, I kissed the floor, then walked away with lowered eyes and lowered head and lower self-esteem.

Probably I should have held my head up high and said, "Sister Directress, if you did not make such unreasonable and ridiculous demands of me, I wouldn't be like this. You are destroying my self-esteem and self-confidence. The independence I developed while working for a year after high school is disappearing, thanks to you!" But I couldn't even think such thoughts without feeling guilty.

The Seminary was taking an emotional toll on me, and I believed I could do nothing about it. I struggled hard to hold on to the optimism I had grown up with and not allow pessimism to take its place. I did not understand what was happening to me—nor why.

That June my sister Carole graduated from high school, and I couldn't wait for my summer visit with her and all of my family. I congratulated Carole when I saw her and wished my brother "Godspeed," when he announced that he had joined the Army and would be leaving for boot camp soon.

I thought back to the happy times we had enjoyed at home—and funny experiences too. Like the time when Mother and Dad had gone grocery shopping and a dispute arose in the kitchen between

Carole and Mel. Carole was at the end of her rope with his teasing, when she turned around, opened the ice box, and slung a slab of meat at him. Instinctively, Mel ducked and the meat shattered the china closet glass, landing inside. It wasn't funny at the time, but years later we would laugh about it.

And I recalled good times at Carlin's Amusement Park. How we loved having fun on the rides and swimming in the pool there in the summertime.

Shortly before I left for the convent, Carole, Melvin, and my younger sister Anne had insisted on taking me to the amusement park for one last fling.

I discovered horses that day. After flirting with the attendant, I spent the afternoon riding a horse around the course over and over again for free. Knowing it was my first exhilarating experience of the kind and probably my last, I wanted to ride and ride and never stop riding.

It was too bad we had to grow up and go our separate ways. I was finding my way as a Sister, at least trying to. Mel was going off to God knows where in the military. And Carole was on the verge of making a major life change. She broke the news that she would be getting married.

"Can you come to my wedding?" she asked. I felt a tearing in my heart, as I tried to hide my emotion.

"You know I can't, Carole." I wanted to add how much I wished I could be there to share her big day, but I stopped myself. I was supposed to be detached from my family by now, not have any desire to be part of such gatherings that the secular world celebrated and I was forced to reject.

When the time came to part, I hugged each one, not wanting to let them go. My heart went out to Mother and Dad who had three losses to deal with in less than two years. Anne too would be affected, losing her three siblings. It seemed cruel and heartless to leave her at home without either of her sisters, when she was just an eighth grader with so much growing up to do.

I wanted to be at home for Mel's departure party and for Carole's wedding. My two hiking companions with whom I had shared so many wonderful hours of innocent fun were going off on their own, and I couldn't be there for their ritual send-offs. The pain cut deep.

I found myself wishing I could be at home to console Anne in her lonely moments, listen to her teenage problems, and offer advice from my own experience. I wanted to be there to help her dress for her proms and affirm her choice of a career. I was her big sister after all—the oldest girl in the family.

It was excruciating not to feel like a member of my family anymore, and it was so hard to conceal my feelings that day. I was torn between my love for my family and my belief that God wanted me to make whatever sacrifices my new life demanded of me.

Still, pleasant memories refused to be subdued. I thought of the times I paddled the canoe with Dad and picnicked at Loch Raven with the whole family. I remembered splashing in the water at Rocky Point with Carole and Melvin; and teaching Anne a "peanut song" I ad-libbed, as I held her hand and walked to a neighborhood store for a loaf of bread.

I recalled walking that same route with my brother and sisters to get a five-cent ice cream cone at High's. And I remembered roaming the area around our home trick-or-treating each Halloween, and sleigh-riding down our street in the snow.

I could still see Mother helping me to get dressed for my proms and giving me perms at home. And how could I forget the Thanksgiving and Christmas celebrations with my family, including Mom Mom— Dad's mother who lived with us, and special feasts at Aunt Elsie and Uncle Ed's house.

So many memories refused to be erased, despite my attempts to forget them. The tension between family ties and the bond my new Community was forging with me was agonizing—I felt cut in half.

Sister Directress had a Vincentian advisor. Tall and robust and in his thirties, he was all-intellect as he began to teach us Theology. Everything was "black and white" in his teaching and, as he reinforced

Sister Directress' instructions, he emphasized the Community's interpretation of the vow of obedience.

"Don't think about what you are told to do. Just do it, because that's what you're told to do. When Superiors speak, believe that they speak in God's Name." He was preaching blind obedience.

As I reflected on the priest's words, I found myself in disagreement on some issues. It didn't make sense never to evaluate what I was ordered to do. Human beings could make mistakes. They were not perfect. But guilt set in once more. I was not supposed to doubt or wonder about my Community's teachings or any of the Catholic Church's doctrines, for that matter. So, I bowed my head in submission and put a stop to mental questioning.

One day, in passing Sister Leo's office, I heard that same priest talking to her inside the room. "I'll be gone for a while," he said. "I'll be going home to visit my mother."

That shocked me. Here, the priest who was training us to obey blindly—which meant never going home even for a short visit—was giving himself that joy. What a contradiction!

It was the first time I noticed the double standard for Saint Vincent's priests and sisters.

Another priest was sent to teach us Theology, this time from Mount Saint Mary's on the mountain nearby. One day the postulant Mildred got him off on a tangent by asking about the Hungarian Revolution. She had overheard someone talking about it outside the Seminary wing and wanted to know more of what was going on in the world outside.

Now, we should have known this would get reported to Sister Directress, either by Sister Margaret James, who always sat behind us during class, or by one of our number. And, sure enough, the next time we assembled for an instruction in the Seminary Room, Sister Directress gave us a tongue-lashing. She harangued about our blatant disobedience in inquiring about the secular world and discussing topics off limits to the Seminary Sisters.

In her way of thinking, all of us were equally guilty of this "crime" that must never be repeated. "Never again!" she cried out. And her message came through loud and clear. No one dared to repeat that transgression.

Many years later, I would learn that in America there were other revolutions taking place at the time. A woman named Rosa Parks had sparked what would be called the Civil Rights Movement. And a man by the name of Elvis Presley had ushered in a revolution in music, giving birth to what the world would call "rock and roll."

Being sequestered from secular society, I knew nothing about any of this. I couldn't rejoice in the advancement of human rights. Nor could I enjoy the evolution of a new kind of rhythm. No one mentioned these or other significant happenings to us.

The world scene and the American scene with their evolving history and culture would become a blank in my mind for years to come. I was living in a vacuum now, and I was supposed to accept this as God's Will for me.

Was it part of a bigger plan to annihilate my feelings? In being deprived of the love of family and the love of a man, and being denied any access to the outside world, what was left for my emotions, except to wither and die?

A naive nineteen year old, I simply adopted this practice of severing ties with secular society, of turning away from the world that I was taught to believe was full of evil and could only taint the goodness I was striving for.

The convent books on holiness bombarded our ears with that philosophy. Thomas a Kempis, a thirteenth-century monk whose writings in the Imitation of Christ were constantly read to us, and our own founder Saint Vincent dePaul, whose seventeenth-century conferences to our first Sisters were repeated over and over again, kept preaching those ideas to us. And my ears listened until I could almost recite the words verbatim.

Much of what I was being taught confused me. Still, I struggled to keep myself focused on one thing: the belief that God had called me to religious life—had bestowed on me a vocation and expected me to carry out His Will as it was communicated to me by my Superiors.

The docile student in Catholic schools had evolved into the docile little Sister in formation. It was a logical transition, given the thinking that prevailed in the 1950's in American society and in the Catholic Church.

I turned twenty that winter and my Seminary training was drawing to a close. For nearly two years I had lived within the massive walls of a fortress-like structure that reflected the coldness and loneliness that now enveloped me.

My Superiors had forged me like molten steel and poured the contents into a mold of their own making. They had succeeded in controlling my thinking until I believed that, in turning my life over to them, I had placed myself in God's Hands.

On an appointed day, I lined up with the other Seminary Sisters and waited. When my turn came, I approached Sister Directress timidly, knelt and kissed the floor—then asked the big question: "May I receive the Holy Habit?"

It was an awesome utterance that put me at a crossroads. Either reply would set me in a radical direction. I would become a nun and devote my life to God's service. Or I would be sent home—free to pursue my own interests and set my own goals, free to follow my heart and fall in love again.

No longer capable of making my own decisions, I placed my future in Sister Directress' hands. And so I listened intently when she spoke up.

"Sister Grueninger, you are still far from the perfection God demands of you. A lot of work has to be done before you will be fit to have the Community use you in God's service. I'm going to allow you to receive the Holy Habit, knowing that your band will have another year of formation here at the Provincial House."

"Thank God you are privileged to be in the first band to have a third year of training, a year that will ensure your readiness to go out into the world while being faithful to all you've been taught."

Sister Directress' "yes," even with conditions, gave me the answer I needed. I would go forward, believing I was doing what God called me to do, what He kept me alive for.

Still, these two years had changed me. I was no longer the independent, carefree young woman I once was. My feelings were now submerged under the garb of a Sister. A part of me felt caged, like I was in a prison. Surrounded by scores of other Sisters in the Provincial House, I felt alone, isolated.

Although I worked and prayed as a Sister in a family of Sisters, I felt like a woman without ties—exiled—distant from the members of my own band. Did being a Sister mean living in solitary confinement on meager rations of moral support? The life—full of losses—was choking me. I felt like I was dying a slow death.

But weren't these thoughts mere temptations? By taking each day one at a time I had made it this far. By continuing to follow that pattern and rely on God's grace, I would make it up that rugged mountain I would have to climb.

621 days had passed since I left home. I missed my brown-shingled house and all its memories. Above all, I missed my loved ones.

4.

The Final Smelting

Staring at the monotonous medley of inkspots that ran aimlessly across the linoleum floor, I stood there. I could hear the faint sound of snipping scissors, as I moved forward in a line that was growing shorter. Somewhere in the distance a clock chimed the hour, probably the clock outside the chapel that communicated the time every fifteen minutes all day long everyday. Since we lived by a schedule and wore no watch, chiming clocks were crucial.

"It's your turn, Sister Grueninger." Sister Directress' voice broke into my mental meanderings. I followed her into a room and sat in a chair she pointed to.

"Remove your coiffe, Sister."

As I watched her put my coiffe aside, I took a nervous deep breath. An uneasy quiet surrounded me. I felt her lift the long braid that now hung down my back. For the past year and a half I had washed my hair monthly, but no haircuts were permitted. I had kept my hair braided, according to instructions, and wrapped it in a coil, before securing it with bobby pins and forcing it into the coiffe I wore.

Since mirrors were considered the devil's source of temptation for women, I rarely saw my reflection. But I could remember how my hair looked when I curled it, and I never forgot how it felt when Bob would run his fingers through my hair leaving me with goosebumps. Here in the Seminary I occasionally glided my hand along the braid before putting on my night cap and I could imagine what it looked like.

Sister Directress spoke up, "Are you willing to have this done?" Grasping scissors in her hand, she waited for my answer.

I snapped back to reality. Was she going to trim my hair or cut it all off? I still didn't know what to expect. I responded with a simple "yes," keeping my questions to myself.

Sister Directress went to work with her scissors. First, she cut off the whole braid, then trimmed my hair very short. I heaved a sigh of relief. She didn't shave all my hair off.

As I got up to leave, I glanced down at the box of braids at Sister Leo's feet. They were a mixture of blond, brown, red and black. For a moment I visualized my hair becoming a wig for a doll. While my hair would make an inanimate object more attractive, it would no longer frame my face and make me feel good about myself. And it would no longer be an expression of my personal identity—a symbol of who I used to be.

A week later the Sister-in-Office took over the hair-cutting chore. I was shocked when I watched her plug in an electric razor and proceed to shave my entire head with no explanation. How humiliated I felt! Was she angry with me? Would I have a bald head for the rest of my life?

The shaving of a Sister's head was a practice that had come down from the Middle Ages, I soon learned. Without hair, a woman could not be vain, and that proved true for me. I hated to have to keep my head shaved.

Was it meant to reinforce my anonymity? Was it a way to remind me that I was merely a cog in a wheel, subservient to my Superiors? At the time, I could not answer those questions, much less ask them.

From then on, I would have to wear two hats to bed, a knitted white watch cap to keep my sheared head warm and a plain baby bonnet that I tied under my chin to hold the inner cap in place.

The next day in the Seminary wing, the big event—Habit-taking— took place without ceremony and without onlookers present. First, I opened my trousseau and put on my new undergarments. My anticipation mounted, as I gazed down at the main parts of a Sister's Habit.

70

It was hard to believe that I was actually going to wear that Habit and dress like the other Sisters who came before me. Even in 1957 there was a mystique attached to the wearing of the revered Holy Habit that dated back three centuries. Although humility was supposed to be one of my Religious Order's hallmarks, the Sisters wore this Habit with a sense of pride. It was distinctive and made our religious congregation stand out among all others.

Now, throughout my training I had heard over and over again that pride was sinful and no attachments would be tolerated. But in this case an exception was made. Our Holy Habit signified who we were—that we had a special Call from God. So, pride in our wearing apparel could only reinforce the gratitude that should fill our hearts and souls for the wonderful gift of vocation. That's what my Superiors seemed to proclaim.

I had seen Sisters dressed this way from my earliest years at Saint Dominic's. Still, I never reflected that the garment was French; never considered its origin, seventeenth-century dress of village girls; never noticed its color was navy blue, while most Orders of Sisters wore black.

Our founder Saint Vincent de Paul had been exposed to the horrors of poverty, injustice and cruelty from his earliest years as a priest. When he was traveling off the southern coast of France, pirates seized his ship and made him a galley slave. Eventually, he was sold into slavery in Tunisia, before being freed years later by a merciful master.

He never lost sight of the images of people savagely treated. Back in France, he was appalled to see still more horrors. Hospitals squeezed sick people in overcrowded beds, while others lay on the floor waiting to grab the place of a newly-expired patient. Beggars drew attention to themselves on city street corners by mutilating foundlings that lay abandoned. The poor, especially girls, had no chance of getting an education. Poverty led to rampant crime.

Determined to right the wrongs he saw around him, Saint Vincent organized wealthy women into Ladies of Charity. When he observed the women sending their servants to do the dirty work, he began to assemble and train country girls. Wanting to create a new Religious

Order of women out of this nucleus, he was determined to get around the Catholic Church's Canon Law of the day. It mandated that nuns take permanent vows and live cloistered lives out of public view. His Sisters wore the gray—blue attire of village girls with a distinctive provincial headdress, instead of veils; and they took temporary vows that would be renewed annually. He called them Sisters to distinguish them from nuns. In this manner, he wanted to ensure that no member of the hierarchy could force them into a cloister. He was determined to use his Sisters for active work ministering to the needs of the poor.

He persisted until the Pope approved his plan and made his Order of Sisters a papal congregation not subject to any bishop or archbishop in their internal affairs. The Pope, ultimately, would be accountable. That was in the year 1633.

But, as time went on, the letter of the rules often became more important than the spirit of the rules, and no adaptations to changes in culture were made. Male dominance remained fixed. And, while Saint Vincent also created an organization of men who would be priests and brothers, a double standard for the men and women evolved, reflecting the thinking of society at large.

But on May 22, 1957, 1 was just twenty and very gullible. I was ignorant of the ways of the world and the role politics played, even in Religious Orders. I was brainwashed in how I was to think and act and speak. So, as I looked down at the Holy Habit I was about to wear for the first time, I anticipated the event.

I put on the navy blue woolen skirt that reached down to the floor, noticing the deep kick pleats in the back that made it extra heavy. Next, I picked up the stiffly-starched white collar that was intended to cover my torso, and I pinned its tail to my waistband in the back with a straight pin. Then I pulled the woolen chemisette with its long bulky sleeves over my shoulders, slipped it under my collar that hung down in the front like a starched dickie and secured it with hooks at the closure.

I was relieved not to have to keep it closed with straight pins, as I did with the seminary dress. But I did have to pin shut the stiff neckband of my collar. For this I used a straight pin that was thick and long, unlike any I had seen before.

All that was left was to put on the long matching wool apron and the headdress. After tying the apron on, I watched as a Habit Sister showed me how to pin together the first three pieces of the cornette, until they fit snug on my head. I observed in amazement, while she bent the long, starched rectangle of white linen and pinned it to the inner part she had just put together. Picking it up, she forced it onto my head in its cumbersome form.

She "pulled" my first cornette until it took shape and hugged my face. Then she lowered and extended the wings on both sides. Kneeling in the Seminary Room for that ritual, I felt a sense of exhilaration. This is what all my training was leading up to. It was a privilege to dress like the Sisters of the past three centuries, and it felt good and right as I basked in the emotion of the moment. I reached up and ran my fingers along the wings that hovered over my head.

"I am finally a Daughter of Charity!" I thought. "My life will get better now that I am a Habit Sister."

Still, I would have to learn to do a balancing act with such large and bulky headgear, and I would have to get used to having my face partially-concealed and locked in place. In the coming days, I would have to relearn how to judge distances from people and things. For a while, I would have to consciously think about keeping my head upright.

As I resumed my life in my new attire, I found it a challenge. My eyes were now shielded on two sides, as if I were a horse wearing blinders. I had to turn my head fully to see from left to right.

Before long I developed a terrible headache. Eventually, I figured out that the inner three-piece frame was too small, making the cornette painfully tight on my head. Although I had a petite body, my head was large and I needed a bigger "bonnie."

Even with that accommodation, I usually developed a headache on Sunday, the first day I wore a newly-pulled cornette. After the starch gave a little in the course of the week and was not so stiff, the cornette relaxed on my head and was not so uncomfortable.

It took me an hour to put together a new cornette, so I "pulled" it on Saturday afternoons and tried to make it last a whole week by avoiding birds flying overhead and the rain.

It took time to get used to the feel of my Holy Habit and adjust to a different way of walking and carrying myself. I was afraid of having my cornette fall off and being ridiculed for having no hair.

I had heard that a Sister did lose her cornette in public. She was riding in the back of a Sisters' station wagon in the summer with the windows wide open, when suddenly the wind lifted the headgear off her head. The cornette went sailing through the air into the lane of traffic behind her.

The thought of such a thing happening was horrifying. I could feel the Sister's shame in being seen with a bald head.

I was wearing navy blue and white now, the only colors I'd be wearing for the rest of my life, I thought. There would be no variety in the color or type of clothing I would wear. Not anymore.

My days of donning my favorite red brocade dress for dances at the Alcazar ballroom were long gone. So were my summer dances in my black halter dress on the moonlight cruises in Baltimore Harbor.

And my feet would no longer strut in fancy high heels strapped at my ankles. I would be restricted to wearing low-heeled shoes—Sisters' footgear that tied with shoestrings. It was unbelievable that I could make such drastic changes in my life!

Soon, we lined up for a private visit with Sister Visitatrix. It was an event we looked forward to, since she was the one who would officially give us a Community name. At that time, Sisters in our Province either kept their baptismal names or received a combination of their parents' names. With Mother's name being Annie Carroll and Dad's being Melvin Albert, I hoped I would be given my own name. But that might be a problem. There was another Patricia in my band.

When my turn came, I entered the Provincial Superior's office looking awkward and feeling like an unworthy servant. I knelt beside her where she sat and tried to kiss the floor. But now, wearing a protruding cornette, I could no longer bend that low.

Sister Visitatrix handed me a holy card, while wishing me holy perseverance. And she called me by name. I was no longer Sister Grueninger. My community name was now Sister Patricia Anne, my own name. I felt relieved. Soon after, I learned that the other Pat became Sister John Mildred.

Later on, after taking a good look at my name as Sister Visitatrix wrote it on the holy card, I discovered that the "e" on Anne had been left off. To me, that "e" was important, since Anne was a family name. Timidly, I approached Sister Directress, who was still our band's Superior, and I explained the problem.

"I was baptized Patricia Anne with an 'e' on Anne. Its omission when Sister Visitatrix wrote it down was probably an oversight. May I put the 'e' back on my name?"

"Sister Patricia Ann, take the name Sister Visitatrix bestowed on you and be satisfied," she responded. "It shouldn't make any difference. Practice the obedience and humility you've been taught."

And so, I would have to keep on misspelling my name, until years later when Sister Eleanor would become Visitatrix. Then I could ask again and finally receive permission.

The distraction of the misspelling made me overlook an important implication. Giving my Provincial Superior the authority to name or re-name me was giving her power over me. Many decades later, I would learn that the biblical meaning of "naming" something gave power over it.

A major event was imminent. We were about to be assigned our Community work or what externs called their career. I had always hoped to be a social worker. But, as blind obedience was drilled into me, and I became aware of the Community's need for teachers to keep costs down for pastors who were ultimately in charge of the parish schools, I began to have misgivings.

I held my breath, when Sister Directress assembled us for the big announcement. And I listened hard to her words as she spoke.

"The two nurses among you will be assigned to a hospital. Sister Mary Eileen, who has had some college training, will be sent out in a short time to teach. The rest of you will begin a course of study in education. When you finish, you will be missioned to elementary schools to do God's work as teachers. Thank Him!"

Thank Him? I couldn't believe my ears! I was being put into teaching, after all! I was speechless! The last thing I wanted to do was become a teacher. Again, I remembered my strong reaction the time my Mother suggested that I become a teacher. I had shouted back, "I'll never be a teacher!"

And here I was at another crossroads—with no choice, I believed. With no redress, unable to question the decision of my Superiors to arbitrarily make me a teacher without giving me the opportunity to have input or even respond.

At the age of three Mother had promised me to God, set me on a path over which I believed I had no control, giving me a direction in life without asking me. Now, after almost three years of formation, my Superiors were repeating that pattern by putting me into teaching and giving me no say in the matter—simply telling me to accept it as God's Will and just do it.

I had gone through fire, so to speak, in order to make it through my training. I had accepted everything and anything that came my way. The pain. The humiliation. The loneliness. The homesickness. And what did it get me? A lifetime as a teacher? My heart sank, as the realization soaked in.

The notion of blind obedience had been pounded into my brain. Deep down I knew what that meant and I had feared being assigned to teach. But I had kept myself in a state of denial. After all, hadn't Sister Andrew emphasized the diverse works of the Community when I mentioned my disdain for teaching, before agreeing to be a Sister? Had she not led me to believe that I could become a social worker, maybe?

"Dear God, please don't do this to me!" I should have cried out. Better still, I should have marched myself to Sister Visitatrix's office and said simply, "I won't do it. I refuse to be a teacher! If I have no other choice, I'll leave. I'll go home."

Instead, I went to the chapel and prayed, "You know how I hate the thought of becoming a teacher, Lord. It feels like a sentence worse than death. Is this really your Will for me? Can you be so unfeeling that you keep inflicting suffering on me time and time again? Give me the answers I need! Stop being silent, when I'm in dire need of your help! Please, Lord!"

Visiting day came in June, when my family would see me for the first time since Habit-taking. It was a sweltering day, and I could feel my layers of clothing cling to my skin. As I perspired, the starch of my cornette wilted against my cheeks. I knew what that meant. My "wings" would flop and fall lower. Even my high-necked collar that was starched so stiffly would become soft from sweat and stick to my neck.

Despite my discomfort, I let myself feel a sense of pride, as I looked into the eyes of my parents and my siblings—eyes that were filled with awe. I had made it to this point overcoming most of the obstacles. In the eyes of the world, even my own family, I was now a nun.

I took a long look at Mother's countenance. Off and on through the years I had felt angry, enraged that she had promised me to God. Yet, deep down I knew that everything she ever did for me, she did out of love. When I lay dying, she had poured out her agony to God. She wanted to buy me more time—time to live—by offering me to be a Bride of Christ. And God evidently agreed, because here I was, fulfilling that promise.

I reasoned there must be a plan in Heaven that was beyond my understanding right now.

I looked at my Mother with compassion. My good Mother. And I hoped she saw the forgiveness that was in my eyes. It must have been hard for her to see me dressed in the Habit of a Sister. Although her faith was deep, she must have realized that, in giving me to God, she had lost her first-born daughter in a very real sense. For I would no longer be at her side, except for these rare and special moments when she came on visiting days.

She could not pick up the telephone and hear my voice. Mother could not even pour out her soul truthfully to me in a letter. And she would never cuddle grandchildren who came from my flesh.

As always, Mother succeeded in covering up her heartache, in suppressing her pain. And I was doing likewise.

My family had been there for just an hour, when the bell tolled. That meant I would have to join the other Sisters for noon prayers and dinner, leaving my parents and siblings to picnic without me. Not sharing a meal that would symbolize our love was a heart-wrenching sacrifice. Still, I had to go off for an hour, before returning to continue our visit. When the bell would ring again for evening prayers and supper, I would have to say goodbye for a few more months.

I noticed my Dad carrying his camera, and I reminded him I was not allowed to have my picture taken. He honored my request until my former high school teacher, Sister Gerald, came along.

"Don't worry about it, Mister Grueninger. Take all the pictures you want. That way you'll have something to remind you of Pat when you can't have her near you."

Soon after the visit, the college registrar sat down with each of us to formulate a course of study. Sister Robertine was a kind Sister who conveyed a lot of empathy, and I liked her.

She tried to take into consideration our aptitudes and preferences, as reflected on the tests she gave us. Although we were becoming elementary teachers, we had to have a major and a minor other than education.

I watched her write down French for my major and math for my minor, and I was grateful. Having a facility for foreign languages, I had studied Latin for four years and French for two years in high school. I was enthralled with French culture and hoped someday to visit Paris with its artists' quarter, and the south of France bordering the Mediterranean Sea.

I had wanted to explore the French countryside too, especially the Loire Valley with its romantic castles and its exciting river. France sounded so wonderful, and I loved everything about it!

What irony! I entered a religious community that was based in Paris, yet observed antiquated customs that inhibited my once-free and creative spirit. But maybe this was a blessing in disguise. If I had to be an educator, teaching French wouldn't be so bad.

In the next fourteen months, all of our time was crammed with courses that barely left us any time to breathe. We ended up getting fifty-three college credits during that period, probably the result of an order from higher Superiors who wanted us to have most of our courses in teaching methods completed, before they sent us out to teach in August of the following year.

I knew that Sister Robertine was too considerate to have overloaded us with coursework, but she too was bound by obedience.

At the same time, we began a new phase of training called the Juniorate. It was something new to our religious congregation, and we were going to be the first band of Sisters in our province to experience it. For Sister Marguerite who was put in charge, it was experimental, and she had to use her own judgment in determining how strict it should be.

While stressing our spiritual development as we took courses with the college girls, she did not allow us to mingle with those young women. Nor could we mix with the younger band of Seminary Sisters we had just left, or even the other Habit Sisters of the Provincial House.

Banning communication with anyone except our own band was devastating to me. Overwhelmed by my coursework and the multitude of prohibitions, I had to struggle to hold onto my sanity.

That first summer, living as a Habit Sister turned out to be an unimaginable challenge. We had to do all of our schoolwork in an assigned room before the days of air-conditioning. We were not permitted to study under the trees and enjoy the breeze or take any break outside. Sister Marguerite even declared that the long porches that lined the northside of the Provincial House were off limits.

This stage of our training ended up being more rigid than the Seminary. The atmosphere was brutal! Sister Marguerite approached her duty with excessive scrupulosity, as if she could assume responsibility for the spiritual progress of each of us in her care. She acted as if she could make us perfect by the sheer force of her iron will.

We couldn't slow down between classes and meals and spiritual exercises. And when we could fit in a half hour or hour of recreation, it always had to be taken with the group, making it stilted and stifling.

I longed to go off alone, maybe take a leisurely walk down the dusty road that cut through the Sisters' old farm. How I wanted to watch a sunset and listen to the birds without guilt. I hungered for a buffet of beauty, as I starved aesthetically.

Still, I tried to give my new Superior the benefit of the doubt and believe she meant well. She did manage to get permission to organize a bus trip to one of Baltimore's wide-screen theaters that was showing the film "Around the World in 80 Days."

It was the first time we had left our home base to go any distance and I would have been more grateful, had I not developed a bad case of motion sickness along the way. I had to consciously use mind over matter to keep from vomiting all over the bus and the theater.

What luck! I finally get the chance to leave the college and my life's rigidity, and I end up being nauseated the whole time!

But maybe there was a deeper reason for my illness. I had heard Sister Directress tell us so many times that satisfaction was wrong, that enjoying anything was an imperfection. Now I found my emotions a mess of tangled feelings, with guilt dominating.

I didn't know how to deal with lifting my eyes and seeing nature's beauty, as the bus driver took us through western Maryland's countryside. And I struggled to beat down memories that reminded me I was traveling through my own county, just a few miles from the place I used to call home.

In the theater I felt an invisible wall separate me from the other patrons. It was a strange and awkward feeling. I was an insecure child again, not a woman. Above all, not a mature woman. I felt lost in the universe, not belonging anywhere.

Back in Emmitsburg, I immersed myself once more in my studies, glad to be distracted from my inner confusion. Then, one day, a fire engine siren filled the campus air. It was an unfamiliar sound that caught my attention. Later on, walking to class in silence, I listened to the conversations around me, hoping to learn what had happened.

This is what I overheard: a Sister home for the summer started a fire, while she was smoking in her room in a dormitory building. Unbelievable! A Sister smoking was unheard of! It wasn't allowed. Ever. It was against our rules. A subsequent rumor said she was no longer among us.

An announcement was made. We were about to be the first Sisters to have a summer Habit. All the layers of clothing would remain the same, but the outer garments would be made of gabardine instead of wool.

I could not imagine how the Sisters who went before me ever survived the heat and humidity buried under that heavy Habit year round. Gabardine was an improvement, but I soon found out that the summer Habit was still uncomfortable to wear in hot weather.

Sleeping on summer nights was not pleasant either. We had to wear our white, long-sleeved, floor-length nightgown topped with the night fichu pinned over our chest, and we had to keep wearing both night caps. We had to cover ourselves up with a sheet and a summer blanket. Never were we permitted to kick off the blanket and sheet and enjoy the occasional night breeze. It would be sinful to seek such forbidden pleasure and enjoy the feeling of wind against our body.

The following winter I turned 21 on a cold January day. It was my third birthday since leaving home—the third birthday I couldn't celebrate. I should have climbed the nearby mountain and shouted to the universe that my big day had arrived.

"I am 21 today!" I should have screamed.

I should have celebrated as the real person I was or used to be. But that "explorer-adventurer-artist-musician-philosopher" all rolled up into one, was nowhere to be found.

Superiors had drained out of me that inner part that was my core, like someone sucking the egg out of an eggshell.

Where was the real ME that day? I felt robbed and cheated –conned out of my own life.

The anguish of not revealing to anyone that it was my birthday, my 21st, stung deeply. I had always believed that the day I was born mattered. For Mother, it was significant enough to record the details in my Baby Book that she kept with so much care, even keeping some of my golden locks of hair.

As I was growing up, Mother would occasionally pull out that Baby Book and take me down her memory lane, recalling the events surrounding my birth.

"Doctor Zuravin was on call to bring you into the world. My doctor was going away, so he arranged for a substitute to deliver you. That doctor was anticipating his first delivery, and he appeared at our door early on January 20th. He kept getting in my way, and I had work to do. So I told him to go home and wait for your Dad's call.

"In the middle of the night, Doctor Zuravin got that call, but it was rainy and foggy. He could hardly find his way across Baltimore City. To save time, he decided to take a shortcut through Wyman Park, and there he got lost.

"Your Dad called a neighbor who was a nurse. Her name was Emma Leimbach. At 4:55 a.m. she brought you into the world. You were a beautiful, blue-eyed infant 22 inches long. You weighed eight pounds and twelve ounces, and I remember the first time I held you in my arms. I felt so proud!

"I never forgot the day of your birth. And every birthday after that was special. See, I even kept many of your birthday cards from the day you were born and your first birthday and your second birthday. There's Mom Mom's card and your cousins—the Wards and the Marsletts and the Sissons. So many people loved you from the start, Patsy. The day you came to earth will always matter. Remember that!"

My every birthday was a joyous occasion from then on. A family celebration! My coming into the world was truly an event worth taking note of, I believed.

But not anymore. To celebrate, even enjoy, the remembrance of my birth was now considered an imperfection. As always, my Religious Community wanted to make sure the Sisters had every opportunity to become as perfect as Superiors thought possible. They wanted us to become Sisters who would earn a high place in Heaven in return for stamping out human satisfaction and human joys—in order to give ourselves more completely and more selflessly in the service of others. That was the rationale they communicated.

As I tried to go along with that line of thinking, even on my 21st birthday, I had to force myself to suppress the pain that threatened to overwhelm me and cover it up with justifications. I could no longer take my Mother's advice and believe that the day I came to earth mattered.

I found my peace in the chapel during prayer time. There I thanked God for giving me life. And I asked for strength to live my life as He wanted me to live it. I begged for the grace to keep in mind that God had a Plan for my life—that I needed to be here as a Sister in order to fulfill His Will that was so difficult to understand. It wasn't necessary for me to know the reasons why He had called me, I told myself.

I struggled to make my faith overcome my feelings. Still, the rigidity of my life and its regimentation made me feel like I was merely going through the motions of living. Not having the physical and emotional outlets I needed increased the pressure that was weighing me down.

I should have talked this out with someone. But we weren't allowed to confide in those who would be the best sounding boards. Even as Habit Sisters, we were still forbidden to unburden ourselves to our families or our own Sisters. We could only go to Superiors and, most of the time, those women did not inspire my confidence.

Besides, inner turmoil in a Sister was not acceptable. I found my Superiors doing what my parents did. What they could not deal with, they evaded or denied, a symptom of the distorted thinking of the times, perhaps. And it was easier for Superiors to mold Sisters into subjects who kept their humanness under lock and key, subjects who lived by a rigid code of silence.

As a result, I became more and more enmeshed in the unhealthy practices of repression and suppression. I threw myself completely into my studies, as repugnant as that was, and the manual duties I was assigned to perform—not realizing I was merely compounding my problems.

One day, while I was doing a science assignment in the college library, I became overcome with curiosity about the male anatomy. Although I was very affectionate in my dating years, I was deeply influenced by the Christian upbringing my Methodist Dad and my Catholic Mother gave me and by my education in Catholic schools. These factors kept me from exploring the world of sex and becoming pregnant. Still, I had mixed emotions about sex, probably stemming from a bad experience I had had as a six-year old, when I saw a man's penis and held it unwillingly.

Thinking we needed a male role model when Dad was away fighting a war, Mother started taking us to the home of a man she considered to be a "pillar of the church." Since he was president of the Knights of Columbus, he was a man whose reputation was impeccable, she thought, as she took us to visit him and his family. What she didn't realize was that his apparent love for kids covered up a sinister vice.

When he organized games of hide-and-seek, he would corner me behind a bush and touch me in ways I didn't like. I was terrified to go to his house and afraid to tell my Mother why. One day he convinced her to leave me there, saying he'd bring me home later. He did drive me home. But all during the ride, he forced me to hold onto his penis that he had pulled out. I was terrified the whole time, and I became filled with horror and guilt.

Years later, I could hardly control my ecstatic joy when Mother announced that Mr. C had died. For the first time, I blurted out what had happened to me—how that man had terrorized me when I was only six years old.

I wanted her to hug me and hold me and tell me how sorry she was—that I shouldn't feel guilty, that it wasn't my fault, that God's justice would deal with this man who could no longer abuse children. Instead, she hushed me up saying, "Don't ever let your father hear about this," and she dropped the subject.

Later on, I came to realize that Mother's reaction was something she had learned in her own upbringing. When she started her monthly periods, her Mother had shown alarm and made it clear that her nine brothers must never know about it.

Even when she married Dad, it was he who had to tell her about sexual relations. So my Mother's reticence about discussing or dealing with the subject of sexual abuse was an honest reaction, the only way she knew how to deal with the revelation that her own child had been molested. For my part, I would bury those memories in my subconscious.

As curiosity overwhelmed me that day in the college library, I looked for an anatomy book after checking that nobody was near. Finding one, I opened it surreptitiously and stared at a diagram in the chapter on male sexuality. Realizing what I was doing, gawking at male genitals, I was suddenly overcome with guilt.

What horrible thing had I done? Here I was, a Sister wearing the Holy Habit, giving in to sexual curiosity, wanting to see what a man's private parts looked like. I was sinning in the most degrading way a Sister could, I thought.

How many times had I heard it said in Catholic schools how terrible sins of impurity were. Impure thoughts, words, and deeds had to be shunned with all our might, the nun repeated over and over again. And look at me! Privileged to be a Sister, I was sinning!

As a youngster, my poor sister Carole had gotten into trouble with our overbearing pastor when she couldn't think of any sin to confess, as she stood where her teacher put her in line. Father Donlan, whose booming voice could always be identified, yelled at my sister and chased her out of the church.

What had she said to enrage him? Needing something to confess, she had picked up a prayer book in a pew and looked up sins in the Examination of Conscience section. Finding a sin she hadn't confessed before, she entered the pastor's portable confessional, then blurted out to the priest, "Bless me, Father, for I have sinned. I committed adultery." Hardly able to pronounce the word, she had no idea what she had said to evoke the pastor's wrath, what it was that made him run down the aisle after her.

Father Donlan instilled fear in me too, and I dreaded having a Sister put me in his confessional line on our monthly jaunt to church for spiritual cleansing. I grew up hating to go to confession.

Now, as a Sister, I would have to confess my sexual sin to the assigned priest who would know I was a Sister. Why hadn't I stopped to think of that before giving in to my curiosity?

The days until the next confession day dragged by slowly. I was in agony in Holy Agony chapel awaiting my turn to enter the dark confessional. Which priest would be there? Would he be merciful and understanding? Or would I enrage him like my sister had angered our pastor so many years earlier?

When my turn came, I pulled back the dark velvet curtain and knelt down. As he pulled open the slide, and I saw the dark silhouette of his head, I began nervously:

"Bless me, Father, for I have sinned. It has been one week since my last confession. I looked for an anatomy book in the college library. I leafed through it until I found an illustration of a man's body and I stared at it."

"What do you mean, Sister, when you say you stared at it? What did you stare at?"

I cleared my throat and replied timidly, "His sexual organs, Father."

"Are you saying that you deliberately looked at a picture of a man's naked body, Sister?"

"Yes, Father."

"Go on with your confession, Sister. Is there anything else you want to add?"

"No, Father, that's all." I hoped my shaking voice would elicit his compassion. Silence followed.

Finally, the elderly priest spoke up sternly, "How could you, Sister? How could you do such a terrible thing against your vocation? God privileged you with His Call and you knew full well what He expected of you. You gave up the outside world with its enticements, yet you gave in to temptation, you have sinned, Sister!"

I felt humiliated. Here I was, a Sister struggling to live a life foreign to my deepest aspirations, trying to accept all of its built-in degradation, a life that was messing up my mind. And I have a man on a pedestal, God's representative I was taught to believe, making me feel like the "scum of the earth!"

"Don't ever do that again, Sister!" he said with authority. "For your penance, say an extra rosary today."

Incapable of assessing the situation objectively, I bowed my head in submission and believed what the priest said about my behavior: I had failed as a Sister. He succeeded in lowering my self-esteem another notch.

After that unpleasant experience, I repressed any sexual curiosity that arose. Later, when my sexual drives made themselves known and plagued me, I tried to suppress them as well. What I didn't realize at the time was that sexual curiosity and sexual drives were neither good nor bad. They were part of nature, part of being a human being, regardless of the Habit I wore. I just needed to learn how to handle those feelings in a mature manner, as a Sister who had to sacrifice her womanhood to God.

What I should have done was confide my frustrations in another woman who would understand. But I couldn't find that person. Besides, using such a solution would only serve to compound my guilt. So I adopted the practice of denying my feelings and urges. I threw myself more deeply into the tasks at hand; hoping that, by ignoring what I felt, my deepest drives would somehow go away. I came to appreciate my schedule that was crammed with work and prayer and left me too tired to care when nightfall came.

Days turned into weeks and weeks into months. I acted like a puppet, going through the motions of living, turning control of myself and my faculties over to someone else.

I looked forward to scheduled visits with my parents and siblings. Despite the restrictions my Superiors held over my head, I basked in the love my family radiated while we were together. I felt like a baby that just wanted to be held in their arms, a child starved for a hug.

The love for life I once had was disappearing, and my Mother must have noticed this. One day she proudly presented me with a package she had carefully wrapped.

"Open it up, Pat! It's something that will make you very happy. Something you'll love having with you. Actually, it was part of you before you left home and should continue to be with you, not with me."

I had to stifle my horror, as I peeked inside the bag. Mother had brought my easel and what I had produced at the Maryland Institute of Art.

I had already accepted the fact that I had to give up my past, that I couldn't look back. I had steeled myself against the temptation to want the life I used to have. Now, I had this to deal with! Seeing my easel and what I created reopened a wound. And I would have to report this to Sister Marguerite whose response would pour salt in the wound.

"What's wrong?" my Mother asked. "These are your wonderful sketches and charcoal drawings from art school. I even brought the beautiful portrait of Mrs. Binebrink that you made with pastels. You certainly remember doing all this lovely work, don't you? And I know how much you loved your easel. All of this belongs here with you, Pat, and I want you to have it."

I suppressed the emotion that wanted to burst out of me, as I tried to keep my composure and look grateful.

"Thanks, Mother. You're really thoughtful," I said and I gave her a big hug. I really wanted to add, "Take it away from here fast, before it gets lost or destroyed!" But I wasn't allowed to say that.

Afterwards, when the time came for me to give an account of my family visit, I tried to explain simply, "Sister Marguerite, my Mother brought my easel today and left it with me. And inside this bag are my drawings from art school."

I wanted to add, "Please, Sister, don't make me give up what my Mother brought. Let me keep what means so much to me!" Instead, I kept quiet and listened.

"Since you won't be needing it anymore, I'll take the easel off your hands. The college art department will make good use of it. And you know what to do with your artwork. Keeping it around would be a temptation to pride. Fortunately, our rules protect you by making you part with such things that are attachments and don't belong in religious life."

"Yes, Sister. I'll tear up my work and throw it away."

And so I did. But as I tore up each piece and watched the bits of paper fall into the trash can and mix with the debris that was already there, I could feel my heart being torn up, along with my work.

My creations not only reminded me of art school, they reminded me of a dream I once had—my dream of letting the artist inside me burst forth and blossom. Even more importantly, they represented ME. They WERE me!

Still, I was the one who allowed this to happen. I believed what I was told, that it was God's Will that I stamp out my dream—and so I destroyed my work.

Maybe, instead, I should have stepped back and uttered a profound question: How could a God of love ask this of me?

The Juniorate was drawing to a close. Sister Marguerite stood before us holding a list in her hand and directed us to kneel down, while she read aloud our new assignments. I held my breath. She was about to reveal the schools where we would be sent to fill needs.

"Sister Patricia Anne Grueninger will go to Saint Ambrose School in Endicott, New York. Sister Lawrence Marie will go with her." When she finished reading off the names and the destinations of each Sister in our band, she instructed us to kiss the floor in submission.

As I bent forward as far as the point of my cornette would permit, I felt dehydrated emotionally. Still, I was anxious to get on with a new chapter of my life, even if it meant going off to teach somewhere. I was ready to throw myself into convent life.

1,077 days had passed since I left home. I missed my brown-shingled house and all its memories. Above all, I missed my loved ones.

II
The Life

Annihilated For God

5.

Convent Beginnings

I stared holes in the double doors that towered above the Sisters, as I stood in the vestibule of the Provincial House. Three years earlier I had walked through that doorway for the first time, shutting the door behind me. It shut out my mother, my whole natural family, and the world as I knew it. I lived my life since then within these massive nineteenth-century walls, fitted to the mold of a Sister.

Waiting to board the bus, I could feel my Holy Habit wet with perspiration clinging to me. Although it was 1958, I stood there dressed like a seventeenth-century village girl in France, struggling to block a message from my brain that wanted to shout out, "It's August—hot, humid August—and look how we're dressed!"

Glancing up at Sister Rosa, I watched her check off names, while she tapped her foot impatiently. This woman who was Sister Visitatrix's assistant looked tall, even somewhat obese, under the many layers of her Holy Habit. Today her job was to make sure the "Summer Sisters" boarded the right busses to go back to their convents. Bound for my first mission, I was among them.

I figured it was simpler for her to arrange for Sister Visitatrix's travel. As a postulant, I had seen the Provincial Superior ride down the "avenue" in a sleek, black, chauffeured vehicle. Surprised, I asked about it, before I learned not to ask questions. Since she was the highest Superior of the Eastern Province, it was deemed proper, I was told. Besides, a businessman had donated it. Probably a Catholic who wanted to score points with God.

But that practice of accepting expensive cars had been discontinued. And the car she now used was much less conspicuous, more suitable even for a Superior, since she was no less obliged to practice humility and poverty than the rest of us.

Sister Rosa herded us through the ominous doorway and onto the busses that were waiting outside. Before giving the drivers the signal to leave, she double-checked busses and recounted us. Was she afraid one of us might run away and become a deserter?

My heart felt heavy as I looked out the bus window at the entrance to the Sisters' world. I couldn't erase the memory of that last embrace between Mother and me, that last hug as Mother's child.

Although I was leaving for my first mission as a Habit Sister, this place would always be referred to as home. And I would be coming back over and over again, regarding the Sisters as my primary family, struggling to blot out feelings for the relatives I had left behind.

To the driver peering at us through the rear view mirror, we must have been an odd assortment of passengers. Tall and short, fat and thin, we had one thing in common: a Religious Habit topped with headgear that looked like boat sails.

I tried to get comfortable for the trip expected to last nine hours, but the tailpiece of the cornette made leaning back an impossibility. I moved forward almost to the edge of my seat, wishing I were allowed to ease the strain on my back with a cushion.

After three years of intensive training, I was finally going out "on mission," beginning my first assignment. I knew I needed to go far away from this place that had made me feel like an abject prisoner. So, despite my aversion for the career assigned to me, I looked forward to a new start.

Riding north on Highway 15 across the Pennsylvania border, stretches of fertile farmland flashed before my eyes. I cringed when the bus paralleled the Gettysburg battlefield. The memorials I saw reminded me of the intense suffering that soldiers fighting on both sides during the Civil War endured. It was the feeling I used to get in cemeteries, a kind of lingering sadness that was hard to shed. The whole town was a graveyard that decried without words so many senseless deaths.

Several months earlier, Sister Marguerite took us there for a field trip. It was Vow Day for the Habit Sisters who were over five years' vocation, a day of celebration which we shared by having our classes and studytime dispensed with.

Sister Marguerite wanted to make our day memorable by arranging a tour of the historic battlefield, something that left me filled with confusion. How could a visit to such a tragic site be a way to celebrate? I returned to the Provincial House that evening feeling like I had been to a morgue—overcome with sadness.

But maybe there was a deeper reason for this. The thought of war always made me shudder. My young life was put on hold when Uncle Sam whisked Dad away to the Pacific to fight World War II and kept him for over two years.

As a family we worried and prayed together, looking at Dad's empty place at the supper table where Mother set out his plate each evening. I listened breathless to every letter from Dad that Mother would read as she gathered us around her. And I huddled next to Grandmother Grueninger and my siblings, with black shades drawn, whenever the air raid siren blared.

I sat in the dark all the while, worried about my mother who was an air raid warden roaming the neighborhood to make sure all the neighbors had their lights turned off, wearing her white helmet with its bright insignia.

I sat there praying that no bombs would drop on Mother or us or the neighbors, like they were falling out of the sky on people in other countries. And I begged God to let Dad stay alive and come home. "Please! Please! Please! I'll be good, God! I promise!"

When Dad returned, the war had changed him. He was no longer the outgoing Dad who was fun to be with. He was like a turtle hidden in its shell. Every sound, every squabble, got on his nerves. And he would tell Mother to shut us up.

So she started hanging a leather belt on our bedroom door as a warning—that she'd use it on us if we got too noisy. I wanted my real

Dad back. Although the war was over, I still had to go on missing him.

We were too young to understand the horrors of war. We could not begin to imagine the hell Dad's life had been for over two years, how many fellow soldiers he had seen die, how he felt when he bayoneted men called the enemy, how he hated living in snake-infested jungles. Dirty, grimy, unable to bathe, yanked away from his family to fight, his home was a bug-ridden foxhole.

And Mother needed time to heal too. When Dad was drafted, she was pregnant with Anne. Dad was given 30 days to dispose of his small business and get his household in order. He gave Mother a quick course in driving, before leaving her in charge of his mother, three children, and a fourth child yet unborn. They were both 29. Married soon after the Depression, they now had a war to contend with.

I remember agonizing over Mother having to go down into the cellar in the middle of the night to shovel coal in the furnace. I knew what **a** fearful place that was. Even in daytime, its dark recesses would murmur frightening epitaphs. How many times my heartbeat raced, whenever I had to go down to the basement for anything. Poor Mother!

She had to do everything now from budgeting rations that the government divided among families—allowing for frugal food supplies, shoes, limited fabric for clothing—to paying off the house mortgage, laundering our clothes in an old-fashioned washing machine, cleaning house, taking us to school, helping us with homework, and struggling to keep us smiling while her own heart was breaking.

When the war was over, she had lost the husband she married. Fighting overseas had drained the life out of him, if not his blood. And she lost three dear first cousins, the Winkel boys. As teenagers she and her sisters Jenny and Marie had palled around with Charlie, George and Tom at their church carnivals. All were around the same age. Like Dad, they had gone off to fight a world war, two in the navy, one in the army. And all three sacrificed their lives for their country, never again to be seen on this earth.

They were my second cousins, although they looked more like uncles. How could God let the life be snuffed out of all three of them, brothers? It seemed so unfair! I hated what war did to them and to Dad and our family life. Where was the God I was taught to love? To believe in? Why was he hiding, when we needed Him most?

Passing an historical marker, I remembered reading the Sisters' stories of that period of history when the Confederates, then the Union soldiers, encamped on their grounds. Fearing an eruption of violence around them, the Sisters had begged God to protect them, praying that no fighting would take place near their residence in Emmitsburg.

When the battle broke out ten miles north, some of the Sisters climbed a high tower with the boarding school students to watch. Still others gathered in the chapel to pray amid the muffled booms.

When the sounds of war stopped, a priest assembled the Sisters with nursing skills and drove a wagon to Gettysburg. Upon their arrival, the Sisters were horrified to discover the entire battlefield strewn with human bodies writhing in pain or motionless, alongside dead and wounded horses. Having their work cut out for them, the Sisters labored tirelessly in churches that became makeshift hospitals, saving as many lives as they could.

When I read those poignant accounts, I felt proud to be a Sister among such selfless women. It was the same feeling I got whenever I read the lives of the Sisters who preceded me. In wartime and when disease epidemics raged, they always rallied to the aid of people in need, regardless of the personal risk.

Florence Nightingale had been so impressed with them during the Crimean War that she modeled nurses' caps after the cornette, according to stories passed down in our Religious Order.

And how could I forget the story of our international Superioress, called "Most Honored Mother," who governed our Community during World War II? After the Nazis invaded the French capital, she was interrogated, then thrown into prison, for refusing to divulge the names and locations of European Sisters who were hiding Jewish families.

I was proud of this Sister whom I had never met. She was a heroine in my way of thinking for risking death to save her Sisters and the Jews that Hitler wanted to annihilate. Fortunately, she was still alive when the Allies liberated Paris.

Certainly, I was in a Religious Order I could be proud of. History proved that its members were valiant women who gave their all. I wanted to follow in their footsteps and carry that torch of courage forward to future generations. Still, I found our way of life so stifling—deadening even—that I wondered if I could spend my entire life being faithful to the charism of Saint Vincent without faltering. "Dear Lord, please help me," I wanted to cry out, "if this is your Will for me."

A voice chanting the rosary brought me back to the present. And for the next fifteen minutes we prayed aloud, one Sister leading us by reciting the first half of each prayer and the rest of us finishing the repetitious words.

Before I knew it, we were in Harrisburg, where the bus started weaving its way like a snake along the west bank of the Susquehanna River, passing through the small communities of Sunbury, Selinsgrove, Bloomsburg and Berwick. We were well into coal-mining country, when the bus cut through Wilkesbarre and Scranton.

Riding along the water, I should have been ecstatic. Growing up in Baltimore and spending so many hours on picturesque rivers and lakes, I couldn't bear to let any amount of time pass without being near water.

I still remembered the adventure with my friend Jeanie and her father on the Eastern shore of Maryland the summer before our freshman year of high school. We had to go north to Delaware, then travel south on the Delmarva Peninsula, before enjoying spectacular views of the Chesapeake Bay. Our destination was Ocean City, Maryland, with its quaint apartment houses facing the beach. Upon our arrival, Mister Mangione rowed us out to Assateague Island's Ocean Beach, where he wanted to look at land for sale.

I never forgot my experience there. I found a paradise of white sand on a beach untouched by humans. The white blanket extended as far as the eye could see, until it reached a distant horizon where the land joined the Atlantic Ocean in breathtaking beauty. I stood as if glued to the spot, lost in the panorama that lay before me, while seagulls flew overhead sizing me up, perhaps wondering what manner of sea creature I was.

It was hard to tear myself away from the ocean that day. I knew I belonged there, that the sea and my soul were one. I would be forever grateful to Jeanie and her father for showing me a world I could not have imagined. The trip had been a rare treat!

But more often my rendezvous' with water took me to rivers: Paddling the canoe with Dad at Loch Raven or with Mother and Mel as part of a small convoy, picnicking at Pierce's Cove or beside a stream, swimming like a fish at Rocky Point with Melvin, Carole and Anne—then later at Beaver Dam.

Now I was riding in a bus alongside a river. For three years I had been away from all waterways, except for Tom's Creek on the Sisters' grounds—water that was nearby, but inaccessible. And somehow, the feelings were gone, as if someone had pulled the plug and allowed them to disappear down a drain.

What was left, as I watched the Susquehanna pass me by, was a kind of emptiness that was hard to define. Sister Directress' teaching that feeling satisfaction could have no part in a Sister's life had sunk in deeply and taken root. A coldness and insensitivity to beauty now coated my heart. My sense of awe and wonder had all but vanished, or so it seemed.

When the river veered off to head northwestward, we remained in a direction due north, until we crossed the New York State Line. We were getting closer to our destinations. And, as my thoughts turned to my first assignment, I felt anxiety that I couldn't banish.

Remembrances of my experiences with Sisters in years past emerged. People put Sisters on pedestals, expecting them to be perfect, to act like angels instead of women. How could I live up to everyone's expectations of me? It was hard enough while I was in formation, when I was under the watchful eye of Superiors. Now I would be working out in the world——a world that was so evil I heard Saint Vincent say over and over again in his conferences to the first Sisters.

Working with externs now, even men, I would be exposed to new temptations. But I would have my Order's rules and policies to keep me safe: I could not go anywhere without permission. I would always have to travel in twos. I was forbidden to look a man in the eye under any circumstance.

My prayer life would have to be my fortress—beginning and ending each day in the chapel. I knew the chapel would always be my safe haven, a place to be alone with the Lord whom I had chosen "above all others." Why, then, should I fear?

But what about my repugnance for teaching? What kind of educator would I be when I hated the thought of working in a classroom? I had tried so hard to stamp out negative feelings, but it didn't work. Why had I allowed persons not related to me by blood make me become a teacher? After all, I hurt my own mother by refusing to take her advice that I choose teaching as my career.

My questions did not matter. Neither did my struggle to deal with them. I was a Sister now, obliged to live by blind obedience. For better or for worse, I had to bend my will and do those things I would never have done, had I not become a Sister. God is going to bless me for those sacrifices, my Superiors had insisted.

I could not let myself lose sight of those teachings. To do so would be selfish. Besides, I could not turn back. I had invested too much in the last three years. God called me to labor in His vineyard, and that was that.

The bus stopped abruptly, jolting me back to the present. First, we dropped off Sisters at Saint James School in Johnson City. Next, a few Sisters got off at Lourdes Hospital in Binghamton. Finally, I arrived at my new home in Endicott.

I walked beside my new companions—the other Sisters who were assigned to Saint Ambrose School and Seton High School. Watching the bus pull away to continue its journey to Syracuse, Utica, Canastota, and Oneida, I felt the pangs of the new uprooting. I would have to get used to life in a strange city, until I was re-assigned elsewhere.

The convent was—of all things—a brown-shingled house. The structure, although a Johnson family mansion of the early twentieth century, was a far cry from my family's humble brown—shingled house built in the same era. Homesickness resurfaced and, for a moment, I was back home sitting on our front porch railing, sketching away without a care in the world. Wiping away a tear, I walked forward.

No people were in sight that day, except for the Sisters picking up their single piece of luggage before entering the Sisters' House. I could see that the Sisters who lived there the previous year were anxious to get to work preparing for the opening day of school. Struggling to smile, I hoped their enthusiasm would somehow be contagious.

I was assigned to teach at the elementary school next to the Catholic Church a quarter of a mile away. Walking back and forth would be welcomed exercise at a time when Sisters had to ask permission just to walk around the block. Some of the Sisters would work at the high school next door to the convent. But all of us would live under the same roof and share the same Superior, who was principal of both schools.

Tall and slim with a ruddy complexion, blue eyes, and dimples deep as craters, Sister Monica was our Sister Servant—the title given to local Superiors by Saint Vincent. This Sister had already gained a reputation for being a model Sister—gentle, gracious, and kind at all times.

A Sister who had pudgy cheeks that seemed to accentuate her friendly personality hurried to catch up with Sister Lawrence Marie and me, the new teachers. Looking skinny, even under her bulky habit, she was not especially tall. Speaking up, she welcomed us to the convent and offered her services, should we need help in getting ready for our first day of school. We appreciated her kindness.

Always humble, this eighth-grade teacher, Sister Honorine, diverted attention away from herself and focused on our Sister Servant, whom she idolized. "Sister Monica's the best," she would say. "Don't expect all your Sister Servants to be like her!" Over the years I would discover that Sister Monica was, indeed, a rare treasure.

This Superior worked tirelessly to make our local community of Sisters a united, joyful one. Deeply spiritual, she seemed to possess the wisdom of Solomon, when it came to the letter of the law versus its spirit. Never breaking a rule, she knew how to bend some of them for the common good or what she considered the welfare of her Sisters.

Realizing the therapeutic value of soothing music, she placed a hi-fi record player in the hallway outside the community room. On feast days and times when she thought the Sisters needed to unwind, she would play relaxing music. She even bought Mitch Miller records and led the Sisters in singalongs during recreation time on special occasions.

Now, according to the rules we lived by, no source of music could be in the community room. While Sister Monica made sure that was true for our community house, she managed to give us music from the nearby corridor at her discretion.

She mounted a bulletin board in the same hallway, posting newspaper clippings to keep us apprised of local, national and world events she judged to be important for us to know, since we were still not allowed to read newspapers.

We lived our lives mainly in three areas, when we were not in school: the community room, the chapel, and the study where we prepared our lessons. We could not loiter in the bedroom area during the day.

The community room was plain with the usual white walls that were bare, except for a large crucifix and portraits of Pope Pius XII and some of our major Superiors. Besides the long, L-shaped conference table and wooden chairs that were sufficient in number for all of us, there were unornamented bookcases of dark color. In a corner of the room, I saw a small table on which a statue of the Blessed Virgin Mary stood——reminding us of her role as our protectress and guide. The hardwood floor on which we would frequently kneel was uncarpeted.

Books that had accumulated over the years were limited, for the most part, to lives of our deceased Sisters and histories of our Order. The books on spirituality seemed outdated, expressing theology of centuries past. Bibles were not available for our reading, since Catholic Church officials, at the time, feared the individual interpretation of Scripture and discouraged Bible reading. Besides, they considered Bible study too Protestant.

At home, growing up with a Methodist Dad and Grandmother and a Catholic Mother, I was well aware of that difference between our religions. Only Dad and his Mother read the Bible, while Mother and the children read from other prayer books.

Dad never interfered with Mother, when it came to matters of religion, since Mother could not get a dispensation to marry him until he signed a promise to let Mother bring the children up as Catholics. And Dad, with his deep sense of responsibility, kept his word. Their wedding took place in the priests' rectory, since "mixed marriages" could not take place in a Catholic Church.

As a family we rarely prayed altogether, except for the grace before meals. On Sundays Dad drove his mother north on Harford Road to Hiss Methodist Church, while Mother went with us children to Saint Dominic's Catholic Church in the opposite direction. Even in the house, Mother usually prayed privately with the kids. I got the feeling that something was wrong with Protestant prayers.

Tension over religion got worse right before Christmas. Mother would ask us to pray with her that we'd get a miracle—that Dad would come to Mass with us on that one day—Christmas. That would be the best Christmas present of all, Mother would say.

Year after year we repeated the same request, begging God to let it happen this time. Was Dad misled, because he was Protestant? Yes, according to the pastors and bishops, and he was even in danger of losing his soul. But my Dad was such a good man, how could that be? And I worried about my Dad's soul. I wanted my whole family to spend eternity together in Heaven.

It was ironic that, after Mother agonized over her wish for Dad, he finally relented and went to Mass with us——the Mass for me and the other postulants from my high school. It was my "farewell to family" Mass.

Although no words were uttered aloud at home about the two religions, the underlying tension plagued my growing-up years.

The hierarchy's distorted teachings produced mistaken attitudes and behavior on the part of Catholics, leading them to believe

Protestants needed to be converted to Catholicism—saved in and by the Catholic Church.

Where was the concept that faith is personal and there are many roads to God? Isn't God the one who speaks directly to the souls of persons who are sincerely seeking the truth? At that time, there was not yet the understanding that "God is Love."

And, in those pre-Vatican II days, Catholics were taught to believe that the fullness of truth resided only in the Catholic Church.

It would take an old Pope—John XXIII—to pave the way for the action of the Holy Spirit by convoking the Second Vatican Council ever. Only then would come the realization that shared faith was more important than differences in religion.

The misunderstandings that still persisted in the middle of the twentieth century caused unnecessary anguish to children like me and their families. It divided our homes and our hearts, while causing immense division between churches of different denominations.

On the convent bookshelf I found additional copies of a book we were required to read often in the seminary. Written by an apparently-holy monk named Thomas a Kempis in the thirteenth century, The Imitation of Christ conveyed what I considered a very morbid theology, out of touch with mid-twentieth century America.

The monk urged followers of Christ to flee the world that was full of evil and live in seclusion, concentrating only on the here-after. To him the world had no redeeming qualities. Taken to the extreme, his thinking led to the rejection of all pleasures—including the exhilaration of a spectacular sunset and the joy of family love.

The other Sisters and I were products of the "be seen and not heard" generations, growing up not questioning our elders, just listening and obeying—a philosophy that female religious congregations had assimilated. So there was no discussion of readings or instructions given by Superiors, no exchange on the meaning of spirituality or the essence of faith. The term "dialogue" would not be used until years later after Vatican Council II mandated it for Religious Orders.

We sat in assigned places, according to age in vocation, in the community room. Being one of the two youngest, I always sat at the lower end of the table, where we had to keep our fingers busy as usual—sewing, darning, or knitting. It seemed to me that my stockings were always developing holes from so much standing, walking, and kneeling on hard surfaces. So I ended up darning darns a lot.

All of us shared the responsibility for keeping the clothing and linens we held in common in a usable state, as our vow of poverty required us to use everything until it wore out completely. This included our chemises and corsettes, and the individual parts of our cornettes, in addition to towels, washcloths, napkins and tablecloths, sheets and pillowcases.

Once those tasks were out of the way, Sisters could knit afghans and sweaters for the Poor, but never for relatives. Our vow of poverty restricted us from giving presents to family members.

We spent the hour before night prayers having recreation at the community room table. Sister Monica allowed other diversions on Saturday and Sunday evenings. We could play card games like Rook or 500 Rummy, while the Sister in charge of the community room was allowed to serve refreshments like soft drinks and ice cream or baked goods.

In warm weather, our Sister Servant provided recreation time outside on the patio under the trees. Sister Monica loved to draw our attention to the pink clouds that followed the setting sun—calling the magnificent sky God's reminder of the heavenly reward awaiting us, if we persevered in our holy vocation.

Her words were full of sincerity and she lived what she preached. She always kept her head in the clouds, but her feet on the ground. She was the best example I would ever witness of a Sister in human flesh living and acting like a real angel.

I wanted my first day of school to go perfectly. Decorating our classrooms and controlling its atmosphere was an important priority for all the teachers. The sample wallpaper I begged for at a local paint store gave a colorful background to my bulletin boards and the cork strip over the blackboards in front of the room. Not having classroom funds, I knew I had to get used to begging. It was for the children, so I shouldn't be ashamed.

Before the children came in that first morning, I had nervously checked the long rows of desks, pushing and pulling until no desk was out of place: six rows of eight and one row of seven. The room looked crowded and the aisles narrow, but it would have to do.

I should have been used to seeing fifty-five children file into a classroom. My own grade school classes numbered as many. And I had already spent eight weeks student teaching in the parish school in Emmitsburg. Those students were seventh graders. Teaching a large class of third graders should be simple, I told myself.

Still, my heart pounded the first time I gazed down at all the children sitting in those desks looking at me so trustingly, with hands folded Catholic-school style. But, as the day progressed, a shrill siren screeched and broke into my nervousness—forcing us to exit the school fast.

As we stood on the cement playground looking up at the red brick building, I wondered why we were having a fire drill on the first day of school. Was it somebody's idea of a joke? I had learned, during my own elementary school days, that pulling a fire alarm was never funny.

We waited in silence—the teachers like good Sisters and the pupils like good children. It was the first day of school, after all, and nobody wanted to get in trouble on the first day of school—at least, not my third graders whose shiny smiling faces communicated their desire to please.

And there I was, a brand new teacher, a Sister eager to do the right thing—wanting the first day of school to go perfectly. I was learning another lesson: no matter how perfect I tried to be—acting obediently the way I was trained to act—life itself made the final decision. And life itself was far from perfect!

Later I would find out that we were on the verge of an electrical fire that first day of school. Fortunately, for all of us, disaster was averted.

At the start of my teaching career, I was determined to give each child the best possible education, tempering firm discipline with caring compassion. Reflecting on my own school days, I did not want my pupils to fear me or be subjected to harshness. I still remembered clearly the teachers I liked and those I disliked.

Sister Mary, my first grade teacher, had been a treasure. I would never forget the feelings of well-being her kindness evoked in me.

Sister Mary Ambrose, my third grade teacher, was just the opposite. Deep in anguish over Dad's absence during the war, I worried constantly. Memories I used to block the pain distracted me. Sometimes I would leave home so engrossed in my thoughts, I'd forget to pick up my homework from the night before.

Eventually, Sister Mary Ambrose let impatience prevail over pity. She called me to the front of the class one day, while the other fifty-four students sat staring at me in the mandatory silence that enveloped all of us. I could feel the tension in the air.

My timidity mushroomed, as I walked forward—not knowing what to expect. I saw my teacher pull a chair in front of the blackboard, centering it where all could see her. Then, she sat down. I stood at her side dumbfounded.

"Don't just stand there, Patricia. Bend over," she ordered.

Curving my small body over her lap, I froze with fear, as she started spanking me. Finally, she told me to return to my seat and learn obedience. Tears rolled down my cheeks, as I sheepishly crept up the aisle, humiliated.

What was that spanking for? Was I being punished for missing Dad—for daydreaming about him? For being so worried I forgot my bookbag that morning? Although Sisters didn't have to justify their harsh disciplinary methods, I wished she had shown some compassion.

Then there was Sister Stephen, nicer than some of the others, as long as no one came within six feet of her precious ferns by the windows. If they did, her voice would bellow throughout the school, putting the fear of the Lord in me. I always believed she liked her plants that got the morning sun better than her pupils. But I was too young to realize she didn't have anything else in her life to love.

Pondering my experiences made me want to make certain my students always felt safe, secure, and happy in my classroom. I found a chapter on mental health in the back of the third grade science book and gave it intense scrutiny. The writer spoke of the three A's all human beings need in order to grow into happy, productive adults: affection, acceptance, and achievement.

I considered this lesson to be extremely important, so I taught the children about their emotional needs—hoping that the grownups in their lives would assimilate what the chapter was saying.

Taking these lessons to heart in my dealings with the students, I worked hard to make each one feel loved and appreciated, accepted by his or her peers, and I tried to remember to praise my pupils for the smallest amount of progress. Affirmation of my pupils was an important priority—the focus I tried to keep.

I became convinced of the philosophy of Catholic education that stressed the parents' role as primary educators of their children. The parents were merely delegating to me part of their own responsibility to give their children the best possible education——not relinquishing it. I tried to keep in close communication with them, reporting the good things their children were doing, as well as problem areas. I sometimes gave these updates in person, happy that my religious community encouraged us to make home visits in order to better assist our students.

One of my third graders, still in the tattling stage, informed me surreptitiously that some of my pupils were making fun of me behind my back, calling me a nasty nickname.

"What is it?" I whispered.

"Fatty Patty," Suzie replied.

"Is that the nasty nickname?"

"Yes, Sister. I thought you should know."

"Thank you," I replied.

Now I had heard teachers called all kinds of names in my growing-up years. So, I thought that nickname was pretty mild. I decided not to let my other students know that I knew.

Since people could not give the Sisters personal gifts—only things that could be shared—our convent always seemed to get a lot of fruit baskets and boxes of chocolates. Our Superior was always passing candy around at recreation time in the evening, and we were encouraged to "eat up." In fact, we could not choose to eat no candy at these times.

It seemed to be a tactic to get us filled sensually, so we wouldn't seek further sensual gratification—an apparent contradiction to what Sister Directress taught us about seeking satisfaction. Of course, in this instance, chocolates were eaten for energy, not for gratification. That was the justification, I think.

I knew I was growing fatter, even though I did not have access to a scale. I really was becoming a "Fatty Patty" and the many layers of my Habit accentuated my look of obesity. Besides, overweight Sisters were considered happy Sisters. So I had to be humble about the weight matter and not concern myself about what I weighed or anything my pupils might call me.

As Sister Directress had said, we were just lowly, simple servants of the Lord. We should be glad to be humiliated and treated like servants deserve to be treated—much less than our masters. "Remember," she added, "those you are sent to serve are always your masters. Don't forget that! Welcome unpleasant treatment like the saints did!"

My biggest adjustments came with convent life. Sister Lawrence Marie and I were products of the first Juniorate with its excessive rigidity that depleted any common sense we had brought to the Community with us.

It seemed as if our Superiors believed that Sisters with only two years' formation were too lax after they went out on mission. Therefore, they came up with the idea that most Sisters should have a third year to live an ascetic life wearing the Holy Habit. That way they should identify austerity with being a Habit Sister.

Sister Lawrence Marie and I arrived in Endicott terribly immature and devoid of any critical thinking skills, unable to make a rational decision on our own. We were true products of our training.

Sister Monica and the others seemed confused by this phenomenon and Sister Monica had her work cut out for her. She had to take us as we were and lead us to greater maturity—a real challenge that was actually "damage control."

In the chapel, without realizing it, the two of us were creating problems. The chapel itself was small. And being the youngest, our assigned seats were in front. Some of the older Sisters were grumbling that they could not see the tabernacle, the focus of their prayers, because we were such a distraction jumping up and down. We were continuing the Seminary and Juniorate practice of standing up any time we started falling asleep.

Between the emotional strain of life in a religious community and having to get up with the rising bell at 5 a.m., we couldn't manage to keep ourselves awake during morning meditation. We had become like "jumping jacks," kneeling for the first half of meditation, sitting for the second half, and standing up whenever our heads would start bobbing; then sitting, and repeating the cycle all over again whenever we dozed off. We just couldn't manage to stay awake for thirty minutes of silent prayer at that early hour.

Finally, Sister Monica found a solution. She told both of us to start sleeping late until 5:50 a.m., then say our vocal prayers and make our meditation after Mass and breakfast before going to school. That way we could get some extra "shut-eye" and have the chapel all to ourselves. This solution proved satisfactory to all of the Sisters.

Afterwards, we would rush to school to prepare our classrooms for the students **or** take outside playground duty when assigned. At lunchtime we hurried back to the convent to say our noon prayers, use the restroom, grab a quick bite of food in silence in the refectory, then rush back for playground duty—all within the allotted half hour.

Not having classroom aides we could take no personal breaks during the day, even for five minutes. In mid-morning and mid-afternoon we would take the children out for recess. It was important that they run off the nervous energy that built up, while they were confined to their seats in a packed classroom.

One day a week we scurried back to the convent after school for mandatory confession to the assigned priest. Another day we darted out of school to meet an assigned partner and "do up" our linen in the convent basement. That meant heating up a cauldron of thick starch to the boiling point, dipping our collars and cornettes in it, then smoothing out the pieces on specially-made "tins." It was difficult to get all the air bubbles out, so we would have to rub and rub until the palms of our hands were ready to blister.

The metal forms for the cornettes were shaped like rectangles, about twenty-six inches by forty inches. The collar tins were shaped with an indentation for the high necks and a smooth area for the front of the collar that extended over a Sister's bosom. We called the metal tin, but it felt heavier like steel.

It was usually a rush to clean up the mess we had made and get to the community room in time for spiritual reading. We would leave the tins with the attached linens to dry for a few days in the cellar—hoping we had prepared enough collars and cornettes to last a while. Then we would sit in our assigned places in the community room trying to wind down as we sewed and listened. For me, it was an extra effort to ignore my wet layers of clothing.

Weekends in the convent went by fast. There was no time to slow down. On Saturdays, besides Mass, spiritual reading, and other scheduled prayers, we had assigned convent chores, the "pulling" of a new cornette for the coming week, and many hours in the Sisters' study—preparing lesson plans, grading papers, and making flash cards.

On Saturday evening before recreation, Sister Monica would unlock the supply closet, while we lined up nearby. When our turn came, we could ask for necessary supplies, such as soap, toothpaste, kotex, and homemade deodorant—a combination of cornstarch and baking soda. "Sister Monica, may I please have?" was the repetitious phrase I used.

Sundays were busier, even without the "servile" work. We'd sleep late—until 5:50 a.m., say our vocal prayers together, then hurry up the street for our first Mass of the day with heads lowered and hands joined and hidden in our sleeves. We'd hurry back for breakfast and cleanup, make a half-hour meditation in the chapel, and rush back to the parish church for the mandatory second Mass of the day.

Upon returning, we either went right to work on lesson plans or focused our attention on our other spiritual exercises—making the Stations of the Cross, saying our daily rosary, or just sitting in the Chapel meditating peacefully. Amassing indulgences was still in vogue.

Once school started and its pressures on us showed, Sister Monica made a surprising announcement. We would start playing basketball on Friday evenings, when the high school gym was available and the building unoccupied. Our Sister Servant borrowed some of the "white gowns" used by our hospital Sisters in Binghamton. She allowed us to wear the lightweight garment in place of the outer layers of our Holy Habit—thereby making us more agile.

My old repugnance for participating in team sports remained with me. But, lacking other outlets, I threw myself into these games. In so doing, I would show Sister Monica my appreciation for her efforts to make our rigid lives more bearable.

Running around the court wilted the starch out of my cornette where it hugged my cheeks and out of my collar that encircled my neck. Although I hated that soggy sensation, the games broke the monotony of my daily life and gave me something to look forward to. Of course, Sister Monica and the other tall Sisters scored the most points.

What a sight this would have been to externs, had they been permitted a glimpse of the Sisters awkwardly playing basketball with floppy headdresses!

But beneath my efforts to show some enthusiasm, I was suppressing inner yearnings that screamed out for fulfillment. New York's state map revealed so many places of fantastic beauty: lakes, rivers, mountains. I wanted to go canoeing or take a swim, hike a trail, or just stand breathless before nature's miracles—go outside and breathe free! As hard as I tried, I couldn't submerge the part of me that wanted—needed desperately—to experience the simple pleasures of life.

As the holidays approached, I did what I was trained to do. Ignoring my homesickness, I made myself smile, while trying to believe the external act would seep in my soul. Then, before long, I should start feeling happy, I was told. But that mental process was not working for me.

Struggling to come to terms with my life's new meaning, I was learning that the religious goal imposed on me—that of being perfect—was not realistic. Life was filled with unpredictability and stress, without adding unnecessary burdens.

In a horrifying way, this lesson was about to "hit home" for me and all American Sisters. A tragic, but predictable disaster—given the convent mentality of the times—was imminent.

1,183 days had passed since I left home. I missed my brown-shingled house and all its memories. Above all, I missed my loved ones.

6.

Blind Obedience Uncloaked

The year was 1958—the month, December.

I glanced up at the overcast sky, so typical of Endicott, New York mornings. Standing on the concrete playground dressed in my archaic French Habit, I shivered as I supervised the children at play. I marveled at their frolicking antics and carefree spirits—oblivious of the piercing cold.

Yanking my black shawl higher in the back, I tucked it between my stiffly-starched headgear and the white turtleneck collar I wore, also heavily-starched. At the same time, I felt a torturous chill penetrate my unpadded cornette and wrap itself around my bald head. I distracted myself by watching a puff of cold air resembling smoke pour from my lips.

Some of my pupils gathered around me. Clinging to my long, many-layered skirt, they started chatting. In accordance with our rules, I gently pulled aside my apron and stepped back.

Suzie with her freckled face and pixie smile put her hands, trembling from the cold, in her pockets. She spoke up, "Run with us, Sister; you'll feel lots warmer that way."

"Let's hurry up and go inside," Molly joined in. "I won't complain about a hot classroom today."

"The bell will ring any minute," I said.

Just then, the principal appeared, clanging a handbell.

"See, Molly, I was right," I called out, as my pupils walked quickly to line up. Children and staff anticipated the comfort of a warm school building on that cold December day.

Although teaching was not my choice of a career and my Superiors never asked me what I wanted to do, I loved those children. I felt privileged to care for them like a visible guardian angel. I liked my Religious Order's philosophy that our reward for sacrificing biological motherhood was spiritual motherhood.

Taking a moment, I whispered a prayer: "Dear Lord, make me a good teacher—worthy to watch over your little ones. Keep them safe today and always. In Jesus' Name, I pray."

My third graders—all fifty-five of them—marched up the stairs with me and entered the classroom. I watched and waited, while they organized their books for class, then sat down and folded their hands on their desks. I called them row by row to hang up coats and put away lunch pails.

After saluting the American flag and saying our prayers together, we were ready to begin a new day. I gazed down at my crowded flock of pupils looking up at me with innocent, trusting faces—waiting for me to set the tone for the day.

It was my first year of teaching. A twenty-one year old Sister, I too was young and innocent.

A thousand miles away in a midwestern Catholic school, Sisters of another Religious Order were going about their teaching duties, just like me. The Chicago cold chilled bodies to the bone, so the warmth emanating from the school's heavy- duty, stoked-up furnace was greatly—appreciated by everyone inside the building.

The activities of the school day were not unlike my own, until the heat got hotter and hotter—excessively hot and suffocating—making classrooms feel like ovens. Teachers started shutting doors, waiting for the principal to resolve the situation. Inside the classrooms on the second floor, the little ones became frightened.

Terror replaced fright, when smoke began to pour through transoms. Panic-stricken students froze in their seats. Sisters led students in prayer, begging God to protect the children under their care. Meanwhile, they waited for someone else to alleviate the problem.

Starting to gag, some children asked permission of their teacher to stand by an open window, so they could breathe better. Others ran to the windows without waiting for permission. Taller students climbed up on windowsills in a last-minute effort to avoid the impending disaster. Shorter students unable to reach up cringed near the floor. Still others remained in their seats with hands folded—as if glued to their desks.

Finally, a Sister—concealing her horror—led students through the corridor to the only fire escape. It was locked. Her heart sank.

I was horrified when my Superior gathered us together after school and delivered the tragic news. "Close to one hundred children perished in a fire today," Sister Monica said. "Pray for their families and the Sisters in whose care their parents placed them. Pray too for the little ones who survived and are in hospitals."

How horrifying was the senseless loss of those innocent lives.

I knew nothing of the fate of the Sisters, because all details were hushed, as soon as they started circulating along convent "grapevines." It didn't occur to me in those days that Church officials covered up what they judged not to be in the best interest of the Catholic Church. Was their spotless reputation more important than revealing the truthful details?

Still, two rumors did slip through the secrecy. A boy had sneaked down to the basement of the school lighting a fire under the stairwell. I didn't know what became of him.

The other rumor involved the Sisters. They did not pull the fire alarm when smoke reached their nostrils. Why? Was it because the principal alone was allowed to do this? I knew that an obedient Sister would not dare usurp her Superior's authority. This is how we were trained, how our Superiors controlled our minds and our behavior. And this tragic event underscored the fallacy of such a philosophy that resulted in the brainwashing of Sisters.

For me, the story had agonizing ramifications. I wondered what I would have done in similar circumstances. Would I have behaved differently? Certainly I never evaluated what I was told to do. I no longer did my thinking rationally. I was trained for three years to practice blind obedience and submit to my religious community's policies, which required me to ask countless permissions. So if I found myself in a like-situation, I knew how I probably would have acted—and that knowledge was frightening.

As I silently mourned with the families of the victims, I felt compassion for the Sisters who thought they were doing the right thing—and I grieved for them, too.

I wanted to learn more details, but the "grapevine" withered. Nothing more was said. Forbidden access to news reports, I had to wait for over three decades to read the actual facts in a documentary written by David Cohen and John Kuenster.

Their book not only revived memories of the horror I felt at the time of the tragedy, it compounded my sadness. For the first time, I learned that three Sisters had died in the fire with the children. In the end—trapped—the Sisters proved their heroism.

But had the Sisters and their students died martyrs for the distorted notion of blind obedience? Had "mind-control" been the real killer? Was no one at all held accountable?

It seems to me that the 1958 tragedy at the ironically-named Our Lady of Angels School was, in actuality, a proliferation of tragedies—of such magnitude, we should never forget that event and its ramifications.

What we read in the prophecies of Jeremiah and again in Matthew's Gospel should remain imbedded in our very souls forever: the story of Rachel bewailing her children who are no more and who cannot be consoled. There's bitter weeping in Ramah, the Bible tells us. Was it an evil occurrence that should never have happened in the first place or an accident? That's the big question, isn't it?

Three weeks later, it was Christmas—not a joyful one that year. Sister Monica's gift to each one of us was a porcelain statue of Blessed Mother sitting in a chair, holding the Infant Jesus on her lap. At her feet knelt two small angels. Although nothing more was said about the fire, the images sealed the remembrance in our hearts. For me, those two angels represented many "Chicago angels" celebrating their first Christmas in Heaven!

Sister Monica worked hard to lift spirits—not only of our own Sisters in Endicott, but our Sisters in neighboring Johnson City and Binghamton. Periodically, on special feast days, she and the other two Sister Servants would coordinate a "picnic supper" in one of their community rooms. There we would gather and eat together, but not in the customary silence. It was called a meal with "talk."

I enjoyed those gatherings with Sisters I didn't see everyday. It broke the monotony and drudgery of our normal routine. For a little while, it was a needed "escape."

On the other hand, we could never mix with Sisters of another Religious Order. That was taboo. At diocesan Department of Education conferences, rooms were set aside where teachers ate their bagged lunches. There was a room for lay teachers, a second room for Sisters, and a third room for OUR Sisters.

I found it hard to understand why we could not mingle with Sisters of other congregations; since they, too, lived a vowed life. It gave the impression that we were snobbish or better than others. Were we being the simple, humble, charitable Sisters Saint Vincent intended us to be? Or were our Superiors guarding us from other ways of thinking that might "taint" us?

I desperately needed someone to love, and I found that person in darling Mary—the ninety-year old grandmother of one of my pupils. After visiting this dear lady and finding her legally-blind and living alone, I easily received Sister Monica's permission to visit Mary regularly to check up on her, even without a companion.

I could still remember my paternal grandmother Carrie Grueninger who lived upstairs from us in the brown-shingled house, until she passed away when I was a high school freshman. In our backyard garden—not far from the apple tree that shielded us from the summer heat—Mom Mom, as I called her, used to plant rhubarb for the pies she liked to bake.

I developed a taste for her pastries, but her special-occasion sour beef with dumplings topped the list of her contributions, in my estimation.

Carrie Louis was born in Baltimore. But after their mother died, she and her brothers grew up in a German Methodist Home in Berea, Ohio. At the age of 18 she returned to her hometown and, in 1900, she married Will Grueninger. Will died in 1927 in the brown-shingled house—ten years before my birth.

When Mom Mom lay on her deathbed, ravaged by arthritis, I loved relieving my mother who spent hours at her bedside—comforting her and praying. I cherished my final moments beside her. That was eight years ago.

I knew that my maternal grandmother was still alive in a nursing home somewhere in Baltimore. Grace Kirby had given us her golden-oak, upright piano that I treasured. As a child, I used to climb up on that magnificent musical instrument and run my finger along the delicate flowers engraved on it.

When I turned eight, it opened doors to much more in my life. My cousin Carolyn, and then Mrs. Raymond, gave me piano lessons. Finally, I studied chords under a third teacher. I took cello lessons, too, and loved being part of my high school orchestra, which was conducted by the fatherly and able Mr. Hipp.

Now, my precious piano was gone and the music I cherished was out of my life.

But the dear grandmother who made those joys possible was out of my life, too. Although she was alive and in her late eighties, I was denied the privilege of visiting her. Both of us had to sacrifice the joy of those visits, and we would never see each other again on this earth.

Nevertheless, I was glad our religious community encouraged us to visit the sick and the poor—with special emphasis on old folks. I loved my walks to Mary's house, where I would climb up the rickety back stairway to her second floor apartment and spend time cheering her up.

Here in New York State, I was given someone else's grandmother to visit. And when the cold weather set in, I was alarmed to discover Mary's only source of heat was her oven. She closed off the front of her apartment, using just her kitchen, bathroom, and a nearby bedroom. Then she turned on her oven, opened its door, and let it stay on day and night.

I worried about this sweet lady whom I came to love dearly. Yet she had one big fear—that she might die before she paid off her funeral expenses. How shocked I was, and sad, that an older person who had lived a long life and given so much of herself to her family and her fellow Americans could not just enjoy her old age without unnecessary worries. Something wasn't right about this system that seemed so unjust. How could people like Mary be set aside and ignored?

Finally, one severe winter, she landed in the hospital. When Mother and Dad came to visit me, arriving in a blizzard, I told them my worst fear. "Mary is dying. Please, Dad, take me to her. I have no other way. I must see her one more time," I said, fighting back tears.

Despite my irrational request, my dear Dad listened. He got the three of us to Mary's bedside, where Mary and I smiled at each other one last time—and kissed each other "farewell." Without words, we spoke volumes in that last conversation. And I hugged her like I had hugged my own Grandmother Grueninger on the last night of her life, when I was fourteen. That was the last time I saw Mary alive, and I knew she was so special that I would keep her in my heart.

That first year working with people in secular society, I discovered that wearing a religious Habit made people trust me. On the streets, passersby were friendly and gracious, regardless of their religious affiliation. The Habit inspired, not just respect, but also confidence. And so, people would come to the convent door for counseling and to pour out their problems—even their life stories—believing that Sisters could solve any dilemma.

Not having any formal training in counseling, I listened and affirmed, before offering any suggestions. And I made a discovery. Most people just needed a shoulder to cry on, someone who would allow them to pour out their heart and soul—without judging them. Once they reached that point, most people would begin to see their own solutions. Relieved of the emotional baggage they were carrying, they could see more clearly the action they needed to take, the steps toward resolving what had seemed like an impasse in their lives.

I felt happy every time I saw a person leave the convent with renewed hope, with the confidence they could change what needed to be changed and find more joy in life. Perhaps this was part of God's Plan for me: that people on the verge of giving up would start healing or renewing themselves with God's help through me. Maybe someone ready to give up completely would tie a knot and hang on, because I was there to help.

Wasn't that the final factor in my decision to become a Sister? That if one person's life would be better, happier, because I was there, then it would be worth the sacrifice of my own needs and wants? I had to keep this thought before me, especially when I felt like I was at the end of my rope. And I had to remember what I had been taught: Jesus sacrificed much, much more when HE laid down His life for me and for others!

One year Mother, Dad, and my sister Anne—still in high school— asked permission to visit me in Endicott for Thanksgiving. Now, I expected to receive "no" for the answer, since my family had never been able to visit on a holiday or holyday. I was thrilled to receive a "yes" from Sister Monica. It would be great to be together on such a big family day!

The day seemed perfect, until the noon prayer and dinner bell rang, and I was made to abide by the Community's practice of not eating with externs. Unfortunately, my family would be regarded as "outsiders" for most of my twenty-two and a-half years in the convent. I sent them away to look for a restaurant.

Upon their return, they said nothing about their meal. It wasn't until years later that Mother would reveal what happened. They drove in circles, unable to find a decent restaurant open on Thanksgiving. Finally, they gave up their search and reluctantly ate at a greasy-looking establishment that served a meal that was not very palatable.

I felt guilty for having such a nice, traditional holiday dinner, and I felt terrible that I had to shut them out. Our rules prevented us from being kind and considerate to the very persons who had given us life and nurtured us. It seemed like such a contradiction! And how painful for all of us!

The following year Mother and Dad celebrated their silver wedding anniversary at home on Thanksgiving Day. I wanted so badly to be with them and share in the festivities, but I knew that was out of the question. My vow of poverty did not permit me to buy a gift or even a commercial greeting card.

In this case, Sister Monica found a solution. She allowed me to use my art talent and make my own card. I poured a lot of love into that undertaking, then sent the card, along with my heart. I struggled to submerge the pain of separation which seemed to intensify my homesickness that day—and make me more aware than ever of the family love I had lost.

Winter passed with another Christmas in New York—far from my Mother and Dad, Melvin, Carole and Anne. Hearing Christmas carols play outside our community room was a mixed blessing. The songs brought back so many memories of Christmases past—but the rendition of "I'll Be Home for Christmas" made me feel like a dagger pierced my heart. I wanted to beg to make a phone call, but it was still not allowed. I had to force myself to be stoic, and I believed it would always be this way. That was hard—agonizing even!

Soon spring came and brought about the rebirth of life. I watched the flowers shoot up again, and high school students get bitten by the love bug—as I passed them by, after school. At prom time, Sister Monica said we should show our interest in the young people by appearing at the prom for a little while. So we filed into the handsomely-decorated gym, then hugged the wall near the exit. Standing there, watching the juniors and seniors dance to romantic and rhythmic melodies, I heard someone call the music "rock and roll."

It was difficult to stand there staid and motionless. And before long, I found my feet tapping to the beat of the music under my long skirt. I was actually enjoying rock and roll—wishing I were out there dancing, too. Better still, wishing I could dance to my heart's content on a moonlight cruise in Baltimore once again. But then I had a horrible remembrance of the night I almost died—or could have.

I was only sixteen, a junior. A young man in his twenties had smiled at me. He was good-looking, and as we danced on that moonlight cruise, he made me feel attractive. Then he asked for a date. "I'll pick you up, but not at your house," he said. "How about meeting me in front of the Arcade Theater up the road?"

In my naiveté I agreed. And I met him a mile from home at that spot, excited about going out with such a handsome guy. No one else knew where I was going or who I'd be with. I got in his car, and he drove off to a nightclub in an unfamiliar part of town. Happy to pass for being much older, I sipped a Pink Lady slowly and enjoyed the attention of an attractive man who seemed so nice. Then we left the club.

He drove down the highway and suddenly turned off on a gravel road in a warehouse neighborhood. Then he stopped the car and turned off the motor. When he started kissing me, I responded at first—until his hands began to explore my body. I froze and tried to push him away. Ignoring me, his roaming hands got rougher.

"No!" I shouted. He refused to let go of me. And I began to fight him furiously. As we struggled, I prayed like I never prayed before. Finally, he issued an ultimatum.

"Either I am going to get in your panties or you are going to end up at the bottom of the quarry outside."

I looked toward the window. It was dark outside.

"Yes, believe me! That's a quarry! And that's where you'll be soon, if you don't give in! Nobody knows where you are! I didn't even tell you my last name."

How stupid I was to go off with a stranger! Now he was offering me just two ways out: to die or stop fighting him. Neither was an option in my mind. I was a virgin, and I intended to stay a virgin until marriage. But I didn't want to end up murdered, either. I had my whole life ahead of me, and I wanted to live it! I wanted to become an artist, then a wife and mother.

My thoughts reprimanded me for getting into such a mess. Why had I lied to my family about where I was going and who I'd be with? How could I leave home without telling anyone the truth? I could end up dead, and it would be my own fault!

I remembered the Miraculous Medal I was wearing around my neck, the medal that was made after Jesus' mother Mary appeared to a member of the Religious Order of Sisters who were my teachers. People had called it a miraculous medal, because of Mary's powerful intercession with her Son. And its name stuck, because of all the miracles people claimed they received while wearing it. Mother insisted on sewing one of those medals on all of our bathing suits, before allowing us to swim as little children. She said we wouldn't drown, if Mary knew we wanted her protection.

I clutched my medal and prayed harder. "If anyone ever needed a miracle, it's me, Mother Mary!" I shouted under my breath. "Please help me!"

I kept refusing to let him have his way with me, and we were at a stand-off when it happened. Out of the darkness, I watched a light coming toward us, getting closer. Then it stopped at my "date's" open window, and I saw a hand flash the light on both of us.

A man's voice boomed, "What are you doing here? This is private property! Get off this land now!"

No answer.

"I'll say it just one more time. Leave, or I'm calling the police." My heart pounded. I wanted to speak up, but I was afraid.

Saying nothing, the driver turned the key in the ignition. The motor started, and he pulled away. I held my breath, not knowing what he was going to do next. At the main highway, he turned and kept driving, until we were in familiar territory again. I heaved a big sigh of relief.

He pulled up at the Arcade Theater in Hamilton where I opened the door, got out, and kept walking without looking back. When I got home, the house was quiet. I crept to my bedroom, and—afraid to make a sound—got undressed and slipped under the sheet. Too shaken up to sleep, I thanked God I was at home... alive! And I thanked Mary for her miracle!

Later that year, I started a steady dating relationship with Reds, a poor boy who lived in the projects near the foot of Broadway. His poverty didn't matter to me. He was cool and hung around with a cool crowd—the rebels of 1950's Baltimore with their D.A. haircuts. They were fellows who wore pegged pants and blue suede shoes—just the opposite of the "squares" with their crewcuts and white buck shoes.

Reds and his friends were clean-cut and morally-good, and they showed their girlfriends respect. I liked Reds who was affectionate and sincere, and never went beyond the limits I set. We frequently double-dated with my best friend Theresa and his best friend Harry, who played the sax—my favorite band instrument. The saxophone...

.

"Sister Patricia Anne, are you there?" a voice asked. "The saxophone Bill's playing sounds good, doesn't it?"

I snapped back to reality fast. "Yes, yes, it was always my favorite instrument in the days when I..." What am I doing? I almost thought aloud. Better shut up and remember religious decorum.

"Yes, the musicians have a lot of talent."

I stopped my foot from tapping in rhythm and slapped a serious look on my face, as I filed behind the other Sisters who turned to leave.

That night I lay awake for a long time. I thought that the almost fatal date that took me to an abandoned quarry was long forgotten. So was Reds, whom I liked but broke off with, after he landed in jail on my senior prom night. It hadn't occurred to me that he wouldn't have the money to rent a tux. And the irony was that I had just met Bob and really wanted to ask him to escort me to my prom. There I was, reminiscing about guys. Why was I still remembering the past?

As a teenager, male companionship had come to mean a lot to me. Yet, here I was, after five years in the convent, still having to struggle night after night with my female drives. My body wanted me to let it react like a woman—to love and be loved, to feel a man's touch.

I yanked the pillow out from under me and sat up against it. No! No! No! I wanted to scream aloud. You can't do this! You'll go crazy. You have to fight your feelings. Your vocation demands it! You made your choice—now live with it!

Soon, Sister Monica started preparing Sister Lawrence Marie and me for the taking of our first vows the following year. By then, we had to have our "Vow Catechism" memorized and the questions answered to her satisfaction. I listened to Sister Monica's instructions, already having more than an inkling of what the vow of chastity involved, with its terrible battles against the flesh.

In a roundabout way, my Sister Servant reminded me I had to give up men, dating, intimacy of any kind and, of course, sexual love. In answering God's Call, I was expected to forfeit my right to bear children, to be a mother, to be a grandmother— regardless of the personal cost to my human nature which, after all, every Catholic had to subdue because it was flawed, I was told.

In pondering the vow's deeper meaning, my mind insisted on wandering. These sacrifices had expensive price tags. I had graduated from high school knowing I wanted to marry and have children. I had fallen deeply in love with Bob, delighting in the thought that one day we would be able to express our love to the fullest and bring forth children out of that love. How could that be wrong?

Still, God had extended His Hands to take back my dreams, much like my father when I was eating a cookie without permission. God had his own Plan for me. That's what Sister Andrew said, when she persuaded me to follow her into the convent. So did all my Superiors who insisted they spoke to me in God's Name.

Pleadingly, I prayed, "Dear God, it's so hard to live like an angel, when you've left me with all the feelings and drives of a woman. Is it some kind of game to test me? Why me? Why not others who won't find these sacrifices so agonizing? I'll change places right now, if you'll let me." But God never answered. And I chided myself for asking such questions.

Next, I listened to instructions on the vow of obedience. Blind obedience. I must cooperate fully with Superiors: carry out their will, as if God Himself were speaking to me.

I already experienced how difficult this was, when I gave up my desire to be an artist, then a social worker, and when I submerged my will that wanted art and music and the outdoors in my life.

In obedience, I would have to go wherever Superiors told me to go and remain as long as they wanted me there—and do it without complaining. I would have to turn my back on all my yearnings to have contact with my family more often—even when my heart was bleeding for them. I would have to turn my back on all avenues to human love.

"Are you really asking me to obey blindly, when it doesn't make sense, even? Dear God, are you so tough and heartless? Tell me, please! Everyday is another day that my life is slipping away, like the salt in the egg timer at home. It's gone forever.

But, there I go again, questioning instead of accepting your Will and fully trusting those in authority who serve in your place, as they give orders. Give me the grace to do whatever you ask of me, Lord. I'll make that my prayer, whenever I have doubts—at least I'll try to.

"Then there's the vow of poverty. You want me to work for no pay, without the thought of financial security, without considering the future. To own nothing, to say 'ours' instead of 'mine' when speaking of material things. To live as much as possible like a poor person, like the poor person Jesus of Nazareth was.

"You know, Lord, I can't help having a thought that makes me want to laugh. Maybe it could be our own inside joke. Every time I say 'our Holy Habit,' I think of the number of years I have worn it, perspired in it—airing it out but not washing it. It isn't 'holy' by anyone else's standards. Nobody would ever want to claim it as theirs, that's for sure! I guess there is humor in my life, if I open my eyes to it!"

Week after week Sister Monica asked me the vow questions and listened to me recite the answers, much like I had done as a child in my parish school. The pattern was the same: Memorize the beliefs and practices required of you as a Catholic. Memorize the beliefs and practices required of you as a Sister. Learn by heart what you must do. Then, just do it.

I raised questions when Sister Monica instructed me on the fourth vow I would take: to serve the poor.

"But, Sister Monica, I'm not serving the poor here. Most of my students come from middle class homes."

"Sister Patricia Anne, they are poor intellectually. By teaching them, you are making them richer. They need you."

"But there are so many poorer people out there, with more serious needs. I'd like to be serving them."

"Sister, you have a good heart, and God will reward your generosity. For now, your religious community wants you to accept the philosophy that, wherever you're sent and whatever work you're sent to do, that is God's Will for you. Leave it to your Superiors to decide what 'serving the poor' means for each Sister."

"I heard a conversation that disturbs me," I said. "It's about the Sister in India who taught at a boarding school for the rich and couldn't stand seeing the poor die under her window without dignity or compassion. Mother Teresa then left her Order to minister to the dying. I was shocked to hear two of our Sisters criticize her saying the Sister in India was arrogant to think she knew better than her Superiors. But Mother Teresa did what she believed God wanted her do. Wasn't that God's Will for her?"

Again Sister Monica spoke up, "That Sister is doing good work. But you must remember that when you do your assigned duties without complaining, you are serving the poor. You are being a good Sister. You will be rewarded for your humble obedience. So don't trouble yourself over this vow, Sister Patricia Anne."

"Sister Monica, I always wanted to make the world a better place. Even before I became a Sister, I wanted to relieve the burdens of the oppressed. That's where my heart is."

"You are a good teacher, Sister. You are doing a fine job, and the children love you. God will bless you for your efforts—even more so, since it 'goes against the grain,'" she responded.

"You are preparing to take your first vows on the Feast of the Annunciation of Mary. Like Mary, you are opening your heart and soul completely to Jesus. Focus your attention on the great privilege soon to be yours. Offer yourself totally to God without any reservations. Trust Him to help you to be faithful."

And so, on March 25, 1961, in Emmitsburg, Maryland, I officially became a Bride of Christ when I pronounced my first vows aloud. Although my vows would expire at the end of the year, I intended to renew them for life. In my heart, my vocation was a permanent commitment. That is what I was taught and what I believed.

Back in Endicott, our convent was a kind of Camelot under Sister Monica, as far as community living went, but it was too good to last. High school administrators made the decision to extend the school to the end of the block. Since the convent, an old building, stood in the way, it would have to be razed.

Our Superiors decided the time had come for each school to have its own Sisters' residence. A high school convent would be built behind the school. And a house near the elementary school would be renovated and made into the other convent. Each school would have its own principal and each convent, its own Sister Servant.

My heart sank, as I listened to Sister Monica announce the decision of higher Superiors that she remain Sister Servant of the high school Sisters. An older high school teacher was appointed Sister Servant for the rest of us. How I was going to miss having Sister Monica as my Superior and friend!

The news about Sister Louis was startling. True, she seemed to be a good Sister. But she was abrupt and uptight most of the time. And she had not been a Superior before. I could not imagine that Sister becoming a Sister Servant and running a convent. But I kept my mouth shut and said nothing. Still, I gulped in disbelief.

While we were still together in the old convent, Sister Monica thought about the chapel in the new high school convent that was in the planning stages. Her deep aesthetic sense wanted appropriate stained-glass windows depicting the mysteries of the holy rosary. She asked Sister Joseph Marie to come up with designs for the glorious and sorrowful mysteries. And she directed me to design the five joyful mysteries with a window for each.

On weekends and evenings I worked on the project, researching Marian symbols used down through the ages. I came up with a sketch for each mystery and gave her my five samples when they were ready. Sister Monica, delighted with the final drawings both of us gave her, submitted them to the architect. When the chapel was completed, Sister Joseph Marie and I were happy our submissions were used exactly, with no alterations.

But then, the "old tapes" of Sister Directress from the seminary took over. "Sisters must be humble and never take satisfaction in what they do." So after that, I did not tell visitors I was the designer of any of the windows. Except for my family, on their next visit, I volunteered the information to no one.

It was a good exercise in humility, before splitting up with the high school Sisters and going off to make a new beginning. My life under Sister Louis was going to take all the humility I could muster. Life under the new regime would be inundated with self-denial beyond the call of duty, I feared.

Summer brought me back to Emmitsburg for assigned studies and my annual retreat of eight days, before I started that new chapter of my life.

2,066 days had passed since I left home. I missed my brown-shingled house and all its memories. Above all, I missed my loved ones.

7.

The Test

My intuition was right. It didn't take long for Sister Louis to show her true colors. Abrasive in her reactions, she became an insecure, threatened authority figure. Once again, my life became intolerable. It was already austere, but Sister Monica had taken the edge off hardships. Now, I found Sister Louis compounding them.

I struggled to accept my new Sister Servant and obey her orders. But it took a real act of faith to be subject to her. She was so unapproachable that I hated to go to her with all the permissions I was required to seek. And before long, the inevitable happened—my medical and dental problems mushroomed.

Previously, I could always find solace in the chapel, but now I found convent practices sabotaging my haven of peace. Our new chapel was tiny, with only three pews for the nine of us. On feast days, the small space reeked with the aroma of flowers on the altar—lots of them—lilies and roses especially. Although beautiful to look at, they triggered my allergies, making it almost impossible for me to breathe, and often I ended up suffering from migraine headaches.

On feast days, the priest saying Mass would implement the ritual of "incensing," right where I was sitting in the front pew. It was a challenge to stifle my cough. Still, I had to find a way, as coughing was not acceptable. I didn't want to be accused of seeking attention or disrupting the prayers of the other Sisters by my coughing.

All year long the Sisters praying wanted air. Lots of it! So they opened the chapel windows and let in what felt like frigid air. Those bolts of morning drafts hit me like knives and stirred up arthritic problems. I should have put on my shawl at such times, but I didn't want to be subject to the criticism of the others who might say, "Here, the youngest Sister of the house is acting like an old Sister. How pitiful!"

When my pains became unbearable, I swallowed my pride and approached Sister Louis. She sent me to a doctor who gave me a shot of cortisone and fitted me with a back brace. After that, I overcame my "human respect," which Sister Directress in the Seminary had called my "predominant fault." I put on my shawl, as soon as a blast of cold air stabbed me in the chapel. But even so, the shawl did not prevent the cold from reaching my bald head—which was covered only by the thin layers of the cornette.

I also started regular visits to a dentist for toothaches and abscesses that began plaguing me—not realizing that all my ailments were probably related to my emotional state. At the dentist's office, I had to remove my cornette in a secret room and put on my night caps. That way I could put my head back in the chair and allow him to get to my mouth without a lot of contortions.

I always felt awkward having a strange man's face so close to mine. I would close my eyes in order to avoid letting our eyes meet— although that dentist did not attract me in the least.

Like most dentists, the man talked a lot. He revealed that his mother forbade him from charging the Sisters for his services—the same woman who insisted he become a dentist despite his opposition. I thought it strange that a grown man had let his mother choose his career for him. But didn't I do the same thing when I let my Superiors put me in a field of work that was repugnant to me?

For dental and medical appointments we had to find another Sister to accompany us. If the Sister did not drive, we would have to ask a woman of the parish to take us. It was humiliating, since most women of the parish had families to take care of. It was an imposition to ask for that favor. Inevitably, they felt obligated to say "yes" to the Sisters. In fact, certain mothers already had a reputation for always being willing. So, those women were most often approached by us.

Once at the doctor's office, we had to keep our hands busy while we waited—not look around or read what was available for the other patients in the waiting room. Since it was an endless struggle to keep up with my students' work, I usually brought along test papers or worksheets to correct.

I couldn't imagine the thoughts circulating in the other patients' minds, as they watched two Sisters sitting side by side, working like wind-up toys—never raising their eyes from their work.

One day when I sat in the gynecologist's office, I felt uncomfortable seeing myself surrounded by pregnant women. What made it worse was that a restless toddler started going around the room repeating the same question to everyone: "Are you going to have a baby?" The closer she came to me, the more awkward I felt. Finally, the child lost interest and stopped making her rounds. I was greatly relieved!

It was baffling to me that some people registered surprise at seeing a Sister in a gynecologist's office. Didn't they realize that Sisters had the same body parts as other women? I, for instance, developed chronic problems with my monthly periods the longer I remained in the convent. The flow would become so heavy and long-lasting that I would have to cover my sheet with a plastic fabric on those weeks of the month. I hated the heavy flow with its accompanying cramps, especially since I could not slow down and throw myself across the bed when the pains became severe. Throughout my convent years, my Superiors sent me to gynecologists, but the problem was never really resolved.

The strain of my lifestyle on my emotions apparently revealed itself through my dysfunctional periods. Yet I was completely unaware of the connection at the time. I always struggled to be stoic and in denial of the pain.

Before long, it became a regular practice for Sisters to get their drivers' licenses and join a pool of drivers for the convent station wagon. I thought about it and decided that driving would be good for me. So, after mustering my courage, I approached Sister Louis to ask the needed permission.

"Give YOU permission to drive? No one would want to ride in a car with you, Sister! You're much too nervous!"

"I don't think I'd be nervous as a driver, Sister."

"Well, you would! So, the answer's NO!" Sister Louis said in her usual tone of voice to me.

I would have to wait ten more years before getting up the nerve to ask permission of a different Sister Servant and finally get my license. I wasn't a nervous driver, and I found that most Sisters were overflowing with gratitude to find a willing chauffeur.

Occasionally, I found humor in my life. One day, Sister Margaret Cecilia and I obtained permission to walk downtown—a few blocks away—and go to the "five-and-dime" store. We were used to people's reactions to our seventeenth-century headpiece with its starched white wings. So we would accept whatever came our way as we walked along the street.

Upon entering the store that day, we went about our business, until a toddler turned up our aisle and stopped in her tracks, speechless. I noticed the child staring at us wide-eyed. Then, as her mother started up the same aisle, the child tugged and tugged at the hem of her dress, pointing to us and gawking in disbelief. Finally, unable to contain herself, she yelled at the top of her lungs, "Are dem pirates or somethin'?"

The face of the embarrassed mother turned crimson, as she tried to quiet her daughter. We assured the mother, "It's all right."

I found it hard to keep a straight face at the time. Later, when we were out of everyone's sight, we laughed ourselves silly. That was a "first". We hadn't been called "pirates" before!

Monthly we had to go to the Sister Servant's office to give an account of ourselves and our adherence to the rules. I dreaded this practice all my life, as it kept me in a state of introspection and guilt. This was in addition to our mandatory weekly confession to the priest assigned to our convent, the public Friday night Conference of Faults with our fellow Sisters, and the annual report of our behavior to Sister Visitatrix during our eight-day silent summer retreat.

I didn't need the constant examination of conscience that kept me fixated on wrong-doing. After all, what could a Sister do that was so bad? We were nit-picking over the smallest imperfections and beating ourselves up over nothing—becoming emotional basketcases. At least, I was.

My training had impressed me with the fact that our Sisters could not get sick. So, usually I taught my classes regardless of severe headaches, cramps, or even the flu, as long as I was able to stand up. But one day when I was sick, that became impossible.

As I was teaching, I knew the worst was about to happen. I was going to vomit. And all the will power in the world was not going to prevent it. Although I was not supposed to leave my class unattended, I scribbled a work assignment on the blackboard and ran out of the room. I lost all sense of religious decorum, as I flew down the stairway just making it inside the principal's office, where I planned to use her private restroom. But I didn't make it far enough. I threw up all over her floor, too ill to care. When I finished using her restroom, Sister Louis sent me back to the convent—to bed—without an argument.

1963 turned out to be an historical year, in more ways than one. Higher Superiors notified us that our American foundress was going to be "beatified" in Rome on Saint Patrick's Day—the last step before canonization. Three Sisters of the Tri-Cities area would have the privilege of attending the ceremony, including our own Sister Edith and Sister Gabrielle from the high school down the street.

I was happy for Sister Edith. If anyone deserved to go to Europe, she did. She had been assigned to teach seventh graders in her old age. With her ruddy complexion that made her face look like a weathered block of stone, she often came back from school looking like she was going to burst a blood vessel. But she never complained. She accepted her "cross" with a stoic front.

On the day of her departure, while the rest of us were teaching, she hurried down the stairs to meet her driver and go to the airport. But she never made it to the car. She collapsed, never again to walk or talk, paralyzed down her right side.

It didn't seem fair that this poor woman who had given her life to God should end up like this. Missing her trip was one thing. But spending the rest of her life on her back at Saint Michael's Villa—the nursing home for our Sisters—seemed a cruel twist of fate. Her body, and maybe her mind, too, had given out—surrendered.

Did she prefer a new kind of pain, immobility, to the daily suffering her life as a seventh grade teacher of a class of 55 students had thrust upon her? Maybe she was totally unprepared for the prospect of a trip to Europe in her old age. Still, a gift offered by God, why was it taken back? Was it Divine Love in disguise?

Sister Gabrielle, the high school librarian down the street, joined the others and went abroad. She returned from the pilgrimage bursting with excitement. She had visited our Motherhouse in Paris, stayed in Rome for the religious ceremony honoring Mother Seton, and was allowed to visit relatives in Ireland before coming back.

She delighted my mother with a special gift, a sapphire-blue enameled Miraculous Medal that she "touched" to the "chair" Blessed Mother had sat on during one of her appearances to Sister Catherine Laboure in 1830. That chair, formerly used by the priest during Mass, was still there. Visitors placed religious articles on it for a moment, believing that the chair held an aura or power that would somehow bring them blessings.

Mother was thrilled! From that day forward, she started wearing the medal around her neck, trusting that Mary, from Heaven, would protect her from harm, even illness. And she resolved never to take it off.

For the following decades, well into old age, Mother would suffer no serious illness. She even boasted that, in her entire life, she never had a headache. Did Mary, indeed, watch over her? Her answer was always a definitive YES!

Several months later, our Provincial Superior sent an unusual announcement to the Sister Servants of New York State. "A special Mass honoring Blessed Elizabeth Ann Seton will be celebrated in Queens, New York, at the World's Fair. Send all the available Sisters to this event," her letter said.

A bus was chartered and off we went to the World's Fair. Unbelievable! After living sequestered from the outside world for eight years, I was suddenly being thrown into the midst of regular people—lay people. And I was supposed to act like this was a normal occurrence.

As I took my first subway ride, squeezed up against a crowd of people, I struggled to hold onto a pole while shielding the back and sides of my cornette—hoping no one would get poked in the eye. We spent two nights in a hotel in the big city, two Sisters to a room, each having our own bed.

That first night my thoughts kept me awake. I had been to New York just once before, when my sailor Bob took me to meet his mother. Now all those feelings for Bob were numbed. I had finally succeeded in burying all memories of the wonderful times we spent together—or so I thought.

Having been a Sister for so long a time, I allowed no sentiments of romance to surface. I had learned to act like my body was a fortress surrounded by a moat, whenever I yearned for affection. Quickly, I would yank up the drawbridge for protection—before "temptations" could seep into my heart and soul.

As I tried to blend in with the crowd at the World's Fair, onlookers stared at the flock of us Sisters resembling birds with our odd headdresses. I was in a quandary. Here I was, mixing with strangers—externs my Community called them—smiling, as I practiced politeness and graciousness.

This seemed easy, at first. I had grown up in Baltimore, the "city of hospitality," where the atmosphere was usually welcoming. But I had been shut away from ordinary people for three years in Emmitsburg. Even in Endicott I lived in seclusion from the real world. I was not equipped now to mingle at the World's Fair with people who walked elbow-to-elbow alongside me.

As I strolled among them with a partner, I only knew how to act like the Sister I was trained to be. I felt like a caged bird that was set free to get a "taste" of freedom—but only for a little while—and under strict supervision. The experience left me feeling more unfree than ever, and my life fragmented and confused.

Before long, we were back at school, and I had to refocus my energy. It was fall. Thanksgiving would soon be here, and I had a lot of lessons left to teach before the holidays.

Suddenly, I heard excitement in Sister Louis' voice, as she scurried down the corridor giving a message to each teacher. When her face appeared at my doorway, I could see tears in her eyes, as she blurted out:

"The President's been shot!"

"Is he all right?" I asked.

"I don't know. He's in a Dallas hospital. Just pray. Have your students pray."

A pall fell over the school and the convent, when we learned that JFK was dead. He had been the first Catholic president and had emerged as a great leader, according to all we Sisters were told. He had kept the nation unified when he led us through the "dark cloud" of the Cuban crisis.

I still remembered the evening we sat on the closed-in porch of our new convent for recreation. There was tension in the air, as Sister Louis sat at the head of our group and turned on the radio she carried in her hands. I had not listened to a radio since I left home, but tonight was different. Our beloved President was about to address the nation. JFK began his speech solemnly, then explained the reason for the Cuban crisis. He urged citizens to pray, even as he tried to allay fears and prevent panic.

I froze as I listened intently, understanding that we were in the midst of a grave situation that involved Russia and Cuba. We all breathed a sigh of relief later, when the Russian ships bound for Cuba turned back, and life in America and the convent resumed its normal pace.

Our Sisters revered our President highly, along with all the Kennedys, as they had been generous donors to our social service and medical institutions. They were wealthy Catholics who gave large donations to the Sisters' works that focused on helping the disadvantaged and lifting the poor out of poverty.

I believed that the matriarch Rose was responsible for that phenomenon. It was a gift she had passed on to her children as their mother, I thought, proving the powerful influence mothers had on their offspring. How her heart must be breaking today!

We too mourned the loss of this man—our president and friend whom we loved like a family member. In this instance, I found it difficult to repeat the over-used expression Sisters often uttered, "It's God's Will."

I knew that murder couldn't be God's Will. It wasn't God who pulled the trigger and assassinated our president. Already as a Sister I was limiting the times I would tell people an event was God's Will. In the face of an evil happening I would say instead, "God did not want this, but He will bring something good out of it."

I had come to honestly believe that God does bring good out of evil. Still, the tension between good and evil was a mystery I didn't want to dwell on. Delving deeply into that arena of thought could drive a person crazy.

The solution, I concluded, was to muster one's faith and believe that a Higher Power was somehow in control of our lives and the destiny of the universe, as the cycle of life, growth, and death was repeated over and over again until the end of time. To me as a Catholic Judaeo-Christian, Jesus the Son of God was the answer. I had always found my peace and equilibrium in Him.

Our school closed down for the funeral, and we were told that the prohibition against watching television would be lifted for a few days. We could join the nation and the Kennedy family in grieving and in celebrating this man's life and presidency by watching the funeral and the newscasts on TV.

I remembered I had a dental appointment on the day of Kennedy's burial. I called to inquire, assuming the office would be closed, since the whole country was in mourning. I was shocked when the receptionist informed me that the dentist would have business as usual, and I hastily cancelled my appointment.

I was really heartbroken over the death of this man that I loved—the charismatic president with whom my countrymen and I had bonded. I wanted to be in seclusion with the other Sisters to grieve, so I spent that day watching TV, seeing the President lie in state in the Capitol rotunda with military personnel standing guard.

As I watched the funeral procession proceed slowly down Pennsylvania Avenue, I was deeply-moved by the sight of the flag-draped, horse-drawn caisson, accompanied by a riderless horse carrying boots reversed in the saddle's stirrups.

Looking regal, the President's widow—Jacqueline Kennedy—stood like a statue with a black veil over her face blowing in the November wind. My heart ached especially for the children. I watched little John John, only a toddler, salute his father's casket, with his sister Caroline standing nearby. My tears flowed like a torrent at that moment. In a split second, its memory was etched on my heart forever. It was a tragic scene in every respect.

We had taken this president for granted, expecting him to be with us for a long, long time. And now, he was gone. Once again, we were reminded of life's unpredictability and our own mortality. With love and regret, we said our "farewells."

Earlier that year we had buried another leader, Pope John XXIII. His short papacy was said to be a contradiction. He had been elected as "interim pope" to fill in the gap for a little while—until a suitable candidate could be found. He was a "safe choice." Surely, this old prelate could not live much longer. That was the thinking of Vatican insiders at the time of his election, according to rumors that circulated in the Catholic Church.

But how wrong those officials were! The new Pope shocked the Catholic world by calling for an ecumenical council, only the second one ever. Finally, after four exhaustive years of preparation, Vatican Council II convened in the fall of 1962, its first session lasting eight weeks.

The saintly Pope John XXIII met with great opposition, but insisted that the Catholic Church "open its windows and let fresh air in." He died before the second session opened in September, of 1963, leaving the new pontiff—Pope Paul VI—to bring the work Pope John had started, to fruition.

Pope John's legacy was a renewed Church—a church that had taken a serious look at itself—its essence, its role in the modern world, its Mass and other aspects of the liturgy, including the lifestyle and "Habits" of its priests, brothers, and sisters. It also probed its relationship to other religions, both Christian and non-Christian. In the end, the council produced documents and constitutions that were intended to guide the Catholic Church into future centuries. Evidence of the presence and power of the Holy Spirit, I believed.

The resulting changes and adaptations would affect Catholics—including the Sisters in our Religious Order—on many levels, some traumatically. For us, transition to a radically-different Habit loomed large on the horizon.

With the school year nearing its end, we had to switch gears temporarily and focus on our summer assignments.

"Vacation is not what you think, here in our religious community," Sister Directress had said over and over again in the seminary.

"As a Sister, this is the definition of 'vacation' for you: it is a change of occupation, not time to relax or be lazy." She made it clear that summertime for teachers meant assigned studies for many years. After achieving whatever degree Superiors determined we should work toward, we would be sent to help out at a hospital or social work center of our Sisters.

We could not grow slack in our obligation to work. Laziness or slowing down in the summer would not be tolerated. Any other concept of vacation was for worldly people. We could "relax in the Lord" during our annual retreat of eight days. Alone with the Lord at that time, we could walk nearby, think, and pray; in addition to, mandatory participation in all the scheduled spiritual activities.

We could speak only for our annual confession to the assigned priest and during our annual visit with Sister Visitatrix to give an account of ourselves and how we were living our vocation. Other than those occasions and prayer time, silence was required.

When I started returning to our Emmitsburg Provincial House for summer classes, I enjoyed being able, finally, to sit under the trees to study. The refreshing breezes made it less difficult to wear so many layers of clothing. And it was thrilling to listen to the bird songs and the rustle of the leaves without feeling guilt.

I listened with empathy to the stories the older Sisters told. Those Sisters were frequently bursting to talk, eager to pour out their hearts to younger Sisters. I was appalled at the grief some of the Sisters had carried for years. My heart went out to the Sister who revealed that her brother had died in the World War II Battle of the Bulge.

He had come to the Provincial House to say "goodbye" to her, she said, before being shipped overseas. But she was in retreat that day and could not be disturbed. The Sister Receptionist told him to come back at a later time.

But a later time never came. He went to war, never to return. The anguish of missing that last hug—his final farewell—was deeply imbedded in her soul and she was broken-hearted still. How I wanted to wrap my arms around that Sister so scarred with pain—give her a hug that said I cared—but it was not allowed.

Another Sister spoke secretly of her family and confided to me that she and her relatives in Pennsylvania were related to Clark Gable. Sister Felicita insisted what she spoke was true. In fact, she added, she was in touch with the late movie star's widow who was active at that time with our Sisters' hospital in Los Angeles.

Even though my band of Sisters had been trained not to speak of our families to anyone, I found it heart-rending to listen to the older Sisters. They wanted so badly to hold on to their past and share some of it with the younger Sisters. They were starving to be heard, to unburden themselves before their hearts shriveled up from emotional strangulation.

These Sisters perceived by others as belonging to another world had a very human side, just like me. After years of repression, they needed to reveal their torment. So I was happy to listen. But how I wished that religious orders had not been so negative about our emotional outlets—had not been so afraid to let us be human.

A Sister younger than me spoke of her great-grandmother, Madame Surratt, who ran the boarding house where John Wilkes Booth plotted President Lincoln's assassination. Although the proprietor protested her innocence, she was arrested and hanged. This Sister said her family had passed down from generation to generation the pearls Madame Surratt wore at her hanging and a lock of her hair. "She had no knowledge of the assassination plot," the Sister insisted.

Another story told of the Confederate spy who was arrested on an East Coast train, dressed in our religious Habit. Had one of the girls at our boarding school smuggled out a Habit? Or even one of our Sisters? We had students and Sisters from the North and the South, after all.

I don't think anyone knew the answer to those questions, other than the spy himself and the person who obtained the Habit for him. I never knew what became of him after he was caught. I could only wonder. I guess I didn't want to know.

Then, there were the Sisters who thrived on telling ghost stories—narratives about our Sisters who "returned" after their death. "Did she need to atone for unsaid prayers?" some asked in regard to the Sister who allegedly showed up in the chapel at prayer time.

In another instance, a departed Sister bothered those who were trying to sleep in one of the dormitories. This became such an aggravation that the priest-director, a normally conservative clergyman, set up an altar there and said a Mass of exorcism to get rid of her—a rare occurrence since priests in those days celebrated Mass only in churches and chapels, other than on battlefields.

Did he consider the Sisters "at war" with the ghost who wouldn't leave them alone? Why did the Sister persist in staying on earth? Regardless of the answer, the priest's prayers apparently worked. The disturbance ceased.

One older Sister, a very intelligent and lucid person, kept us on the edge of our seats whenever she recounted the gut-wrenching story that would later be made famous by the book and the film The Exorcist. The Sister had been working in the archdiocese where the incidents actually occurred. In fact, she related that the monsignor who was appointed by archdiocesan authorities to handle the case was brother to one of our Superiors.

The Sister narrating insisted she had obtained the facts firsthand from the priest in charge. She was very conversant about the details of the horrifying case, commenting that, while the core of the story was factual, the book's author had embellished the tale to include happenings in previous cases of possession by the devil. She added that the subject of the book, no longer possessed, was now happily-married and wished to remain anonymous.

I had no reason to doubt some of the ghost stories I heard, as I believed in the existence of spirits of the dead and the possibility of souls not at rest. Still, after knowing the suffering that our rules and practices inflicted, it was difficult to imagine that any dead Sister's soul would not be at rest. How could any Sister not go straight to Heaven?

The day each summer that I anticipated above all others was called "Coney Island Day"—dubbed by our older Sisters from New Jersey and New York who were studying among us. This was the only day when the relatives of the summer school Sisters could come to visit.

On that day the vast lawns of our college campus would be blanketed with people—with Sisters covered up in their "Holy Habits" and throngs of family members dressed for the intense heat, some in shorts. The gathering was hot, but always enjoyable, since our guests were dearly-loved and dearly-missed relatives whose visits were restricted and scheduled sparingly.

Unfortunately, we would have to leave our families to picnic alone, while we Sisters went inside to say noon prayers together and have dinner. Under no circumstance could a Sister share a bottled drink, even water, with her family or go off for a short ride—even on the campus. We still had to remember the invisible boundaries that included emotional distance from our blood relatives, whom our Superiors referred to as "externs."

The notion that my family was included in the broad category of externs should have been impossible for me to fathom. My dear mother had given me life—twice! She and my hard-working dad had guided and nurtured me. My parents, my brother and my sisters had shared love with me in the family unit. Treating them as outsiders was not right. I could not imagine Jesus habitually shutting out his parents.

Should I have rejected my Community's philosophy or, at least, questioned it? Was my silence culpable in God's sight? Or was I incapable of thinking clearly—or even logically?

The summer visit was a mixed blessing for me. Upon my family's arrival in the morning, I exploded with happiness. When I waved goodbye and watched their car pull away in late afternoon, I could feel my heart break in many pieces. Each tearing away hurt more than the previous time—and no amount of stoicism could numb the pain.

It would have been so wonderful in those years to spend a few days at home, even take a short vacation with my family—like most priests did. But, here again, there was a double standard reflecting society outside religious life. All such activities were forbidden to women in convents who, as members of a Catholic Order of Sisters, had no rights.

Our Superiors said we should "offer it up"—put up with hardship that would bring more grace to our souls and earn us a high place in Heaven, our ultimate goal. "Be grateful for your pain," they said. "It's your opportunity to save souls. Embrace your suffering like the saints did. Rejoice that you are in good company."

"But I want to be in my family's company!" I should have screamed out. "Is that so wrong? I love my family dearly. Practicing customs of exclusion only serves to aggravate the pain of separation—for me and for them!"

At such times, I wished I could cry my heart out. Naive young woman that I was, I crushed my anguish and forced myself to comply.

It would not be until decades later—after I was out of the convent and after my father's death—that Mother would reveal to me Dad's heart-wrenching words: "Maybe if we had a body, we'd have part of her."

If Dad had revealed his grief directly to me—had he let me know how tormented he was, would that knowledge have changed my life's direction?

In each other's presence, my family members and I continued to play the "cover-up" game. Smile, cover up the pain, and don't add to each other's suffering. And so it went, year after year.

I had expected to return for my seventh year to Saint Ambrose School in Endicott. I liked the people in that city. The area had grown on me, and I was fond of my pupils. But, on an appointed summer day, I knelt down to listen, while a Superior read the list of changes for the new school year.

"Sister Patricia Anne Grueninger will go to Saint Charles Borromeo School in Pikesville, Maryland."

The words shattered me. "Is this another game, Lord? My destination is changed, after I struggle so hard to adjust—and finally do. What a cruel joke—sending me to my home county, when I can't go home, even for a visit. Although I'll only be a few miles away, I won't be any closer to my family than I was in Endicott. Why, Lord?

"And I won't be allowed to go back to Endicott to say any farewells or even write a letter for that purpose. I'll simply be replaced. Another Sister will be sent to fill my shoes, and I'll soon be forgotten. School will go on. Convent life will go on. Was Sister Directress right when she said we were all dispensable, and we should be willing to be transferred at the will of Superiors who know what's best for the Community?"

"If we're practicing detachment, seriously striving for perfection, we'll thank God for the opportunity to grow in holiness," she had said.

I couldn't bring myself to thank God.

This was my first big change from one mission to another, and I found it scary. But convent assignments and reassignments were to be expected in religious congregations—like the military. My Superiors called it "doing God's Will."

Never were we given a reason, nor were we to question the decision of Superiors to move us around—much like pawns in a game. To do so would have been considered a fault, an imperfection—unbefitting someone called to be a "Bride of Christ."

While I was not given the opportunity to speak face-to-face with my Superior to discuss how I felt, I found it impossible to just stamp out my feelings. Change would always be painful, especially change I believed I had no control over—change that would redirect my life, rechannel my energies, and deny me any choice in the matter.

If there was repugnance for the new location or the new Community of Sisters I'd be joining, I had to bow my head to the Will of God and not react. It was a test of my faith, if it involved a struggle; and that was good for me, my Superiors said. My reward someday would be a high place in Heaven; which, after all must be my major goal in life.

So, silence to pain and silence to personal needs or wants. Nothing mattered, except pleasing God and reaching Heaven. In my Catholic school training that's what I was taught to believe. And the same philosophy pervaded my convent formation. Isn't that what my vocation was all about? I was to place myself with trust in the hands of my God-appointed Superiors who had the authority to do with me what they said was for the best.

As I prepared to relocate, I reflected on the previous six years. During this time-period my health problems mushroomed, while my individuality and self-esteem continued to disintegrate.

On the one hand, people placed me on a pedestal, revering me as if I were from another world, an angel "in the flesh." On the other hand, I wanted to cry out, " I'm human, just like you. I'm a real woman. I have feelings. I have drives. Stop acting like I am in a non-human category. My pedestal isn't worth the price I have to pay!"

I went to my safe haven—the chapel—and had a good cry in secret. Then, in obedience, I bowed my head to God's Will. When peace returned, I got ready to leave for my new destination. Walking past the parked bus the Sisters bound for New York State were boarding, I wished my former companions a good school year. Then I got in the station wagon that would take me to Pikesville, Maryland—a two-hour drive away.

3,267 days had passed since I left home. I missed my brown-shingled house and all its memories. Above all, I missed my loved ones.

8.

Changing Habits

It was 1964, and the autumn leaves were becoming a kaleidoscope of color. I was unaware of what was happening in the secular world, but it didn't matter anyway. September 20th was fast approaching, and all 40,000 of our Community members worldwide were focused on just one thing—our major transformation in appearance.

Vatican Council II had issued a document making it mandatory for congregations of Sisters to adjust to the "changed conditions of the times." The Decree on the Appropriate Renewal of Religious Life stipulated that Habits meet the requirements of health and be suited to the circumstances of time and place.

At our Paris Motherhouse, Superiors had tapped into the talent of a former employee of Christian Dior, now a Sister, to help design a new Habit. The result was a navy blue uniform of polyester that reached to the ankles. A white dickey of soft fabric replaced the starched white collar, while a short blue coiffe covered the head—making the new headpiece resemble a veil. The resulting look was a radical departure from the seventeenth-century dress our Sisters wore for over three centuries.

Our hair still had to be concealed, but we no longer had to shave it off. We could keep it the length we wanted, as long as it did not show. And finally, we could wear modern underwear—panties and a bra—instead of the antiquated undergarments of a bygone era.

Classrooms had to be in order by Labor Day, but our biggest concern was to be ready for the big change—to meet the deadline!

We spent a lot of time that August and September sitting around the community room table, putting the final touches on our new Habit and stitching up seams. One day, when the atmosphere was gloomy like a morgue, I tried to inject some humor into what we were doing. I thought, by joking, I could break the uncomfortable silence and dispel the funereal air, but I was wrong.

"This new Habit is really different from what we've been wearing," I said. "It's going to take some getting used to. At least, we won't have to watch out for birds anymore. The days of birds flying overhead, doing their business on our cornettes, those days are gone forever."

No one spoke up, so I continued. "I love the Habit as much as any of us, but I won't miss the sticky starch melting against my cheeks and neck in the summertime. And I won't miss the long skirt dragging in the dirt, gathering it up."

"That's enough, Sister Patricia Anne," Sister Edwina roared. "Where's your loyalty?"

I wanted to respond and say I didn't mean to sound like a traitor. After all, our Superiors in Paris had ordered us to adopt this new Habit. Where was blind obedience now? The whole scenario reeked of contradiction. Why could we not vent our emotions, instead of always keeping them bottled up?

As if she could read my mind, Sister Edwina added, "Just keep quiet, Sister, like everybody else."

My new Sister Servant had reacted as if I had attacked her personally. You would have thought I had committed an act of treason. It wasn't until this moment that I realized just how attached the older Sisters were to the old Habit and how painful the sacrifice was for them.

I looked around at all the Sisters sewing in silence, not giving voice to their thoughts for or against the new Habit. They were practicing blind obedience as they, too, had been trained. Those who were in pain were suppressing it, just as those who were looking forward to wearing more modern apparel were keeping their anticipation to themselves. How sad that the Sisters believed their only option was to sit there with their mouths shut and their feelings buried.

Now, I had worn the seventeenth-century Habit for over seven years, and I felt some sentimentality also when Superiors announced we would have to change it—obey the Pope and the male hierarchy who recognized that religious Habits, as well as many other things in the Catholic Church, had remained too static through the ages. Those Church leaders had voted for adaptations in order to be more in tune with the demands of a different era.

As I redirected my thoughts, it seemed odd that it was men who had evaluated the lifestyle and dress of religious women, then made that determination. Maybe Sister Edwina had a point to make, that she had no say or vote in the matter. I knew that Saint Vincent de Paul and his successors represented the Pope for us. But even in mainstream society men ran everything, so it should not have surprised me or any of us.

Besides, there was a positive way to regard the Habit change. Although the traditional Habit was picturesque and made us stand out among other religious orders, it was hot—terribly hot—and outdated! Modern young women were no longer from the "be seen and not heard" generation. They would not stand for repressive rules, oppressive policies, and antiquated dress. We had to change our ways or lose the very people we wanted to attract to our lifestyle.

The big day finally arrived. I took off my old Habit that morning, turned it in, and replaced it with my new Habit. I felt strange, changing my style of dress for the first time in over seven years.

I had started out in the Community wearing a postulant's dress for six months. In the seminary I dressed like a "Dutch-cleanser" girl for fifteen months. After Habit-taking, I wore the dress of seventeenth-century French village girls, which I continued to wear for the last seven and a-half years.

Today, I simply took off the old garb and donned my new Habit. I would never again have the cornette "lock up" my head. I would no longer feel anchored to the ground by the sheer weight of the Habit I wore. I had a wider range of vision now, and my neck lost the sensation of wearing a dog collar. The discomfort of having a heavily-starched ring around my neck was gone, along with the stiff headgear that locked my cheeks harness-style.

School had started two weeks earlier. So there was no time for nostalgia or any kind of sentimentality. It was just as well. I got right to work, acting like nothing much had changed. The children sitting in desks before me gawked until the newness of my appearance wore off. For all of us Sisters, memories of the old Habit would gradually fade away, as we focused our minds on the tasks assigned to us.

That same year our Community initiated a practice called "dialogue"—a term I hadn't heard before. Superiors cautiously introduced the concept to us, encouraging Sisters to voice their opinions only after careful consideration and prayer. Selected topics were organized in color-coded sets to control the areas we could explore. Finally, I thought, my observations will count.

Believing that openness was being called for, I spoke up candidly and made suggestions that would improve our lifestyle without compromising it. Although I didn't think I was proposing anything radical, I got the feeling I was being labeled.

It did not occur to me that Superiors in our Province might want change to occur slowly—or not at all. So in my naiveté, I wasn't concerned about repercussions.

In some religious congregations, changes took place rapidly. When Sisters of an Order in Los Angeles began dressing in lay clothes, the local Cardinal and other members of the American hierarchy expressed their shock—even horror. This was not what they anticipated, when they called for adaptations. The abandonment of Habits by female religious was not on their agenda. Those women were an embarrassment to church leaders—out of control in their opinion.

Witnessing this new phenomenon that was "rocking the boat," my Superiors tightened the reins. They reacted like threatened figures of authority, who were afraid to take risks and tamper with the status quo.

So more than ever, they emphasized that the highest priority of each Sister had to be personal holiness and doing the work assigned. Decisions about community life had to be left in the hands of Superiors and no one else.

Contradictions characterized the post-Vatican II era of our Community's implementation of its mandates—despite the introduction of dialogue sessions in local convents. Many Superiors gave the impression that our Religious Order would disintegrate without their control. Perhaps that very attitude was blocking the action of the Holy Spirit in our Community, as well as the Church.

Ignoring all the upheaval, I concentrated on my new assignment— teaching new students in a new school with a new principal.

Sister Edwina was a big woman—not very tall, but quite wide. She had spent most of her life as a Sister working with orphans in an institutional setting, before being appointed principal of our school. Rumor had it she had stepped over the line by flaunting the rule that forbade Sisters from touching people. She had hugged her motherless and fatherless children, despite warnings.

By her stubborn insistence on showing affection to her charges like a real mother, she had questioned the wisdom of her Superiors— not by words, but by her behavior. And, for this, she paid dearly. According to the convent grapevine, she was subsequently removed from the work she loved.

I supposed, at first, that Sister Edwina just had a naturally-grumpy disposition. In reality, torn away from the children she loved, Sister Edwina was struggling with deep hurt. Eventually, I discovered that her gruff exterior hid a warm and compassionate heart.

But I, too, was carrying pain. I had to adjust to an unfamiliar convent with Sisters I hadn't lived with before. The other Sisters also had adjustments to make, so I just had to smile like everything was all right—smile a Sister's smile—and go on with my life.

New at her job, Sister Edwina had made a strange decision that summer. Since there was an overflow of seventh and eighth graders, she would have to create a combination class. She came up with what she considered a "brainstorm"—putting together the brightest eighth graders and the slowest seventh graders. Her rationale was that the smartest students were going to learn no matter what, while the slowest ones were not expected to learn much anyway. She decided further to give the outdated textbooks with dull black illustrations and small print to that class.

Since my student teaching had been with seventh graders, she assigned me to teach all the seventh and eighth graders in a departmental setting. I would teach Social Studies, Music, Reading, and Religion.

I was appalled by her philosophy of education, although I wasn't surprised by it. After all, she had no training in teaching or the administration of a school. And I could see that she was going to use a "hit-or-miss" approach to this job that she didn't really want in the first place.

I tried to give all of my students a good education; but before long, I had a disaster on my hands. Never before did I have discipline problems. But now, they abounded.

With the large class size and the growing number of boys with behavioral problems, I ran out of ways to separate the unruly. Each day became a catastrophe waiting to happen. It didn't take long before the boys seated near the bulletin boards in the back of the room were pulling out straight pins and hurling them at the necks of the students in front of them.

I became terribly frustrated. Classroom discipline was so time-consuming that I could not do a good job of teaching. So, finally, I went to my principal for advice.

"I've never had discipline problems before," I stammered out. "Now, I dread the time of day when that class comes in. They are out of control, and they won't listen to me!"

The solution Sister Edwina offered was not a workable one. She told me to send for her each day when those students came in, and she would sit in the back of the room doing her work.

Despite my misgivings, I obeyed. It worked at first. Students cooperated when she sat in the back of the room. Built like a "bouncer" in a bar, she was the one person with the power to expel them. They always cooperated when she was present. But as soon as she would leave the room to take a phone call or meet with the pastor or a disgruntled parent, the class would go crazy again.

Somehow, I made it to the end of the school year—happy to say goodbye to those students. Under my breath, I added "good

156

riddance!" It would be the only year of my teaching career marked by a negative attitude on my part.

In the spring of 1965, we traveled back to Emmitsburg for the dedication of the new Provincial House. Since the repairs of the old building had become too costly, a decision was made to rebuild nearby.

It had taken three years to construct the sprawling air- conditioned complex with its Spanish tile roof, its four U-shaped stories, and its three wings jutting out—leaving a fourth corner for the chapel that sprang up like an eye—catching cathedral.

Close to four hundred bedrooms and over fifty restroom and bath accommodations were built; in addition to the common areas that included refectories, kitchens, community rooms, retreat spaces, studies, laundries and offices.

Outsiders were impressed with the chapel's hemispherical sanctuary that was dominated by a gigantic crucifix hovering over an elegant marble altar on which the priest could celebrate Mass facing the congregation. Magnificent mosaics put finishing touches on the chapel.

I joined the hundreds of Sisters who filled the pews for the dedication of the chapel that would eventually become a national shrine, housing the remains of our holy foundress Mother Seton, and evolve into a basilica to honor America's first native-born saint after her canonization.

Participating in the ceremonies, while lost in the army of Sisters, gave me a sense of being part of something that was bigger than all of us—a sense of solidarity with women who had followed their Call, who had responded to God who asked them to sacrifice their own will and replace it with His Will. Still, I had to quiet some questions that wanted to burst out of my mouth: Why was so much money spent to house Sisters vowed to serve the poor? It was obviously a multi-million dollar project with special items coming from Italy and other parts of the world. Was it a religious monument our French founder Saint Vincent dePaul would have approved of? Who actually paid for this spectacular specimen of architecture? Did the money come from the combined salaries of the Sisters who never received a paycheck for their hard work? Was the failure to explain these small details honest? Was the building such a distraction that it disguised the Catholic Church's culture of abuse that infiltrated its Religious Orders of women?

But I had not been given the opportunity to question. I had not been asked my opinion. So, as usual, I kept quiet and said nothing. When the day's festivities ended, I returned to Pikesville.

In keeping with Vatican Council II's mandates my new pastor, Father Cummings, wanted to enhance the sacred music of the parish liturgies. He had already asked Sister Edwina to appoint Sister Ann Adele as adult choir director. Now, he directed her to have me organize a youth choir.

He would provide the training—send the two of us to Howard University to learn choral techniques and to the Catholic University of America to study church music. In addition, we would join the other Sisters of the Baltimore Archdiocese and attend the music workshops given by the very talented Sulpician priest, Father Eugene Walsh—the expert on the implementation of the <u>Constitution on the Sacred Liturgy</u> in the area of music.

The following summer I found my name on the list of changes once again. This time I would be going to the cold north country— to Holbrook, Massachusetts. Knowing I had no option other than changing my mindset and preparing to leave, I did just that. Then, word came suddenly that I was to remain in Pikesville, after all. That seemed strange.

Later I would learn that our pastor, now a monsignor, was not happy when the principal told him I was leaving and not being replaced by a Sister proficient in music.

What I did not know, since I never received a paycheck, was that he was giving my Sister Servant a double stipend for the two of us who were directing the church choirs, in addition to teaching in the parish school.

I didn't realize that the pastor was paying me for double duty, and my Superior was using the money to run the convent and buy what she deemed necessary—then sending the balance to our Provincial

Superiors. All of this was done unbeknown to me. Even though I had taken a vow of poverty, was this just? Or was I being used and taken advantage of?

When my Sister Servant informed higher Superiors of the pastor's reaction and the convent's loss of income, they reversed their decision to transfer me. They would keep me working where I was worth more to the Community and find another Sister to send to Holbrook to fill needs there. I would still not receive any of the money I was earning, nor would I even know how much my Superiors were receiving for my labor.

Monsignor Cummings was delighted with the way the matter was resolved. After all, the Sisters served the parish at his will.

But the pastor had other problems to remedy. He was having a difficult time adjusting to some of the changes brought about by Vatican Council II. One was the new funeral liturgy that was supposed to replace the traditional Requiem Mass. Instead of black, white was to be the funeral color. And it was to be a Mass of Resurrection—a joyful send-off to Heaven rather than a morbid ritual. The monsignor refused to implement the change—then he died.

I was surprised that the Archbishop of Baltimore chose to initiate the change in the pastor's own funeral Mass. Our monsignor had been an elderly priest struggling to come to grips with change. Intent on enhancing the sacred music of the parish, he had made his contribution.

Would it not have been more considerate of him, if his wishes had been honored—at least until after his funeral? But enforcing rules and rubrics was a high priority in the Catholic Church at a time when its officials clung tenaciously to their absolute power.

And so, the monsignor's very interment ritual was a slap in his face, as we prayed for the repose of his soul.

Our new pastor, another good priest, was Monsignor Cummings' opposite in temperament. Athletic in orientation, Father Schwalenburg kept company with sports personalities like Brooks Robinson of the Baltimore Orioles and Don Schula, coach of the Baltimore Colts, whose chaplain he became.

We Sisters did not have direct contact with the pastor or his assistant priests. Only the principal met with the pastor regularly to give an account of the school and how it was running. A new superior, Sister Rosemarie, had replaced Sister Edwina, and it was she who started bringing back to the convent stories of the athletes who were the pastor's pals.

She said that Coach Schula always started his days with early Mass and that he prayed especially hard on days when games were scheduled. One day she returned, announcing that the pastor had baptized his friend Brooks Robinson. Many of the Colts' and Orioles' team members frequented the rectory, our Sister Servant said—realizing that a little bit of gossip would break the monotony of convent life.

But it was taboo for any Sister to go to sports events or even cultural activities—other than those that involved the children under her care. So there was an aura of mystery in discussing those topics.

I began to see for myself that there was, indeed, a double standard between the behavior considered appropriate for priests and that of Sisters. While we women could not go out to restaurants or theaters or socialize with externs, the priests could do all of the above—even go off on vacations, pursue their interests and develop their talents. One of Father Schwalenburg's assistants at Saint Charles Borromeo Parish became an actor in amateur theater during his off-duty hours.

As all Sisters at the time, I was expected to accept this as a fact of life—not complain or even question the contradictions. My conditioning at home and in the secular society of the 1950's, then in my convent training, led me to comply.

Deep down, it was painful to keep myself so stifled. Certainly, the priests were aware of the discrepancies. Why, then, did they not speak out for justice?

While my Superiors were considering some suggested adaptations to the emerging culture, an unexpected change was announced. The ban on going home for a visit was being lifted. Sisters could start going home, but it was limited to three days a year—either three days in a row or three separate days.

At first, I had mixed feelings. I left home believing I would never see my house again. I could still remember standing outside, taking a long, last look at my brown-shingled house, while my mother waited by the car—ready to take me to the Sisters' Provincial House to start my training and become one of them.

I thought then of what my house had meant to me—what it symbolized—reminding me of my birth; my mother's promise to God; my growing-up years with their anguish, but also their joys; my emerging as a young woman with a heart full of love for down-trodden human beings and helpless animals; then my first love for someone special—my falling in love with my sailor Bob. With that last good-bye, I thought I wouldn't be coming back ever.

I had closed the "book" on all that had gone before in my life. Now I was re-opening it. And that thought was scary!

After I digested the idea, I considered the ramifications. Certainly, Mother and Dad would be happy—thrilled, I suspected. Carole and Melvin, married now, would be glad. So would my sister Anne—the only one still living at home with our parents.

It would be a most-welcomed event for all my relatives who had missed me over the years. And, of course, a happy event for me. Three special days at home were better than none, although I wished the amount of time I could spend with family members could have been extended and the visits made longer.

I knew it would feel strange. Would I be opening a "can of worms?" Reopening wounds for myself? For my loved ones? After all, each of us had finally—agonizingly—accepted the fact that I couldn't step foot in my house ever again.

I sent my parents the good news and began to look forward to my first visit home in ten years. But, suddenly, my joy was curtailed. Sister Rosemarie, observing the excitement among the Sisters, called us together to give clarification: "Sisters, you are going home to make your parents happy. The visits are not for your own satisfaction. By your vows you live a life of self-sacrifice. Don't let any form of self-seeking enter your soul now. Be detached from the world outside, even your own families."

My Superior's message left me confused. For ten years I am not allowed to go to my home. That policy is reversed. I am happy—and now I am put on a guilt trip for showing some enthusiasm for the concession. Something's wrong with this picture! Please let me express a little bit of human emotion, I wanted to cry out!

The big day arrived and I went home. My heart beat fast when the car pulled up at my house. Wow! I can't believe this moment. Am I really here or am I dreaming?

After greeting the many guests, mostly family members, I sat down in the backyard. Gobs of nieces and nephews gathered around me. Some sat at my feet. I felt like an oddity, seeing so many eyes focused on me—staring like I came from another world.

I realized something for the first time. Carole and Melvin had children now. They were parents, and obviously their families were growing. I was the only one present who didn't have children—would never have children of my own—and I felt a tearing in my heart.

I recalled my high school dream. I wanted love and a husband and children of my own flesh and blood. And, secondly, I wanted an artist's life. But all of that was snatched away.

Trying to redirect my wandering imagination and let joy conquer sadness, I excused myself. "I need to use the bathroom," I said. "I'll find my own way."

Opening the screen door I entered the house. I was alone. Taking a few steps forward, I rounded the bend and started down some steps. My piano was still there. It really belonged to all of us. But—for the moment—it was mine, all mine.

I let my fingers glide over the ivory keys. Then I lifted them higher and ran them along the magnificently-carved flowers of the antique oak piano that I had cherished. So many memories were still on that instrument—sealed forever. I could hear the melodies—hundreds of hours of music that I played and sounds I could still hear faintly. I sighed deeply.

"Go ahead and play it," I heard a voice behind me say.

I looked up and saw my younger sister. "It's good to be here, Anne. Do you play the piano often?"

162

"Not much, since I started working. Do you miss it, the piano I mean?"

"I should have gone upstairs, not downstairs," I said.

"It's all right. This is your home, Pat. There's nothing wrong with missing your piano—or our home, even."

"Anne, I shouldn't really be down here. I'll go up now. I can find my way to the bathroom," I blurted out awkwardly.

Halfway up the stairs I looked back and saw the sadness in my sister's eyes. I wanted to give her a big hug and hold her, but that would have started a flood of tears from both of us. Instead, I smiled, then hurried toward the next flight of stairs.

Suddenly, another voice spoke, "You found your way to the piano, just as I suspected. I can still see you sitting there with Bob, playing 'The High and Mighty.' It was your song, wasn't it—I mean, yours and Bob's? Do you miss him...and us?"

My sister Carole was following in my tracks.

"It's been ten years now. I've taken vows. Of course, you and the family mean a lot to me. But I'd better keep going and reach the bathroom, before the others wonder if I got lost.

At the top of the steps I looked back and whispered, "I love you, Carole, and I do miss you."

I went forward without looking back, hoping she would not see the tears welling up in my eyes. How sad that I could not allow myself to open my heart to my own sister. I should have hugged her at that moment and exclaimed, "I miss you and the others so much I can't stand it!" I should have told her about all my inner struggles—and that I belonged with the family. Instead, I returned to my "act" and put on my fake smile for the rest of my visit.

So many long-lost relatives came that day that I saw little of my parents. Before long, it was time to leave. I had chosen to spread out my three days of family visits, so we said goodbye. We hugged, and a stranger named Pat departed.

Back at the convent I tried to switch gears, as the 5 a.m. rising bell clanged. I could not get my body to move very fast that next morning. Realizing that if I took the time to make my bed, I'd be late for prayers, I shut my bedroom door to hide my unmade bed. I hurried to the chapel and arrived just in time.

After breakfast I rushed back to my room to make my bed, before heading over to school. As I pulled up my white bedspread, Sister Rosemarie appeared at my doorway.

"Sister, you should have made your bed before going to chapel," she said.

"I'm sorry, Sister. I thought I was going to be late."

"Sister," she said sternly, "leaving your bed unmade is against chastity."

"It won't happen again," I replied. As I watched her walk away, I was bewildered. If she had called it disobedience or even bad judgment, I could have accepted her admonition more easily. But an infraction against chastity? I racked my brain, but could not figure out what she meant.

Some time passed, and I received a happy announcement from my sister Anne. She was getting married.

"I'll be getting married at the parish church, not far from your convent. Surely, you can come to my wedding," she said.

I rushed to my Superior to make my request. Hopefully, I could attend Anne's wedding. It was my last chance, since Anne was the youngest sibling. I had missed the other weddings, but by now, that policy should have changed.

The NO that fell from my Superior's lips crushed me. I wanted to yell, "Why not?" What I asked for sounded so reasonable with the changes Vatican Council II was bringing to religious orders.

"I'm sorry, Sister Patricia Anne. That's a policy that remains unchanged."

I should have pursued the issue, pestered the woman. But I was silent. I walked away like a child whose lollipop had been whisked away by somebody's cruel prank. How could I disappoint Anne and my family once more and permit all of our hearts to be broken?

I had missed so many family celebrations in the past ten years. None was insignificant —all the Mother's and Father's Days, all the birthdays and graduations. Then, there were the big holidays: Christmas and Thanksgiving and Easter. Were these sacrifices that hurt so much really God's Will?

As I agonized over what I would tell Anne, I was sent for.

"Anne and Stephen can stop at the convent after the wedding reception. Then you can congratulate them and wish them well." Sister Rosemarie added, "That's the best I can do."

And that's exactly what they did, despite the inconvenience of taking a detour on the way to their honeymoon—a detour to a convent, no less!

I tried to accept the will of my Superiors as God's Will. Then, the unpredictable happened. Just twenty-two days after Anne's wedding, convents were notified of another change of policy: Sisters could now go to family weddings.

I could not believe my ears! Had Anne gotten married a month later, I could have attended! How can such a cruel thing be happening? If it had been a year or even six months later, maybe I could accept this—but only twenty-two days! I wanted to yell and scream and throw a temper tantrum!

Fighting my anger, I threw myself into my work more intensely. Blotting out my frustration, I focused my attention on helping my students.

Among the many delightful children I had the pleasure of teaching was a fifth grader named Sarah. At a parent—teacher conference I discovered that her mother was Sharon, a girl with whom I had graduated from high school.

I gave Sharon a glowing report of her daughter who was a model student—so enthusiastic about learning, so cooperative, a joy to teach. Looking older and somewhat drawn, Sharon was still the bright and attractive classmate I remembered. But I could see that pain had begun to carve its way across her face. Her look of vitality was draining away.

"What's wrong?" I asked.

"It's Sarah. She has cystic fibrosis and there's no cure."

As she told me the bad news, I could see her agony. Sarah was not expected to grow up.

For the rest of the school year, I watched Sarah closely, keeping her mother's secret inside me. I wondered how a child who appeared to be fine and in love with life could have such a dreadful disease. I took every opportunity to make Sarah's hours at school happy ones, until I was transferred.

Several years later I learned of Sarah's death, as well as that of her younger brother. Sharon had lost her only two children. I grieved for my friend who had brought the two children into the world and had to give them back to God so soon. Both died of the same illness, I was told. I wanted to find my classmate and hug her and tell her how sorry I was. But I was not allowed to do that.

I had another student named Charlene. The fifth grader was new in the school and cried everyday. As the days turned into weeks, I began to suspect a reason other than her move to an unfamiliar place.

Wanting to help the child with her problem, I sat down and had a heart-to-heart talk with her. I listened, as she poured out her anguish.

"I sleep in a room next to my parents. And every night they argue. It makes me sad and scares me. I worry about what will become of me and my brothers. I want to make my mother and father stop fighting, but I don't know how."

As I watched tears roll down her face, I wanted so badly to give her a big hug and comfort her. Knowing that was unacceptable, I offered to help in another way.

I sent for Charlene's mother and told her about her child's sadness at school and her frequent crying spells. I was concerned about the girl's unhappiness and wished I could help resolve her pain. I was willing to help out, if the mother wanted my assistance with whatever was going on.

The woman spoke of her own anguish and her frustration with her home situation. She had considered leaving her husband for the sake of the children. I encouraged her to talk about her feelings and the options she had in dealing with the whole problem. I raised issues she might think about and wished her wisdom in seeking answers and the courage to do what was best for her children and herself. I was transferred before the mother resolved the situation.

One day news reached me about Charlene, when she was in high school. A terrible tragedy had occurred. Charlene was dead.

That can't be, I thought. Charlene was just a teenager. Besides, I heard from another Sister that her mother had divorced the man she fought with. She had remarried. What happened?

I was told that one day, while the teenager was in the kitchen doing the dishes, her step-father went after a gun, then brought it back and shot the girl. I went to Charlene's funeral, grief-stricken, wishing there were something I could have done to prevent her death. But as I prayed, I came to believe that God indeed gave Charlene a gift—the gift of peace—no more pain, no more tears. And I felt comforted. I hoped her mother and her brothers felt comforted, too.

I loved my students and wore myself out trying to make their school days happy ones. I discovered that one of my students was never with the others at lunch time. My investigation revealed that he was hiding behind the school, refusing to play with his classmates.

After some long chats with the boy, I discovered he had very low self-esteem. He believed he was his brother's opposite in every way: looks, academic achievement, and social acceptance. Obviously, he needed professional counseling to help him deal with what was troubling him and causing him to withdraw. I could be a compassionate listener, but I knew that wasn't enough. I sent for his mother and referred him to a child psychologist. Gradually, the boy seemed happier, and I was glad to see the improvement.

By now, the list of changes for Sisters came out in the spring, making it easier to prepare to leave. We were allowed to tell the people with whom we worked that we had been missioned elsewhere. So I told my students I was being sent to another school in the fall.

One day, the formerly-troubled boy I had taught the previous year stuffed a note in my hand. I was so touched by what he wrote in the form of a poem that I kept it and still treasure it:

I wish you didn't have to go away

but I will always remember you when I pray.

I know I disobeyed a lot,

but I tried my best to make it stop.

As a teacher I thought you were a mess,

but now I know you are the best.

I hope your plane is very safe

but I know you have a lot of faith.

I want to thank you for all you did,

even though I'm just a stupid kid.

I used to think of you as dirty lice,

but once I know you, you're so nice.

I think you're the best teacher I ever had,

but once you leave I'll be very sad.

I know a lot of people who think your preaching is a bore,

but I think they are as wild as war.

I know sometimes you flipped your lid,

but I know now what some people did.

I know sometimes you were very sore,

but I will now say something I never said before,

I LOVE YOU!

He attached a second page which read:

Dear Sister,

I guess you're wondering why I said "I love you."
It is because you helped me with my problems.
You helped me so much I almost took it for granted.

I know I disobeyed you a lot, but I'm sorry.
I wish you didn't have to leave this year,
but I know you have to go.
Sister, I want to thank you for all you did.
Even way back in fifth grade.
I'll be writing to you when you're in Saint Louis.
And when you are in Seton High School.
I think I passed it a couple of times when I went
to see that doctor.

> *Well, thanks a lot, Sister.*
> *God bless you.*

PS: I really love my parents now, (better) than before.

Because you helped me. Thank you for making our home a happy home.

Before long, another sixth grader I had taught the previous year sneaked a folded piece of paper in my hand, when he passed me in the school corridor. It read:

Dear Sister,

I must write this letter to you, thanking you for the help you gave me. You might not believe this but you were my best teacher I've ever had and I'm glad you taught at Saint Charles.

I appreciated you teaching me and my friends. George says he can't stand you but deep inside he likes you.

When you used to give me lectures about how you were trying to help me with my conduct so I can be safe in sixth grade, I thought it was a lie and I found out it wasn't.

You really helped me out and I thank you not only for this, but also for being so understanding.

You were my best teacher and I liked you the most yet I gave you a smart lip. I just don't understand it and I'm very sorry for giving you a hard time and thank you for putting up with me. I think I'll make it past 6th because you helped me

*realize I must change my attitude and conduct. And so I'm
going to do it.*

*PS: We'll all miss you, and we are sorry you have to leave.
So I hope you have fun with your new career.*

*Well, all that I can say now is GOOD-LUCK and GOOD-
BYE!*

With thanks.

Their letters touched me so deeply that I could not let myself throw them away. They were proof to me that I must be doing something right, that God was using me to help people; that God did have a plan for me, and I was indeed accomplishing it. These letters reinforced my belief in my vocation.

I tucked the letters away in a secret place, so that whenever I felt discouraged or doubtful, I would have ammunition to help me fight against obstacles, especially the recurring struggles with my female drives that cried out for satisfaction and my humanity that battled to burst free from its invisible straight jacket.

The letters would help me fight against those yearnings that still plagued me—the yearning to draw to my heart's content, to relax at a piano, to be in ecstasy at the ocean, to marry and have children, to be loved.

When the war within me raged furiously, I had only to pull out my letters and say, "See, I AM doing some good where I am. My sacrifices ARE worth it. So, shut up all you forces inside me and around me that want to topple my chosen life. I won't listen to you. Understand? I'll fight with all my might to keep the lid on that box where I've relegated you to non—existent status."

Reading those and other notes from former students was my way of "tying a knot and hanging on," when I felt like I had reached the end of my rope.

I carried on and, in the late spring of 1964, I was notified that I would be on the list of graduates of Saint Joseph's College with a Bachelor's Degree in Elementary Education. My band of Sisters had accumulated too many credit hours to wait until our assigned majors were finished.

Of course, we would not be allowed to attend our graduation ceremony. It would only serve to instill pride in us—a vice opposed to the humility that was part of our Community's heritage and spirit. I had heard that rationale repeated so many times I could almost recite it verbatim.

It was better this way, our Superiors had said. Still, we would continue working toward our other assigned major.

And so, I would keep returning to Emmitsburg each summer for courses with the other Sisters. But, in the summer of 1968, our college offered no advanced French courses. I was told I was being sent to take two specific courses at Fairfield University and stay with our Sisters at Saint Ann's Hospital in Bridgeport, Connecticut.

I moved into the Sisters' quarters at a perfect time. A doctor and his family had gone away on vacation, leaving their home and pool available to the Sisters for the duration of their absence. The Sister Servant at the hospital decided to allow her Sisters to spend some time there on a rotating basis for relaxation. Already I could see that this northeast province of our Sisters was much more progressive than my own southeast province.

That same Superior notified those of us in summer school that we could participate too, as much as our classes permitted. It sounded great at first, until I signed up for my pre-assigned courses—"Masters of Modern Novel" and "Conversational French Workshop." I was sent to get undergraduate credits to bring my total up to thirty—the number I needed to complete my major. But I discovered that most of my fellow students were high school French teachers working on their Master's Degree.

I was told that the same course requirements applied to me, even though I just needed undergraduate credits. Since I had taken a vow of obedience and received my summer assignment from those in authority over me, I had no choice but to do as I was ordered and accomplish what they sent me to do. It would be a challenge. That I knew—but wasn't my whole life a continuous challenge?

The doctor's home in Wilton, Connecticut was lovely and the grounds, idyllic. The landscaping with its gorgeous flowers and magnificent plants led to a pond that was always enticing—especially at night when the croaking of the frogs broke the Sisters' silence.

It felt exhilarating to be in such a beautiful setting that had been foreign to me for so many years, but I had very little time to enjoy it. Aside from prayers and class time, I had to spend many hours studying and struggling to keep up with my classmates. Although I managed to get in a few moments of swimming time, I had to sacrifice a lot of pool time and sharply curtail my walks to the pond.

Finally, one night before leaving, I followed the sound of the croaking and sat on a bench near the pond. I delighted in listening to the chorus of frogs and to the water splashing as they jumped from lily to lily. I thrilled to the sensations I felt, so close to nature.

This was a family home, I thought. It belonged to a doctor and his wife and children. If I had gotten married, I would have had a home, probably not this elaborate, but my own home. Maybe not a pond, but water would have been accessible. I would never have lived far from water. I needed it for relaxing, regrouping—for being myself. Without it, I would be dehydrated—not alive.

What am I thinking? I've given all that up. Following my vocation has meant forfeiting such things, and I'm still alive.

"Are you?" a voice inside me wanted to force its way out like the sizzling steam of a geyser. I heaved a sigh and got up. I shouldn't be here. I've got a lot of reading to do tonight and it won't be easy, Balzac in French.

I switched gears. If I do well in my courses, I might be sent to teach French in a high school, since French is about to become my second major.

I thought of the teenagers I'd be teaching. I knew I'd love working with that age group. Back in Pikesville, I had started doing just that. Noticing some neighborhood teenagers living a life without purpose and getting in trouble, I wanted to do something about it. So I went to Sister Rosemarie with a proposal: Let me organize them, tap their music talent and take them to hospitals. I'd like to show them they can make a contribution to society, as much as anyone else. That will surely build up their sense of self-worth and make a lot of sick people happy. I'd like to show them how to pour out their energy in the task of helping others.

"My work as a teacher won't suffer," I assured my Sister Servant.

After she said "yes," I went to work on that project on weekends. I called the group that evolved TPA—"Teen Power in Action." I identified talents and planned programs for the Children's Hospital, the Veterans' Hospital, and state institutions for the mentally-ill and other disabled persons.

The only requirement was that the teenagers use their "gifts" and skills to cheer up the disadvantaged. Neither race nor religion nor police record were considerations.

It was heart-warming to watch the young people give of themselves in service to others. They responded to sick children and the mentally ill with the same kind of generosity. They joked with me about how much at home I acted in a mental ward where I had been a volunteer for four years. I told them they were right: I was very much at home there and I loved the people.

It was a real challenge to face one child in the Children's Hospital. A nurse prepared us for Ella, a seven-year-old who had a rare disease. Under no circumstance could she be allowed to see herself in a mirror, the woman added. Nor could anyone show any reaction in her presence. Still, she needed, and would appreciate, our visit.

The nurse's speech confused me. How could she even suggest we might show a negative reaction or do anything to alienate a sick child. She needed cheering up, and we were there to bring cheer, not discouragement.

Soon I realized why the nurse had been so blunt. The disease was eating away the girl's face, making her look monstrous. It took immense effort to look at her and not flinch. My heart went out to this poor child and her family.

As the teenagers sang to the music of Jim, their guitarist, I glanced around at them and felt proud. They were smiling at the child as they sang—treating her the same as all the other young patients.

On another occasion we went to a state institution for the physically and mentally handicapped. Upon our arrival, a staff member met us at the door and led us to a common room where over fifty persons, young mixed with old, were milling around restlessly. The employee, after pointing across the room to an area we could use to set up, left the room, shutting the door behind her.

As my musicians took out their instruments, the patients stampeded us, snatching us up as dance partners and fighting over us. Alarm bells went off inside me, as I quickly glanced around to check on the reactions of the teenagers I was with. But they were taking things just as they were, dancing with whoever grabbed hold of them.

Before long, someone pulled on me abruptly and began dancing with me. I looked toward the door. Where was the staff member who brought us to that room? Certainly, I could not handle all the problems that might arise.

This experience was a real "eye-opener." The system of dealing with people institutionalized with birth defects was flawed in the 1960's. Society locked them away. "Out of sight" produced an "out of mind" mentality that led to "I don't care." My heart ached for the poor souls we spent time with that day. I hoped we cheered them up, but I knew I could not take the teenagers back. It was too serious a responsibility. So much about the situation needed to be corrected.

Since my religious community did not allow me to get involved, I could only hope and pray that someone with the power to effect change would do something.

Surprising news lifted my spirits. Our Superiors wanted our Sisters represented at a theology workshop soon to be held at Niagara University. This was a Vincentian college and we should support their programs, they said.

Because I was the Religion coordinator for my school's middle grades, my Sister Servant determined I should participate. I jumped at the chance, not only because of the seminar, but because of its geographical location. I had seen pictures of Niagara Falls, and I knew the area abounded in water—lots of it! I could never fully catch

174

up on the years I was deprived of water, but I could try. I was thrilled beyond measure!

As I took my first airplane flight ever, my whole being was flying in spirit. I couldn't wait to get there!

Between sessions, I took advantage of every opportunity I could find to go to the water. The experience of standing at the falls was indescribable. But when I went to Goat Island, watching the rapids surge around me was even more fantastic!

The wildness of the rapids spoke to the adventurer in me, while my heartbeat joined the rhythm of the rushing waters. Surrounded by the ethereal, I touched heaven—or rather, heaven touched me that day. My soul and the water became one. Every moment I spent at Niagara Falls sealed itself in my memory and in my heart.

When the time came to leave, I had to drag myself away. It was hard to say goodbye to the water I had found once again. It had been an amazing experience, and I thanked God for it.

By the spring of 1969 I knew I was missioned to Seton High School. Believing I was going there to teach French took the edge off the pain of another uprooting. I liked the idea of working full-time with teenagers, and I liked the French language, as well as the culture.

But before long, I was notified that I was being sent to Saint Louis for summer school to get nine Theology credits at Marillac College—a Sisters' college that was run by my own Religious Order.

I was perplexed. Surely, that must be a mistake. Why was I not studying for my Master's Degree in French? I learned painfully that I was not being sent to Seton to teach French. "The Community needs high school Religion teachers. You will be teaching that subject—not French," my Superior said.

"But French is my major now, isn't it?" Her answer floored me. French was going to remain my minor and not become my major. This really confused me. I had worked so hard—sweat blood, so to speak, the previous summer to get my thirty credits. I would not have needed those credits. I could have had some fun at Wilton's Pool—swimming to my heart's content.

"You worked hard last summer for God. Now He's calling you in another direction. It's God's Will, Sister."

Her explanation made no sense to me. I was being told that those courses I struggled with were taken in vain. I was not going to become a French teacher, after all. I was being put instead in the field of Theology without any input, without having the opportunity to share my feelings. How terribly disappointed I felt! Was I being treated like an inanimate object—like a pawn?

I could not believe it was God's Will. It appeared as if I was being manipulated to serve a purpose that was unclear to me.

"Why, God, can't I do something that I want to do? Can't I have a little bit of personal satisfaction? Don't you want me to be happy? Not just in the hereafter, but in the here and now?"

Ignoring my feelings of disappointment, I flew to St. Louis, and I studied hard. When the Art teacher, Sister Marie, asked for volunteers to help at the local prison, I signed up without a second thought. Of the three groups, Art, Music, and Bible Study, I chose to coordinate the latter for the inmates.

It was an eye-opener to discover how unjust the "system" was. Those who gathered around me for Scripture were Black men serving time for drug offenses, mainly the possession of marijuana. I thought that on the East Coast, whites found guilty of possession were given probation, not prison time. And I found that no rehabilitation was being provided. It seemed unfair to the inmates, as well as to society.

Before long, my Bible study classes became therapy sessions with the men pouring out their very souls. They were tragic human beings, scarred from not being properly nurtured and guided, once they came into this world. Most had grown up in bad environments without love or stability in their homes.

My heart ached for them and for others born with similar strikes against them. Victims from birth, the worlds they described dragged them down. It was too bad they had no choice about their birth parents, their upbringing, their surroundings—even the values they assimilated from the adults around them.

If only there were someone to lift them up emotionally and spiritually—someone who could restore their self-esteem and motivation, someone to believe in them as unique persons. They needed to see God's Love personified. But why couldn't they? Where were the Christians who should have been helping them?

While doing my best to lift the inmates' spirits and affirm them, those weekly visits to the "Workhouse"—a medium-security institution—became sacred encounters for me.

Seventeen-year-old Lemuel revealed he was addicted to heroine and was desperate for help. Going off the drug "cold turkey" was driving him crazy, he said. I encouraged him to seek the services of the prison social worker.

The following week I asked if he had followed up my suggestion. "Yes," he said, "but I was turned away and laughed at. Who was I to think the social worker—the only one there for three hundred men—had time for the likes of me? The man told me not to come back. I guess I can't get help here."

I said I was sorry and encouraged him to pray and keep his faith in God. Secretly, I was disturbed at the realization that inmates were being warehoused, apparently without any attempts to rehabilitate these men who deserved to be treated humanely and who deserved help. Besides, one day they would be back on the streets. How could anyone expect them to change their behavior without intervention? I hoped my summer visits for "Bible Study" effected some good, deep in the hearts of my new friends. I wished I could do more, but "obedience" was taking me elsewhere.

Flying back to Baltimore, I had to switch gears fast. I had spent six years in Endicott, New York and five years in Pikesville, Maryland. Now I was heading to downtown Baltimore.

By the time I left Endicott, I had migraine headaches, arthritis, and chronic tooth abscesses. Not long after arriving in Pikesville, my allergies became so bad that an allergist started me on regular shots, while the severity of my headaches escalated.

More recently, I had to stop directing the youth choir. A throat specialist discovered polyps on my vocal chords. "From voice misuse," he said. "Stop talking and singing," he added.

As always, I reported the doctor's advice to my Sister Servant. Impossible advice to give a Sister, I thought. But maybe that's why I was being sent to a new place. No longer able to direct a choir, my usefulness to the parish was now limited.

Before leaving Pikesville, I learned that my Grandmother Kirby had died. In her nineties, she was ready for Heaven. Once again I had to face the reality of my religious community's restrictions on gatherings for family funerals. I was not allowed to grieve with my family at the funeral home—only miles away. Nor was I permitted to attend her funeral.

It was so disappointing, but disappointment had become an integral part of my life. I tried to "steel" myself—be stoic—and hope the pain would soon go away.

Before starting a new school year at a new location, I made my annual eight-day retreat at the retreat house we now owned in northwest Baltimore. As I walked the grounds in silence between spiritual exercises, I could see priests and sisters from other Orders roaming the acreage in the distance. I was told they were patients at the Seton Psychiatric Institute that was run by our Sisters. I could see the awesome and imposing building on the hill.

Nothing was said openly about the place—one more of our many restricted topics of conversation. But I had heard rumors that priests and members of Religious Orders came from various parts of the country for the treatment of mental disabilities, nervous breakdowns and problems that were considered "hush—hush." How many were locked up here? And what kind of treatment were they receiving?

I wondered, what happened to their minds? What was it in their lives that would contribute to a nervous breakdown? How could anyone serving God generously end up this way? It seemed so tragic, yet we could not discuss our mental hospital and its secrets that were kept behind bolted doors.

Those poor religious—priests, brothers, and sisters—had answered God's Call, struggled like me to do what they believed was God's Will—and yet, here they are! Would they ever return to their convents, rectories and monasteries? What would become of them? These were additional painstaking reflections during my retreat—and I could not give voice to them.

I got back to my praying. For now, I must seek to be strong mentally and spiritually, and develop a mindset to start anew somewhere else.

5,093 days had passed since I left home. I missed my brown-shingled house and all its memories. Above all, I missed my loved ones.

9.

The Convent School

Riding in the back of the station wagon bursting with Sisters bound for downtown Baltimore, I did not feel free. In the course of fourteen years I had bottled up my feelings and capped them. Still, my emotions struggled to play a kind of tug-of-war game that day. Disappointment and frustration battled my yearnings for my life to encompass more, to blossom into the woman I once was in a seedling. What was supposed to be numb inside me was more real than ever. And I fought to ignore the turmoil that left my insides feeling like a smoking volcano.

My stomach really was churning. I always got carsick in the rear of busses and station wagons where I usually got relegated, being one of the youngest. I had learned years ago not to speak about it, to put up with it. But I had to work hard at forcing mind over matter and not throw up that day.

Riding along Charles Street, I focused my attention on the imposing institution known as Seton High School. More pavement than trees lined the sidewalk out front. Across the street, Saints Philip and James Church seemed in competition with the school to block out nature.

My emotions were mixed. I liked the idea of working full-time with teenagers. If I had no choice but to teach, being assigned to a high school was preferable to working on the elementary level. On the other hand, Seton was my Alma Mater. I remembered the high ceilings and black woodwork. There was nothing aesthetic about the school.

I had known that the Sisters lived in the building, in secret areas off limits to the students. Off and on during the day, Sisters appeared and disappeared, evaporating into the woodwork, I thought. And their lives seemed as fragmented as their living quarters.

I was a carefree teenager then, sketching my way through boring classes, listening well enough to pass my tests with a minimum of studying. I had wanted to join the Art Club but my request was met with rejection.

"This club is just for girls with art talent," Sister Gerald had said, without ascertaining what talent I did or didn't have.

When Sister Andrew approached me and asked me to join the orchestra, I seriously considered her invitation.

"You tried out for a music scholarship, playing the piano. That means you can read music, and I really do need another cellist. Mister Hipp will teach you."

So I signed up and came to love being in the orchestra. Since the others drowned out my mistakes, I could play to my heart's content. My love for music grew still more, as we played Gershwin, Kern, Sousa, and Beethoven.

When the dismissal bell rang at the end of the school day, I'd meet my best friend Theresa in the locker room. We'd change our black-and-white saddle shoes to the popular black "ballerina" shoes, or else cover up our nylon stockings with white socks and put our saddle shoes back on—just to ride home on the city busses. Other than on school days we would not be seen wearing bobby socks, which identified "squares" back then. And that's something my best friend and I did not want to be called in 1950's Baltimore.

I went to dances on weekends with Theresa and sometimes, my sister Carole, unless I had a date. And I continued taking piano lessons. Music was so much a part of my life. I still remembered turning on the radio at home and letting the music and its rhythm thrill every fiber of my being, as I whirled around—oblivious of my surroundings.

But where was music in my life now—or even, rhythm? Silence superseded song in religious life, and the rules, along with my clothing, fettered my body's movements. I wanted to cry or scream over the loss!

The station wagon made a sharp right turn, shaking me back to the present. We parked in the school's courtyard, then carried our luggage inside by way of a porch that hugged one side of the building. As we cut through a classroom, my eyes scanned the high ceiling, then the newly-painted white walls that contrasted with the dark doorways and woodwork.

With its aura of starkness, Seton still looked like a turn-of-the-century industrial school for girls. I could imagine those prim and proper young women sauntering through that same room with long skirts dragging on the floor, wearing long-sleeved blouses with cameos modestly closing the bleached white linen at the neck.

We crossed a corridor covered with linoleum and climbed a steep staircase. At the top some Sisters stood, waiting to greet us. Entering another gigantic doorway framed in black, I knelt down in the chapel—hardly able to breathe.

"Dear Lord," I prayed, "please help me as I start this new assignment. Take away my fears and my reluctance to live in a school building. The thought of how I will feel living such a fragmented life, with constant reminders that I am a teacher scares me to death. I need your help now—desperately!"

Next to the chapel, a Sister opened another black door, a double door that looked eight feet high. The community room I entered was not unlike the ones we had in Endicott and Pikesville. I surveyed the long conference-like tables with their wooden chairs and the dark bookcases that foretold the type of reading materials I would find on their shelves. The room's best and surprising feature was its air-conditioning. Huge windows overlooked the third-floor porch, which would serve its usefulness as a place to air out holy Habits.

A tall, matronly Sister entered with a police dog on a leash. Seeing some of the Sisters raise their eyebrows, I wasn't sure whether their body language was a reaction to Sister Cora or the dog.

"I want to welcome all of you, our new Sisters and those of you who have just returned. I hope you will be happy this new school year.

"As you know, the Sisters' quarters are spread out in this large complex that's almost a square block in size. I keep a guard dog to check out the building before I go to bed. During the night, should I hear any disturbing sounds, I walk the corridors with Simon. Don't worry. I'll keep him out of your way."

Simon really did look ferocious, like he could easily make a meal out of anyone of us. But I supposed that a dog of his size was an asset in our sprawling convent near the heart of the city.

As I trailed the others in a column to the refectory next door, I scanned its predictable white walls with its black oversized woodwork and doorways. A large crucifix provided a focal point, as we said the grace before we sat down in silence to eat at square tables covered with white linen tablecloths. At each Sister's place, there was the usual service—flatware wrapped in a white linen napkin, a white plate overturned and covered with a dish towel. A plain glass completed each place setting. There were no flowers or decorations of any kind.

As a Sister sitting at a small desk in a corner read to us, I watched a dumb-waiter in the wall near the kitchenette. Periodically, a Sister got up and unloaded food, when she heard the muffled sound of a bell ringing.

My thoughts wandered, blocking out the reader's voice with her admonition that, like the saints, we seek to be perfect. How was I going to survive here, living each day in a school building, missing the sunshine—even the outdoor air—calling scattered parts of the school my convent? Already, I found the atmosphere depressing. How could I seek perfection, when my primary concern must be survival?

"Dear God, help me," I was still crying out deep inside my soul. "Obedience is obedience—but isn't this going too far? I'm a human being with feelings, not a 'wind-up' toy for my Superiors to play with!"

What is wrong with me, thinking such disloyal thoughts? I have to get hold of myself. I've had things much more difficult than my surroundings to deal with in previous years—and I've overcome those obstacles. This is just one more challenge.

The Sisters' sleeping quarters were disseminated throughout the third, fourth, and fifth floors. Being the youngest, I climbed a lot of stairs behind a Sister who was showing me the way to the bedroom assigned to me. Reaching the top floor on the rooftop level, I could see the tub room I'd use. It was located between a science lab and a classroom. Around the bend, we approached the mysterious door I used to wonder about when I was a teenager studying biology in the classroom opposite the Sisters' private wing.

Sister John Mary unlocked the door saying I would get my own key later. She walked me to a bedroom doorway, pointed, and said, "You will sleep here. Any questions?"

"Thank you, no," I responded. Then she left me alone.

My room was small, with an attic window overlooking a tar-papered roof. Outside, I could see tops of aged brick buildings and a slice of blue sky above them. Inside, the walls were antiseptic-white, giving the room a hospital atmosphere. I looked around at the furniture: a twin bed covered with a thin bedspread, a wooden chair, a chest of drawers, a small desk with a lamp—and even a little sink topped with a medicine cabinet reflecting light in its mirror. A mirror at last.

As always, there were no closets. Having only two holy Habits, including the one I was wearing, I didn't really need a closet. After all, I had no property whatsoever to store.

I sat for a moment on the chair that leaned up against the bed and took a deep breath. I felt strange. No, I felt lost with nowhere to turn. Fighting tears, I tried once again to pray, "Dear God, please, please help me! I know You're probably tired of hearing me repeat this same prayer, but I don't know what else to do."

Going in and out of the school areas and the convent quarters depressed me those first days. And forcing myself to have a positive outlook was not working. I wanted to run away—feel free and unencumbered—and definitely not live inside an archaic school building. With all my might I battled my negative feelings, as those days turned into weeks and I prepared for another first day of school. It was my twelfth year of teaching.

But then, the worst happened. I began to get a stabbing pain over my right kidney. I ignored it, until it became unbearable. So I went to Sister Cora sheepishly. I told her what was going on and apologized for being a problem. She reacted with kindness and sent me to the emergency room of our Sisters' hospital—Saint Agnes.

The doctor examined me in a cubicle and left me alone for a few hours. Suddenly, a Sister I didn't know pulled aside the curtain and entered. Happy at first, to have someone with me, I noticed a smirk on her face. Finally, she broke the silence.

"So you're the one who <u>says</u> she has a terrible pain."

"I do, Sister. I'm not making it up."

Shaking her head in apparent disagreement, she turned and walked out. What was that all about? I wondered—not actually caring, as I was really feeling awful. Still, I wished there had been someone to comfort me. My own parents and siblings lived in the same city, but I could not contact them to reveal I was in the hospital. I was not allowed to let them console me. I was not permitted to worry them. So they never knew about this incident.

When the doctor returned, he said I had probably passed a kidney stone while there, and I could go back to my convent home. My Sister-driver took me to Seton again, and I joined the others in rushing around, getting ready for the first day of school.

Being a Baltimorean, I knew where most of the lakes and rivers were located. How I wished we could take a day off to relax and sit by the water. But everyone seemed to have a two-track mind: work, pray, work, pray. Was I the only Sister who felt the need to slow down? To catch my breath and gorge my lungs with fresh air? To smell the fishy fragrance of a wonderful lake or river or even the captivating Chesapeake Bay?

It seemed like the right thing to do to break the cycle of oppression that was strangling me like a noose. I was bursting to shout out,

"Please! Can't we relax and stop working ourselves to death for just one day?"

Struggling to put my whole heart in my work and prayers, I tried to accept what life was offering me in that situation. But my anguish got worse instead of better. I felt depleted emotionally. Finally, I went to Sister Cora and bared my soul.

"I'm trying as hard as I can to adjust here, Sister. But I'm unhappy—depressed all the time. And I don't know what to do about it. If I have a vocation, why is it so difficult for me to live this life?"

Sister Cora, whose heart was as big as her plump figure that looked squeezed in her Habit, tried to comfort me. I got the feeling she really did understand, that perhaps she was experiencing some of the same frustrations.

"Wait a minute," she said, before disappearing through the doorway that led from her office to her bedroom. When she returned, she handed me a transistor radio and spoke up.

"When you are feeling down in the dumps, use this. Listen to some soothing music. That should help."

I could not believe my ears! My Sister Servant was advising me to act in a way that was contrary to our Community's policies at the time—to listen to a radio. Of course, I was grateful. I loved music; and, oh, how I missed it. But, deep down, I felt like a prisoner locked in my cell being told that all I needed was music in my life—not freedom.

Maybe it was the free-spirited Pat still lingering in the school building that was screaming out to me, "What you are lacking is your freedom! How can you forfeit your liberty that you used to cling to so tenaciously? Isn't the deprivation of it what is killing you now? Take it back! Don't allow anyone, even in God's Name, to make you give it up!"

What I really wanted to hear my Superior say was, "Fly away, Pat. Be free, before the person you are evaporates or disappears! I give you that permission."

But, as a Sister Servant carefully trained and placed in a position of authority, Sister Cora was restricted in the advice she could give me. She wasn't permitted to offer me my freedom. I belonged to my religious community. Besides, with high school theology programs in a state of turmoil, she was desperate for a Sister who could and would teach it, regardless of personal feelings. She needed me badly.

I went back to my classroom that Saturday and wrote my lesson plan, listening to music. I was determined to make Sister Cora's solution work.

A former monk headed our theology department. Working under him, I discovered there were no written curricula and no guidelines. So I developed my own philosophy on how to teach theology to teenagers.

Since the concept of God was a mystery beyond human comprehension, I believed I should start out with some basic self-understanding and focus on building up the young people's self-esteem. Also, they needed to begin to understand relationships on a human level, before they would be capable of developing a mature faith-relationship with their Creator and His Son Jesus. That became my starting point.

Convinced of the need to put faith in action, I set up community service projects. I had never forgotten the saying of Nietzsche from my philosophy class: "Maybe if Christians looked a little more redeemed, I could believe."

Often Christians failed to let "their light shine." Instead, some easily drifted into habits of materialism, narcissism, even hedonism—so Nietzsche's indictment of the behavior and life-styles of a lot of people calling themselves Christians could not be denied.

I hoped my students, by focusing on assisting the poor and alleviating suffering, would develop into generous adults—more intent on making the world a better place than on amassing a fortune for themselves.

For the upper classmen I set up courses that dealt with the Christian response to social issues; such as, racism, the exploitation of women, poverty, prison reform and rehabilitation, and ecology. Using people like Martin Luther King, Bobby Kennedy, Cesar Chavez, and Mahatma Gandhi, I created a course I called "Modern Prophets." Sex and Marriage, Parenting and Child Psychology were senior courses taught from the Christian perspective. Since I lacked personal experience, I ordered audio programs and brought in lay speakers to make sure they were getting a realistic viewpoint. I also made sure a priest was on our staff.

Concurrently, the school staff was undertaking a self-study to redefine its philosophy of education and seek ways to implement it. I was impressed with the sincerity of the faculty members, both Sisters and lay teachers, who were looking for ways to better serve the student population, while seeking the Middle States' accreditation for the school.

By November it was obvious that my department head could not handle his job. He submitted his resignation, effective the end of the first semester, and his responsibilities landed in my lap. I was ordered to write all the theology curricula for the high school and supervise anyone teaching any theology course. I was assigned to teach most of the classes myself.

In addition, I was named moderator of the orchestra. When I set about inventorying the musical instruments, it was discouraging to discover that most of what we used when I was in the orchestra was in a state of disrepair. I worked to salvage what I could and rebuild the orchestra.

A Filipino woman who was a concert violinist and classical guitarist had been hired that school year as conductor and instrumental music teacher. Celia was competent and easy to get along with. Together we worked hard to give the orchestra the prominent place it formerly had in the curriculum.

She even offered to give me classical guitar lessons. Sister Cora encouraged me to take her up on her offer and begin taking lessons. I followed my Sister Servant's advice for a period of time, but found it difficult to stay motivated and practice while carrying out my duties in school and my spiritual obligations as a Sister.

Finally, fighting chronic depression, I lost interest entirely and discontinued taking lessons from Celia.

My monotonous life with its inhumane expectations of me and the denial of outlets that I needed was draining the life out of me.

It became harder and harder to rise at 5 a.m., get dressed quickly, rush down two steep flights of stairs to the chapel, meditate and say morning prayers with the other Sisters, attend Mass, eat breakfast in silence, go to my classroom, perform my school duties, eat a quick lunch without talking to those around me, return to school for a few more hours, be in the community room on time for spiritual reading before evening meditation and additional vocal prayers in the chapel, eat supper in silence, accompanied by more reading from books considered holy, followed by more time for classroom preparation, then an hour sitting around the community room table—sewing for recreation as I conversed with the Sisters assigned to seats at my end of the table, before final prayers together in the chapel and my final trek to the rooftop wing and preparation for bed.

I would then take my key and leave the Sisters' quarters to find my way to the desolate tub room. By the time I got there, exhausted from my long day of work and prayer, most of the others had finished bathing. I would run my bath water and soak myself in the ghostly-quiet atmosphere on the top floor of the school—feeling lonely and isolated, hearing only the occasional scamper of a caged guinea pig in the dark biology lab nearby. Outside the tub room darkness surrounded me, except for the light that lit the path back to the Sisters' wing.

That was my schedule Monday through Friday. On Saturday and Sunday, when I wasn't praying, going to Mass, having spiritual reading or other spiritual exercises, I spent the major part of those days in my classroom preparing for the next week's classes or grading test papers and essays. I found life teaching at Seton oppressive, to say the least.

In November Sister Cora gave me a break. She sent two of us Sisters to a religious education seminar in Chicago. This was surprising, since the organization sponsoring it was non-denominational. We would stay with our Sisters at their hospital on Lake Michigan and commute daily to the Palmer House, she said.

I was excited as our plane landed at O'Hare International Airport. Following Sister Grace, I watched the crowds of people rushing chaotically around the airport terminal—until I noticed something unusual. A seven-year old girl was standing on her toes, struggling to reach high enough to deposit her dime and make a phone call.

The scene didn't look right to me, so I offered to put the money in the slot for her and dialed the number. That accomplished, I stood nearby and listened.

"Mommy," she said, "you've gotta come to the airport and wake up Daddy."

I took the phone and spoke to the child's mother, "I don't know what's going on, but I'll be glad to stay with your daughter until you can get here. I'm a Sister of Charity."

Having said that, Sister Grace and I trailed the child to a spot where she pointed, saying, "There's Daddy."

Her father lay sprawled out on the floor, apparently drunk and deep in sleep.

"Have you had anything to eat?" I asked the girl.

"No," she answered.

"Why don't we take a walk and find something to eat? Sister Grace will be glad to sit here with your father." I turned to the Sister who nodded.

The child followed me to a restaurant, where she ate a good meal. When we returned to the spot where we left Sister Grace with her father, her mother was already there and proceeded to fill us in.

"My husband was fighting in Viet Nam, when he received word that his father in Tennessee was dying. They sent him back to visit his Dad. Afterwards, he has to go back to Viet Nam. He was here with our daughter to take a flight to Nashville."

I agonized for the man who sat up as if dazed. He had used alcohol to deaden his pain—the very pain that stared him in the face once more. It was one of many instances in my life, when I felt helpless, wanting to alleviate a family's pain but not having a way to do it.

The woman thanked us, and we left. I was grateful for that chance encounter. Hordes of people had been milling around the airport. I was glad the Lord let us be the ones to notice the child's predicament.

Chicago amazed me. I loved Lake Michigan, and I was glad each day began and ended there at the water. Sister Grace and I took frequent walks at the edge of the lake. I discovered that the Sisters' hospital had a solarium on each floor facing the lake. Water was everywhere I looked, and it felt great.

One day, as we crossed the Palmer House lobby heading for the conference room, Sister Grace spied Jack Benny standing alone. Without a second thought, she rushed over to him, shook his hand, and blurted out: "I'm so glad to meet you, Mr. Benny. My mother is a great fan of yours!" Her greeting to the celebrity struck me as funny. She had put him in an older generation's category, not her own! I had to struggle to keep my composure and not laugh.

I suppose I shook his hand, too. But something surprised me. The famous comedian's "poker face" never changed its expression. There was no laugh, not even a smile. He was minimally civil. Yet, I thought afterwards, even comedians must cherish times when they are allowed to relax and frown. Jack Benny probably wished he could be anonymous.

Back in Baltimore, our accreditation went through. And we set about making the changes we had researched and adopted. We modified the Trump Educational Plan and initiated a continuous progress program of study that allowed students to move along at their own rates of speed. Renovations were made so that each department would have a resource center with all the materials students would need, as they worked on learning activity packets, better known as LAPS.

In this program, large group instructions were followed by small group discussions within a ten-day cycle. Once everything was implemented, students could finish the school year early or go on to the next year's work.

The new school philosophy stipulated that every student must graduate with an employable skill, regardless of plans for higher education. A data-processing course was already in place. The staff started speaking in terms of the 21st century, with greater emphasis on critical-thinking and decision-making skills. It was 1970.

A new principal was sent to oversee the changes, and Sister Cora was sent elsewhere. The police dog disappeared too. We heard that he was given away. Even though Sister Cora's dog was a guard dog, he was perceived by some to be a pet. And Saint Vincent was very clear on that subject. Pets would only serve to waste a Sister's time and cause her to develop emotional ties that should not be present in a Sister's life.

How painful that parting must have been—for Sister Cora and for the dog. It was too bad that pets were considered wrong for convents. Perhaps, pets might have made life more tolerable for a lot of us. As always, our higher Superiors were threatened by the notion of Sisters developing emotional bonds of any kind. Emotions, they thought, would only serve to lead Sisters into temptation, even sin.

Sister Adeline, our new Sister Servant, gave me permission to get a driver's license, and I became part of the Sisters' pool of station wagon drivers, at last. That meant getting out more, and I came to love driving.

In the early seventies, our religious community gradually adopted some changes. We could watch television in the evening, mainly news programs and shows like Lawrence Welk that were considered harmless.

Since it was uncomfortable to sit back and relax—dressed in full Habit with our heads covered and shoes on, Sister Adeline allowed us to take a bath and return to the TV room wearing our nightgown, robe and slippers. But always we had to keep our heads covered with our coiffes.

It felt so good to sit in the upholstered couches our Sister Servant purchased for the TV room. And it felt great to wear slippers instead of shoes—after having worn shoes from morning to night for seventeen years, no matter how my feet ached. I was grateful for that concession that was so thoughtful on Sister Adeline's part.

But this was not to last. Someone among us must have reported this departure from our Community's rigidity and fixation on the letter of the rules. Before long, we received word from a higher Superior that what we were doing was an aberration. We must return to the official policy and remain dressed in full Habit with shoes on when watching TV.

After that, I decided that watching television wasn't worth it, if I had to sit there feeling uncomfortable—so wrapped up in fabric, unable to kick off my shoes.

Soon, other changes came about. After having an overdose of white walls everywhere for so many years, we were told our bedrooms could be painted other colors. Once again, Sister Adeline wanted to accommodate the Sisters. She gave us two choices of paint color for our rooms—then saw to it that our rooms got painted.

My choices had been peach or light turquoise, and I ended up getting a peach bedroom. I loved what the new atmosphere did for my mood—I had almost forgotten the wonderful effects of a pleasant color. For this adaptation, I was extremely grateful.

Our reading options expanded. We could now read the Bible, and our community prayer book was superseded by the Church's Liturgy of the Hours for morning and night prayers. In addition, we could start checking books out of the public library and even read novels—appropriate ones.

It was now allowable to buy personal supplies outside at shopping centers. Still, we had to ask our Sister Servant ahead of time for the money we needed. Upon our return, we had to give an account of our shopping trip and hand in the change. Even buying tampons, instead of kotex, became permissible. That was really radical for us as Sisters.

On weekends we could sleep as late as we wanted in the morning provided our spiritual exercises and our schoolwork did not suffer. Attending a second Mass on Sundays was no longer mandatory.

An especially-appreciated concession came when we were informed we could begin visiting sick relatives, if they lived in the area. Also we were now allowed to attend the funerals of relatives and their wakes.

Around this time, my cousin Meredith landed on the cancer research floor of a hospital close by. I visited this daughter of my Dad's brother Herb regularly, after seeking and receiving Sister Adeline's permission.

I admired her bravery, when I discovered she permitted herself to be used as a guinea pig for drugs being tested for leukemia. Only 32, Meredith was married and already had six children, the youngest—a six-year old boy.

I was surprised to discover that her biggest fear was that she might die before finishing all her "thank you" notes. She believed her doctors who predicted how long she would live, and prepared to die, instead of putting up the fight of her life.

Through it all, my heart agonized with her husband and her children. I attended her funeral and grieved with my family—only to learn that another first cousin, Lois—the twenty-two year old daughter of Dad's other brother Ed was diagnosed with the same type of cancer, shortly after her marriage to Elmer—when she became pregnant with her first child. What terrible tragedies, it seemed.

Only God in His infinite wisdom knew the answer to the question "why" that my aunts and uncles were asking in regard to the loss of such young lives cut off too early. I could give no simplistic or even "holy" answers. I could only hug them and do my best to console them in their grief.

When I was missioned to Seton, I was at war within myself. Now over 32, living the life of an angel in a woman's body was harder than ever. Despite the battles I fought, my female emotions and drives still refused to be conquered. Even with the changes my religious community was making, I felt unduly repressed. Was it too little too late?

Chronically frustrated, I kept throwing myself full force into my work befriending my students—spending hour after hour listening to their problems and advising them.

I had first learned compassion from my own mother who was always reaching out to the needy. Years earlier, when I told her about my Biology teacher, Sister Angela, who regularly visited the poor of the neighborhood after school hours, she started sending eggs to school with me.

"Just leave them in the Sister's lab refrigerator with her food for the poor. It's enough that God knows where they came from," Mother would add, never wanting to receive gratitude.

I tried to teach my students that kind of selfless compassion for others, especially in the courses on social issues like poverty and racism, Third World problems, and even the Holocaust.

In teaching about the Holocaust, I held up Viktor Frankl as a hero, using his book <u>Man's Search for Meaning</u>. I had been deeply moved by that Jewish psychiatrist who wrote an account of his life in Auschwitz and other concentration camps, then explained what it was that enabled him and others to stay alive, when so many did not survive.

In conjunction with the course, I showed the film "Night and Fog". Although I found it heart-wrenching to watch the movie over and over again, I knew that its effect on my students would be far-reaching and speak a message better than I could ever tell it.

Man's inhumanity to man in the most horrific manner was indelibly impressed on me through the film, and I wanted my students to feel that impact so they would work hard not to let it happen again. I wanted the horrors of the Holocaust and Viktor Frankl's teachings about survival in the face of incredible odds to stay with them forever.

His philosophy of finding meaning even amid terrible suffering had a direct link to the Gospel message, I believed.

As religious educators struggled in those days to find ways to reach the hearts and souls of adolescents, many of us adopted a multi-media approach. Seeing its value for classroom prayer-experiences and for retreats, I searched for slides depicting people, their lifestyles, their joys and sorrows and accomplishments.

Then I started listening to the teenagers' music in order to find songs with a message that could be put together with the slides to touch them and deepen their faith. The multi-media meditations I created became a reflection on their lives and their yearning to find meaning in a confusing world.

Their over-riding concern was for their brothers and boyfriends whom they thought were being made into killing machines, then sent overseas to fight a war in Viet Nam. What they were dying for was a mystery to many of them, their parents, and to me.

With the hippie movement in full swing, my students searched for its underlying value. Was it an escape mode or was it a genuine reaching out for freedom in a world that deprived so many individuals and groups of their liberty? Was it a reaction to war, or was it truly a return to love?

I found that generation of teenagers agonizing over the very questions. I encouraged my students to articulate their questions, discuss the issues, and seek solutions.

While stressing the need for faith in God and to follow Jesus, I emphasized their personal responsibility to search for truth and meaning in their lives. I could give them no pat answers.

As I looked for music that would touch the hearts of my students, I discovered a singer named Barbra Streisand. Her song "People Who Need People" mesmerized me, and I used it frequently in my slide presentations. I was haunted by the words and the melody, as I listened to the record hour after hour, while I worked in my classroom on weekends between chores and spiritual exercises.

I felt like Ms. Streisand was speaking directly to me, and a side of me wanted to respond and shout out: "Yes! Yes! I am one of those people you are singing about. Without deep communication and closeness to real people, I'll continue to feel dehydrated, exiled from life!"

Sometimes, when my body clamored for the satisfaction of its drives and yearnings, and I felt like I was going crazy, I would rush to my classroom as fast as religious decorum would allow. Once there, I'd play the records my students had brought to class. Above all, I'd allow Barbra Streisand to speak to my heart and tell me I was one of those "people who need people." She was awakening my awareness that the lack of friendship and intimacy with other human beings was at the root of my problems.

Still, when I was tempted to follow that line of thinking to its logical conclusion, I'd be like the driver of a car deliberately turning up a dead-end street. I was in a state of denial. Redirecting my thoughts to my students and immersing myself in helping them, I'd remind myself why I had to beat down what wanted to rebel inside me—why I had to ignore those invisible hands that were trying so hard to yank the steering wheel out of my clutches and force me to go in another direction.

God gave me peace through my students during that tumultuous period of my life. That first Christmas at Seton, Jane alleviated some of my pain of celebrating without my family through a letter of gratitude that gave me food for thought:

> Thank you so much for taking your time to worry about a stupid problem like mine. I was kind of surprised to think you would be worried about it too. Everything worked out just great and whenever I feel the need to consult with you, I won't have any doubts about who to come to. I really did need someone at that time but nobody seemed to care. Thanks a million for stepping into the picture. It's better that I write to you because I don't think my words could express it quite as well. I just wanted you to know how glad I am to have you for a friend. And I am grateful for all the thoughtful things you do and say. Your friend, Jane.

A year later Anita left a touching note on my desk:

> In the beginning, having you for a homeroom teacher and then when you came to visit me when I was in the hospital, I could tell you cared. You have a sense of caring, concern and understanding that's pretty rare today. It used to really bother me that when I would confide my whole life to a close friend, it disturbed them more than I ever thought. It made some of them frustrated because they would say, "I want to help but I

don't know how."

I think it drove a lot of people away from me. But I never wanted it to be like that. Anyway, I got a pretty deep complex and I didn't want to relate to anyone. But you helped me get over that. I now realize that so many people have problems and I want to help. I'm not always sure how but I honestly try. Thank you for really communicating with me. Love, Anita

A few months later in summer school I received a letter from Sarah, also one of my students. In it she bared her soul:

All my life there has never been much love around our house. My father was always getting drunk and beating on my mother and there was always a lot of arguments between my brothers and sister and myself. I always had a terrible complex that others were better than me.

Sarah went on to explain her feelings of inferiority and her first love and her broken heart that followed. After telling me agonizingly about her family trials, she closed her letter saying:

I feel like I'm writing to Ann Landers or something, but it's good to get it off my chest. Thanks for caring. Enclosed is a poem I found that reminds me of myself:

I feel like I'm living in a shadow of me and what was me. I know I can only live for tomorrow and not yesterday. I know I've got to be me and not her, but I don't know who me is and what tomorrow is.

Love was good to me, and I was honest to it, if not noble.

It left me and I don't know where to find it. Everyone seems to avoid me. I'm so confused and alone and cold.

I'm not sure how, when or if I can give anymore. I need someone to give my life direction and value. Maybe you can't get that from the love of a friend. God can help me find it.

Her letter and the poem touched me deeply, and I wrote back to her. A few weeks later Sarah sent a second letter:

Dear Sister, I want to say that your letter is the most beautiful thing I have ever read. You have a fantastic sense of understanding. Your letter really made me stop feeling sorry for myself and it gave me a little bit of confidence."

Sarah proceeded to give me an update on her social life and her family, before telling me about a new song that "a guy named Tom Clay put out."

The beginning starts with a man asking a small child what

segregation, hatred, and prejudice mean. And the child answers with "I don't know." The song then goes on with sounds of marines marching in boot camp, then goes into the deaths of John Kennedy, Martin Luther King, and Bobby Kennedy. Finally it ends with the man and the child talking again. In the background, the song "What the World Needs Now Is Love" plays all through it.

It gives me chills every time I hear it and I just can't turn it off.

Sarah's letter showed me she was indeed searching for meaning—not just in her own life—but in national and world events. I was sorry that Sarah and the other teenagers had to suffer so much pain as they grew up, but I was happy that she was thinking deeply and critically. It made me feel like education was really happening. She was growing in wisdom, as well as knowledge.

One day back in school I found a note on my desk that started with the words, "Try and recognize the handwriting while you're reading." It was from Sherry, whose wisdom beyond her years always amazed me. Her message, more than her penmanship, identified her.

I wouldn't feel bad (about a classmate's outburst).... You gotta remember, trust has to be earned and matured. The world is so impersonal and cold, that we are brought up, from the time we are small, to be on the defensive. To find a really caring person is rare. When you find something you don't know about, don't you like to run it through the mill before you go into it and trust that it won't hurt you?

Look at it this way. You are something rare and beautiful. When you find something of this nature, at first you want to see how much you can get out of it, but each time you look at it, you see it in a new perspective and in a more mature way. Then you realize, one day, that it is priceless, and you clutch it to your heart and place it in your mind where you know no one else can get to it, and that it will always be there. No matter how old, or tarnished, or worn, the trust you put in it is still there.

Think about it. Don't give up now. There are a lot of people waiting for you to make the move. God didn't quit the first time he fell, and he had to die to get that trust!

I was overwhelmed by Sherry's deep perception and her wisdom, well beyond her teen years. Her letter was one of many that renewed my hope, because they made me feel that I was accomplishing something and that I was needed.

As I continued counseling my students, one junior confided that she had just returned from New York City where she had gone to have an abortion. She went on to explain that, suspecting she was pregnant, she went to a planned parenthood agency.

At the same time a staff member confirmed her pregnancy, she advised my student to get an abortion, without offering any other option.

"Have your boyfriend drive you to this address in New York City where abortions are legal. I'll set up an appointment for you."

It upset me to think that the teenager was not given any time to think about her pregnancy and consider alternatives. The counselor had made the decision for her. I was appalled to learn that an agency could do that without her parents having any say in the matter or even knowing what was going on. She was a minor, after all—and being sent out of state.

I spent a lot of time trying to convince her she would feel better if she would confide in her mother. But she balked at the suggestion.

"My mother is against abortion. She'll hate me if I tell her what I've done."

"Your mother hates abortions. She won't hate you," I tried to assure her. You need her moral support," I added.

All my attempts to convince her to tell her mother failed, as far as I knew. Believing strongly in confidentiality, I kept her secret and revealed it to no one.

In two additional cases—one a freshman and the other a sophomore—students approached me and spoke of the abortions they said their mothers had insisted they get. Without judging them or their mothers, I listened to their stories—believing they must have needed to talk about it. Both girls said they were receiving psychiatric treatment.

I did not want to compound their guilt, so I emphasized God's infinite love and forgiveness—believing that they unloaded their secrets on me, because they wanted a Sister's reassurance. Or maybe they wanted to reach a point where they could forgive themselves.

After each girl's revelation, I never brought up the subject again to either girl—although, as part of the curriculum, and my own belief in the sanctity of all human life, I taught my students the Catholic Church's stand on abortion.

I could see that living life as a teenager was anything but simple for the young person or their parents in the 1970's. The teenagers who dealt best with life's unpredictable situations were, in my estimation, those who—with their parents' help—had crystallized their values already.

Armed with high ideals, healthy ways of handling stress, good critical thinking skills and knowing when to say "no," then following through decisively—these young people seemed to have an edge over others who lacked what they had acquired.

Springtime rolled around and with it another junior-senior prom. As I joined the other Sisters who lined the back walls and gaped at the students, I couldn't help but think back to my own youth and recall my senior prom in that very room. I too danced with a sailor, like my student who lifted her head from the shoulder of the sailor she glided by with, to give me a broad smile.

My date Reds had stood me up. And Mother, who had a solution for everything, had called the USO. "Can you find a nice sailor to take my daughter to her prom? Yes, I'll send her in a cab. Just keep him there."

And so I was driven to the USO headquarters, where the cab driver located my sailor right where Mother said he'd be waiting. Then off we went to my prom.

It was uncanny. I had just recently met Bob. He was the sailor I really wanted to be with that night. But I had already asked Reds to be my prom date and I couldn't hurt his feelings. Yet Reds did not show up. And there I was, all dressed up, without an escort. What could possibly have gone wrong?

The USO sailor was nice, but a bit backward and definitely not my type. Later I learned that Reds landed in jail. Was he caught stealing a tux? I never knew the answer. I broke off with him and looked forward to starting a dating relationship with Bob. Reds, unfortunately, would grow up scarred from his impoverished, dysfunctional home life.

As I watched the prom with the Sisters, I could see other sailors dotting the dance floor in their spotless whites. I used to like flirting with sailors. I remembered the very first one—Sam from Mississippi at Carlin's Amusement Park. We kept banging each other's bumper cars, flirting really.

I noticed the beautiful gowns the girls were wearing. I liked the one I chose for my prom. It had a monochromatic color scheme using shades of pink and lavender—halter-style with net forming the halter. I was convinced the dress reflected my personality well, and I felt beautiful wearing it.

Mother, fearing the Sisters might consider the dress immodest, had added two half-inch pink satin straps to go over my shoulders. Still, Sister Raymond embarrassed me in front of my date by pulling on one of the straps and commenting that not much was holding my gown up.

There I go again, taking another journey down memory lane. Was I the only Sister feeling taunted by reminders of what used to be? Of what could have been? I had to force my toes to stop tapping, when I turned to follow the others back to the Sisters' quarters. We were like puppets acting in unison—acting oblivious to the world around us.

The school year was winding down at a hectic pace. Summer school was approaching—my fifteenth year in a row.

Assigned to take specific courses at Providence College in Rhode Island, I found myself waiting in line to register for a Master's Program—far away from my Provincial House in Maryland.

Although surrounded by Sisters, mainly Dominicans in white Habits, no one else dressed like I did. I would be the only one from my religious congregation studying here. I found it hard to believe. It was rare for our Sisters to study apart from the others.

By now, our Sisters teaching in high schools needed to work toward a Master's Degree in the field in which they were teaching. So, most were assigned to graduate studies—except for Sisters teaching theology.

In the period following Vatican Council II, a lot of confusion spread among Superiors of religious orders. Catholic colleges were becoming too liberal in their teaching of theology, some thought. This was making nuns less pliable, turning them into critical thinkers.

Sisters started questioning antiquated practices, and some were leaving their convents—believing they knew better than their Superiors how they could best serve God in the world outside. Were they becoming tainted by the secular feminist movement? This was terrifying to some religious leaders in the Catholic Church. Did they fear the system in place would crumble—that they would lose control?

My own Superiors reacted by pulling the reins even tighter and refusing to assign our Sisters to graduate theology programs. Rumor had it they did not want to lose Sisters to liberal college thinking, which could taint their fidelity and rub off on the other Sisters. The exodus of Sisters would be destructive to the Church's institutions that had kept the Church going for so many centuries—an attitude I found hard to understand in some ways.

When eighty-year old Pope John XXIII opened Vatican Council II nine years before, had he not chided "prophets of doom" within the Catholic Church and stressed the world's need for the "medicine of mercy"? Had he not called for a new openness to the power and direction of the Holy Spirit in the Church? How could Superiors or any one of us let fear take control? Surely, authority figures were not letting themselves become power-hungry or even smug—depending on themselves instead of seeking God "in spirit and in truth." I hope this was not the case.

Be that as it may, my Superiors decided to send me to get my Master's Degree in Religious Studies. They ruled out Washington, DC's Catholic University of America for being too liberal at the time. And La Salle College in Pennsylvania was rejected on the suspicion of creating free-thinking Sisters.

Sister Eleanor, a Bostonian who had succeeded Sister Irene as Visitatrix, believed that the Dominican priests had made Providence College in Rhode Island a safe place to study theology. So, that is where I would be sent.

For the past sixteen years I had lived only with my own religious community of Sisters. Now, all of a sudden, I was being thrown together with Sisters and priests and lay people, all of whom I was trained to regard as externs. I had never before mixed with persons other than those trained to think, speak and behave like me. Maybe I should have been elated—seeing it as a unique opportunity, but I was scared.

A side of me said, "Here's your chance to experience freedom." Another side of me drew back and said, "Remember, you are bound by your rules and community policies, wherever you go. You must not jeopardize your vocation or your vows. Be loyal, no matter what! Don't undo the work that went into your formation."

Before long, I latched on to two other Sisters who were the only ones there from their religious orders. Their companionship became a security blanket for me, making me feel less intimidated. Between classes I made sure I said my prescribed prayers, went to Mass, and took my spiritual reading. Weekly I went to confession to a priest. I was relieved to be free from the dreaded Friday night Conference of Faults that kept me uptight and in a state of tension.

Sister Anna was not much taller than me. She dressed in a black skirt that reached just below her knees and a short-sleeved blouse that was light blue. On her head she wore a short black veil, pushed back, revealing some of her red hair.

Always smiling a sincere but timid smile, she was predictably proper. That whole summer she was homesick for Canada and would not return to take courses at the college the following summer.

But that summer she and I palled around with Sister Julie, who took upon herself the role of Mother Hen. Born and bred in Massachusetts, Sister Julie wore a plain dress that hung straight and reached several inches below her knees. Somewhat stocky, she was taller than either of us and had short gray hair, uncovered, that framed a face revealing her intense sincerity. Her eyeglasses helped to accentuate her intelligence.

Already having a Master's Degree in math and another in genetics, she was working on her third in biblical studies. From the beginning of our friendship, Sister Julie sensed the insecurity of the two of us who acted lost, away from our religious congregations—unable to do anything without a Superior giving us orders.

At first, Sister Julie got on my nerves, as she challenged almost everything I said. But eventually, I saw in her behavior, acts of kindness, and I came to appreciate what she was doing. Realizing I was merely "mouthing" what I was trained to say, she was forcing me to think before I spoke. She was a colorful character whom people either loved or hated. And I would come to love her like my own sister—as if we had blood ties.

When I returned to Seton to teach another school year after summer school in Rhode Island, I found it extremely difficult to re-adjust to my fragmented life there. My battle with my emotions kept escalating. The more I beat them down and tried to suppress them, the harder they fought back and wore me out. The contrast between my life during the regular school year and my life in the opposite environment of summer school made me feel like I was on a seesaw. I lived for my summers up north, focusing on Providence College as my "oasis in the desert."

Meanwhile, my physical problems worsened, and I was sent to a doctor at our District of Columbia hospital who took charge of our Sisters' health. He was the last resort in a chain of doctors Superiors permitted us to see. So many Sisters were under his care that it was hard to get an appointment with him. Finally, my Sister Servant succeeded and sent me to him.

He examined me, listened to my complaints and scratched his head.

"Sister," he said bluntly, "There are so many symptoms you describe, that I don't know what to do with you. I'm sorry, but I can't help you."

After making a few suggestions and giving me a prescription to give my Superior, he sent me back to my convent. I left his office knowing little more than I already knew.

At that time, I had no idea that the frustrations of my lifestyle and my confused mental state could manifest themselves through physical ailments. But the doctor should have known.

Yet he chose to remain silent.

Was it because he was getting a hefty paycheck from the Superior of our province? Did she control him to the extent that he felt unable to give me a direct and honest diagnosis? What did he write in the report she received? And why could I not have access to it? As always, I was not allowed to raise questions.

Nevertheless, our Religious Order began to show awareness that Sisters needed time to relax in body and spirit. By 1970, Sister Servants were given permission to rent a cottage by the water annually, if certain conditions were met: The convent needed to have sufficient funds to budget for it. Only the Sisters of our own Order could participate, and the location had to be as private as reasonably possible. Sisters could not go off and mix with externs. Nor could they go to public places nearby for additional recreation, even for a meal.

It was thrilling the first time I went back to the ocean, fifteen years after leaving home. I savored the emotion, as I walked down the beach squashing the grains of sand with my bare feet. I had to suppress the kid in me that wanted to race to the water and feel it splash all over my body trickling down in streams.

The symphonic sounds of the surf added to the euphoria I felt, as the first wave embraced my ankles, then another enveloped my whole body. It was a great feeling to be at one with the sea again—an almost sensual elation to be back where I always felt at home. And here I was, with the seagulls, even, as my welcoming committee.

The first few times back at the beach left me breathless, until I began to feel deeply the freeing influence of the water that inundated me. The ocean evoked in me a yearning to be free, to be that child who was most herself at aquarian places, the young woman who wanted to spend her life on the water and fly with the seabirds—join a flock somewhere. Or else, just stand immovable on a shore and inhale ever so deeply my beloved ocean! Why not?

Some realizations were seeping through. The concept of together-ness was becoming too much for me. Doing everything with a group of women everyday for so many years had taken its toll. Here I was, at the sea, with the same women with whom I rubbed shoulders day in and day out—the very Sisters I needed to get away from for a while.

I needed the freedom to go off and be alone, to unwind in my own way, to lose myself on the beach, to be transformed—without distractions, without obligations. Was it so wrong to wish for that?

Even at the water, I had to remember all my spiritual exercises: say all the prescribed prayers and take my spiritual reading. I was suffering from an overdose of religion and needed an occasional day to dispense with mandated prayer. Besides, having to teach theology five days a week intensified that crushing sense of being overwhelmed. With so much legislated religion and few physical or recreational outlets, my life seemed lopsided to the degree that one side was dragging me down—perhaps killing me.

Forcing myself to live this way day after day, week after week, month after month, year after year, was not revealing the results I hoped it would. Did God not make a promise in the Bible that those who would leave all to follow Him would find a hundredfold of happiness in this life, in addition to an eternity in Heaven afterwards?

Where was my hundredfold? I would have settled for half that much—at least, more than a trickle. Something was wrong. Radically wrong. I felt trapped in a corner. It was hard enough to deny myself male companionship. But added to that, the mandate to work and pray within a community of women bound by rigid rules was wearing me down.

As always, I tried to "pray out of my agony." I cried out to God, "I keep trying, Lord. But I can't throw off my humanness and live only on a spiritual level. For more than fifteen years I've struggled, and nothing is working. Please, God, I need help!"

I was drowning in frustration. Pulling my hair out, so to speak, as I frantically reached out for ways to deaden my pain. Listening to music was not resolving what was wrong. Throwing myself more deeply into my work wasn't really a solution, either. I wanted to go off somewhere and scream, if I couldn't shed what was choking me to death.

Finally, to keep my sanity I resorted to something I had not done before. At the age of thirty-five I began to masturbate, finding it gave me temporary relief from the struggle.

It released some of the sexual tension I could no longer control, but—in the long run—it backfired. My feelings of self-worth, already eroded, were undermined further—keeping me introspective and believing I was a terrible sinner. Masturbating served to compound the guilt complex that plagued me more and more intensely, the longer I remained a Sister.

Over and over again I would have to admit to the priest in Confession what I was doing. I would feel like a worm struggling to disappear beneath the ground every time I repeated that humiliating admission. Would it not have been better to walk away? To leave the convent? To allow myself to fall in love and marry? At the time, I still believed it was not an option.

It wasn't until years later that I came to realize that other Sisters, Brothers, and priests too, were fighting similar battles with celibacy and isolation in a confining lifestyle that choked off their emotions.

Perhaps, some of them were having illicit affairs or sinning in worse ways. Maybe, all of us were hypocrites—outwardly professing to live angelic lives, while secretly living imperfect or even sinful lives.

The Catholic Church and its officials, the hierarchy, swept under the rug such problems—ignoring the desperation of many of the clergy, Brothers and Sisters. What they did not want to face and admit, they evaded. And far worse consequences emerged inside the Church with repercussions outside.

Perhaps, the greatest sin lay with those who could have brought about change and chose to do nothing. Could they not have listened and honestly sought reasonable solutions? Maybe celibacy was more a hindrance than a help to some. Perhaps greater open-mindedness was being demanded of those holding the reins of authority. Maybe God was calling them to exercise compassion—even empathy—asking them to release their "death grip" on the past and set consecrated souls free from the strangling neckhold of guilt.

Jesus' behavior always emanated from love, never from attachment to power or any other vice. Why could Catholic Church leaders not follow the same pattern? Why could they not try harder to understand the human side of their subjects?

It seemed as if members of the hierarchy were so obsessed with preserving what they perceived as the "spotless" reputation of the Church—that their "victimization policies" were ignored.

Meanwhile, my parents moved north of Baltimore to a place called White Marsh, where they purchased a shell of a home on Bird

River. Together they completed the building project as a labor of love. My fondness for water had originated with them. Now I would be able to spend three days a year visiting them on the river.

At those times, whenever I sat on the pier and inhaled the pungent river aroma, I would be transported back in time to the days when I swam at Rocky Point as a child. It was easy to recall memories of canoeing at Loch Raven with my family and fun picnics beside the water at Mount Pleasant and Herring Run. They were wonderful times that seemed to happen an eternity ago, almost in another lifetime.

Taking in the scenic sights of trees hugging the banks while I listened to the birds flying overhead and the water lapping against the pier gave me a mystical high. Nature that I loved called me to stay.

I wanted to answer, "Yes! Yes! Yes!"

Being there was a mixed blessing—so great while I could enjoy it, so painful when I had to get up and leave. It was the pattern of my life repeated over and over again: Take delight in it, then tear myself away and return to my "imprisoned self" in the convent.

And so, I would go back to my convent feeling like a dog that had spent its day running free through an open field, then had to slink back with its tail between its legs to a kennel to watch the world once again from its fenced enclosure.

This was my life, as another chapter came to a close. After having lived and taught at Seton for only three years, my name appeared on the list of Sisters transferred. Still, I had no regrets. Rather, I was relieved to leave a situation that had left me feeling fragmented and broken. Part of me was amazed that I had survived my "sentence" there with any sanity left.

At the end of six years in Endicott, storms clouds were increasing and becoming darker. Five years later in Pikesville the clouds had given way to heavy, aggravating rains. Now upon leaving Baltimore City I had the storm's fury to deal with.

My studies at Providence College, while giving me sunny respites from the turmoil, had made it more difficult for me to go back to my Order's province and readjust to convent life there.

Still, I hoped that starting anew in Virginia would gradually break through the darkness and reveal a glorious sunrise. I had to believe this was a possibility. And so, I clung desperately to hope.

6,189 days had passed since I left home. I missed my brown-shingled house and all its memories. Above all, I missed my loved ones.

III
The Awakening

Pursuit of Happiness Denied

10.

The Chronic Criticism Syndrome

In 1972 I arrived in the southern city of Lynchburg. The good news was that the Sisters lived in a convent surrounded by trees—apart from the school. I would have a hill to walk down and up twice a day, giving me precious moments outdoors.

The bad news was that I was being sent as a "troubleshooter." Some of the students' parents had turned against a priest and a Sister for teaching religion in a radically-wrong way, in their estimation.

"If it feels good, do it," was the philosophy the priest allegedly promoted, and the students' parents demanded a change. As a result, both teachers were thrown out of the school, and I was sent to repair the damage. In a real sense, I was being hurled from the "frying pan into the fire."

After my arrival, one thing came through loud and clear. Many of the disenchanted parents assumed I would make the same mistakes and not teach "real religion." More conflict in my life was what I didn't need. Hadn't I brought with me frayed nerves and mangled emotions? I felt under siege from the beginning.

Nevertheless, I did my best—continuing to use the multi-media approach, while adapting the curricula I had developed at Seton to my new environment. There was no way I could go back to the question-and-answer method that many of the parents and I had experienced, using the Baltimore Catechism in our own Catholic schools.

Before long, the parents were up in arms again and converged on my principal, who insisted I call a meeting to explain what I was doing and why. When the scheduled day arrived, I woke up with an abscessed tooth.

"There's no way we can postpone the meeting, Sister Patricia Anne. You'll just have to wait another day before going to the dentist," my Sister Servant insisted.

So I dragged myself through the school day, and that night I stood before my audience in excruciating pain. Feeling like a criminal on trial for my life, I explained my method of teaching and answered their questions apparently to their satisfaction.

I was relieved to finally have the tooth pulled out the next day.

At this school, too, we were getting ready for our accreditation with numerous self-studies. Implementing a continuous-progress program similar to that of Seton, I would need to set up a theology resource center. With limited space in the school, I asked and received permission to partition my classroom with the help of student volunteers.

Several of the high school boys planned the project, then came back in the evening to get the work done. As I supervised the undertaking, I found myself enjoying their company. I felt like the mother of a family, as we laughed and talked for a few hours each evening. And I loved the feeling.

It was as if I were given a glimpse of what motherhood felt like. But in the end, I had to beat down the pleasurable sensations that threatened to revive my old yearnings and dreams. They were only temptations, after all. That's what I told myself.

Still, it was thrilling to experience those feelings. Having to forfeit the right of giving birth to my own children, was it not right to enjoy my classroom children?

In the following weeks, as I performed my assigned duties, my feelings of loneliness and isolation mushroomed even more than previously. When weekends came along, I would hurry down the hill to my classroom, after finishing my convent chores and mandated prayers. There I would pull out a record player and listen to music, as I prepared my lesson plans.

Sometimes I would close my eyes and visualize myself driving along Blue Ridge Parkway nearby or hiking a trail—and inhaling the aroma of wild flowers, as I enjoyed the mountain air that gorged my lungs. But such activities were still prohibited.

I found comfort in the songs my students had brought for classroom meditation. I'd let Barbra Streisand speak to my heart, reminding me that "people who need people are the luckiest people in the world."

Listening to the haunting melody and lyrics over and over again reinforced my conviction that I was one of those people she sang about—that I needed people other than those placed around me. While letting Barbra serenade and comfort me, I battled the realizations that those sentiments elicited.

When Richard Bach's book was published, I enthusiastically put copies of <u>Jonathan Livingston Seagull</u> on my resource center bookshelf to use in my theology classes. Jonathan mesmerized me. I found myself feeling at one with the seagull who yearned so much for freedom he went apart from his flock and took risks to fly free.

When the movie based on the book was released, I couldn't wait to take my students on a field trip to see it. My emotions peaked, when Neil Diamond sang his songs on the film's soundtrack. The singer had no idea that his passionate singing about Jonathan's search for freedom was beginning to tear down a wall a Sister had put up to keep her feelings in check. The words he sang touched me deeply.

I looked up at the "lonely looking sky" and, as I started to "wonder why," answers began to emerge. I wanted to "dance to the whispered voice"—yet I felt totally confused, lost even. Deep down, like Jonathan, I knew what I needed to do, but I hesitated—afraid to spread my wings and fly into the unknown.

Living close to the Peaks of Otter, I hungered to be immersed in nature, to feel Mother Earth's healing touch. Lost in God's wilderness, it would have been so easy to unleash what was pent up inside me and grab hold of the answers. Perhaps, I would also have found the courage to try out my wings—to take risks. But I was in a psychological straight jacket, unable to break free.

I kept on spending my Sunday afternoons letting Barbra Streisand and Neil Diamond cheer me up and give me hope. Although I refused to allow myself to act on my feelings and I fiercely battled the truth, I continued to sing with Neil Diamond—deep in my soul—in search of "a voice that was silent."

I trusted that God would clear a path for me eventually. This belief gave me strength to hold on and wait for the ultimate answer.

Meanwhile, I kept my eyes focused on the near future knowing that, if I could make it through the school year, I would have another summer in Rhode Island to look forward to. And so, I went back to Providence College the following June.

As always, Sister Julie welcomed me like a "real sister". In an indirect way she helped me, once again, to get in touch with my feelings and it felt good. I was gradually finding inner freedom using Sister Julie as my role model. She had found freedom in her own religious order that permitted, even encouraged, individuality within the larger framework.

Since my friend knew I wasn't allowed to go to movie theaters unless I was on a field trip with my class, she understood my yearning and walked me to a neighborhood theater one Saturday. There we saw the feature film "Love Story"—the only movie being shown.

Although I found it a terribly sad tale, it was a "first." I had given myself permission to see a movie in a public place, without feeling guilty. Was the noose around my neck loosening?

I couldn't help recalling my growing-up years, when I loved going to Saturday matinees. I'd walk four blocks to the Northway Theater, where I thrived on romance mixed with adventure, musicals, and—of course, I wouldn't miss any story filmed on the water.

Richard Widmark became my hero after I saw him in "Down to the Sea in Ships". And I was infatuated with the swashbuckling characters played by Errol Flynn, Louis Hayward, and Tyrone Power. I never forgot Jeanne Crain in "State Fair" or Gene Kelly in "Singing in the Rain." Yet, for the last eighteen years, I had given all of that up—except for the few occasions when theaters had special showings of "wholesome" movies for Sisters.

Besides putting me back in touch with the world of film, Sister Julie recognized how much I missed the sea. She drove me to the New England coast that she knew like the back of her hand, since she had grown up in Salem. I was thrilled to listen to the crashing surf, as I gazed at the awesome ocean in Gloucester. The statue of the woman looking out to the sea waiting for her fisherman husband to return enthralled me.

In Rockport I loved watching the artists at work, while the salt water tinged my nostrils and the waves lapped against the pilings of the wharf. I wished I could sit among the painters and capture the beauty on my own canvas. And for those fleeting moments I was a child again—breathing freely—wanting so badly to savor the ecstasy and not let it end.

Still, I must have made progress in my inner search for freedom, since I had actually permitted myself to follow the call of the sea without feeling any guilt, on those day-excursions with Sister Julie.

Summer school up North shed the chronic gloom of my life for those months and renewed my spirit. I could see, then, that something remained of who I really was—despite the pressures and frustrations inherent in religious life within the Catholic Church at that time.

But back in Lynchburg one autumn I received bad news. Doctors had diagnosed my friend Julie as having breast cancer. After removing one breast, then the other, the surgeon's prognosis was not very good.

"The cancer has spread to your lymph nodes," he told her. "Fifty percent of women in your condition will survive five years."

I felt devastated. I did not want to lose my dearest friend who had become like a real sister to me, who had lifted me from the dead, so to speak. I was terribly worried about her but lived too far away to visit and comfort her.

While Sister Julie took her radiation treatments, followed by chemotherapy, she was hard at work studying for her comprehensive exams and finishing her required research paper. I knew the testing process at the college was rigorous—a written exam one day, followed by an oral exam the next day. And I wondered why she was still going to put herself through additional agony. I dared not say aloud what I was thinking.

At the time, I continued to suffer from the "believe the doctors" syndrome, when it came to predicting the remaining years of life people with "terminal" illnesses had. As a Sister, I should have known better.

When the appointed days arrived, Sister Julie took her exams and passed "with distinction"—a high honor not achieved by many—a tribute to her brilliant mind. However, in her humility and wisdom, I don't think she believed she deserved adulation for merely using the talents that came from God, after all.

I discovered that Sister Julie's stubborn streak ran deep. She refused to die until she was good and ready. In her mind she had a lot of living to do, and nobody and nothing would ever make her give up the life she cherished. If we could have looked into the future, we would have seen that she would survive another twenty-three years.

Sister Julie was regional coordinator of a Massachusetts Meals-on-Wheels program—a job her religious congregation allowed her to select for herself. Only eight weeks after her operation, she announced she was going back to work full-time. Throwing herself into her work, she was determined to beat her cancer.

As I prayed for my friend and rooted for her, I tried to be optimistic about my own life. Back at school teaching, my frustration deepened each time my students or their parents treated me with hostility. Certain students would speak up arrogantly in class, voicing criticism of my teaching in ways only adults would have expressed it. They must have been repeating what they had heard at home. Obviously, suspicion and skepticism still colored the attitude of their families toward me. Some became constant "thorns in my side," and I was losing patience.

I was doing a job I had not asked for—a job I would never have chosen for myself. And I was performing my assigned duties the best I knew how. I just wanted to be left in peace.

Couldn't they imagine what the life of a Sister was like? How difficult it was to battle the flesh and live like a disembodied spirit, while all the human—even womanly—drives remained? Couldn't they show a little bit of compassion towards Sisters who, after all, had to teach for free—sacrificing their needs and wants—their very lives? Why did they have to complicate my life that was already so fragile?

My heart felt like a dam ready to burst. I threw up my hands, finally, in a gesture of futility and called out to the Lord:

"I didn't ask for this job. I really wanted to teach French, but nobody asked me what I wanted. Teaching another subject would have been non-threatening, and I wouldn't have had to put up with all of these post-Vatican II conflicts of Catholic families.

"I have tried and tried and tried, until I'm sick of trying, Lord— but you already know that! Why aren't you here with me, helping me out? Please, Lord, answer me!"

As I prayed and listened, a solution bombarded my brain. I went to my room and wrote a letter to Sister Visitatrix—now called the Provincial Superior.

Without revealing the inner struggles of my heart, I frantically poured out my frustrations with my work, then made a suggestion:

"Maybe if I could distance myself from teaching and have time to reflect, I could work this out and come back and make a new start. May I have your permission to work full time on my Master's Degree at Providence College?"

I sent the letter and held my breath waiting for the reply. Meanwhile, national attention was focused on POWs returning from Viet Nam. One day the Sisters assembled on the school grounds for a television interview of a local young man who was among the POWs.

All of us shared in the happiness of our country's released prisoners of war. Impressed with the graciousness of the reporter who spent a few minutes speaking to the circle of Sisters, I needed him to ask us how free WE felt.

Wasn't freedom everyone's right, even Sisters? Wasn't it more than just a valuable commodity? As the man turned to leave, my soul was shouting out: We are not free. Ask me about that. But, like the others, I stood there with my mouth locked in silence.

Finally, the letter I anticipated arrived. My whole future and my happiness seemed to hang in the balance. As I ripped open the envelope, a burning question seared my brain: Will it be YES? Please, God, let it be the answer I want—the answer I so desperately need!

Anxiously I began to read:

"With great concern I read your letter, Sister Patricia Anne. I will honor your request and permit you to remain at Providence College for the fall semester after summer school. You will be accountable from a distance to Sister Lourdes, the Sister Servant of the Provincial House. I wish you God's blessing, as you study away from Saint Vincent's family."

I took a deep breath and let the message sink in. I had already spent three summers at Providence College, and I had finally let myself begin feeling free inside—at least while I was there studying and taking courses. This was great news—what I needed to weather the storm.

And it meant Superiors would have to send someone else to teach in my place. I was so relieved! I felt euphoric as that school year wound down. I wanted to shout "Hallelujah," when I finally walked out the door. Let someone else be "trouble shooter" for a while and see how it feels.

Back in Providence my studies made my life simpler. Theology on the graduate level was a freeing experience, helping me recognize I had been living in a spiritual straight jacket.

As I listened to my professors and read the Holy Scriptures, I came to realize that the most basic message of the Bible—the bottom line—was not complicated at all: God is Love, and the Holy Spirit came to set us free!

As I pondered Scripture's meaning, I was glad my Religious Order now permitted me to read the Bible. But soon, I found myself confronted by a question: If living my life is making me feel so unfree, where is the Holy Spirit?

Deep in my soul Barbra Streisand was still singing, reminding me I was one of those "people who need people." And Neil Diamond never ceased haunting me with the memory of my beloved Jonathan— my "gift" from Richard Bach.

Neil's song was a constant push toward my own freedom, as I admired the seagull who risked the flock's rejection. Now I was finding reinforcement in—of all places—my theology studies.

God was calling me to be free. Was the message finally sinking in? Was it finally loud enough for me to hear it clearly?

I began attending Sunday Mass at Saint Patrick's Cathedral, where I encountered the Catholic Charismatic Movement for the first time. This opened me to a type of spirituality that would reinforce all the forces pulling me toward freedom.

I felt a more personal relationship with God through His Son Jesus. And I loved the free-flowing prayer. I was amazed to be greeted with warm hugs, after having starved for a hug for so long a time.

No one placed unreasonable demands on me here, and the atmosphere did not reek of unhealthy guilt. It was a refreshing change of pace, paving the way to wholeness, peace, and eventually, my freedom—although I couldn't see that far down the road to the future.

Still recovering from her cancer, Sister Julie visited me at the college and drove me back to the New England coast. It was thrilling to dine at a restaurant overlooking the ocean in Marblehead. And she showed me Salem, her birthplace, where we toured the Witch Museum and the home of Nathaniel Hawthorne—the great writer.

Once again I celebrated incredible moments beside the water, mesmerized by the aroma of sea creatures, salty air and—of course— the foaming surf. Standing like a statue at the water's edge, I let myself be inundated by the rapturous molecules—almost invisible in the drenched air. And, as always, I gorged my lungs with the incomparable and indescribable experience, making me wish my feet were imbedded in cement, to keep me there forever.

On another sunny day the college staff set up a field trip for students who wanted to spend a few hours at Newport in Rhode Island. Signing up fast, I was thrilled to have that additional seaside excursion.

As I began my trek high above the ocean, a tourist passing by pointed to one of the many mansions that lined the path.

"The Great Gatsby is being filmed there today," she announced excitedly. I nodded, then turned my attention back to the sea that I found much more appealing than a movie set.

I loved the cliff walk where the rough waters beating against the rocks sent electrifying shock waves to the tips of my toes, while I watched gulls fly freely over my head.

For a moment I wished I could rip off my Habit, flap my wings and fly over the sea with them—explore distant shores and "set loose" the adventurer imprisoned within me. The trip was a dream come true.

Back in Providence, I was excited to hear the news that Cesar Chavez was coming to town to speak. I made sure I was present in the audience, as he was one of my heroes. I had included some of his life and work in the mini-course I had entitled "Modern Prophets."

When this humble man finished talking, I was so overwhelmed by the experience that I rushed downstairs from the balcony and went backstage to look for him. The moment I saw him, I threw my arms around him and said:

"Mister Chavez, I can't be this close to you without giving you a big hug. Thank you for what you are doing!"

I had hugged this man without feeling guilty, for he was "my brother." We shared a deep concern for the oppressed, and I knew he was truly a saint. No secular celebrity could begin to reach this man's stature. That I believed. His countenance and the way he carried himself exuded only humility—the bottom line of greatness.

That year I became close to many of the college students and felt like I was doing unofficial campus ministry. Soon after my arrival, I was approached in the library one Saturday night by a frantic student from Long Island.

"Where is the chaplain? I have to see him right away," the young man cried out.

I told the freshman I would search for the priest, then return. Upon learning that the chaplain was away for the weekend, I came back and relayed the message, adding:

"Maybe I can help. I have time to listen."

So I sat with Jimmy and let him pour out his heart and soul to me. He was terribly frustrated and needed a friend at that moment. New on campus, he was having a hard time adjusting to the academic and social pressures of the college. And he was so homesick. I was probably one of the first friends he made, and I felt good about being there when he needed someone to listen to his pain and affirm him.

I made more friends when I attended the campus prayer meetings. One was a Viet Nam veteran recently back from overseas. My heart went out to this young man who returned home a basketcase emotionally. I befriended him and did my best to lift the spirits of this broken human being whose face revealed the ravages of war. It was obvious he had a long journey ahead of him before healing would take place.

War was always a mystery to me. It had destroyed something in my own Dad. And now it was killing the spirit of so many young people and their families. How did the world reach the point where its main solution to problems was killing one another—taking away precious lives—and for what? War made absolutely no sense to me. How could any good come out of war?

Why couldn't human beings use their God-given intelligence to come up with peaceful solutions to conflict—and MAKE them work? This puzzled me. On the other hand, the mere semblance of peace was not enough—without inner peace inside each individual.

I only had to look at my own life to realize that truth. Wasn't oppression just as bad as war? I learned a lot that year in addition to theology through my experiences away from my home base.

As the semester wound down, I wrote to my new Provincial Superior to report that I had finished taking all the coursework required for a Master's Degree. Wanting so badly to remain in New England and continue to be nurtured in ways I would not find back in my religious community, I asked for more time to write my research paper and study for, then take, my comprehensive exams.

Sister Clara Mae's reply was affirmative:

"Yes, you may stay and finish what you need to do in order to get your degree. But then, you must return to our dear province and do the work that will be assigned to you. There will be no reason to go back to Providence anymore, Sister."

I was elated! I had bought myself more time to be at peace and feel free. As a Sister, yes—but not having unreasonable burdens dumped on my shoulders and not feeling the oppression of intolerance. For whatever reason, I felt happier and more relaxed in Rhode Island.

College officials notified me that I could not remain housed on campus, now that my courses were finished. My acting Sister Servant in Emmitsburg advised me to look for a nearby convent that would offer me hospitality for a semester. My Province would foot the bill. And so, I searched.

The FCJs in North Providence welcomed me and offered me exquisite hospitality. The Faithful Companions of Jesus lived up to their name, and I became fond of each Sister who showered me with kindness. Their spirituality, accompanied by graciousness, was truly compelling.

While I prepared for my comprehensive exams, I wrote my research paper and entitled it: "The Outpouring of the Holy Spirit in the Acts of the Apostles." My obsession with freedom had led me to dig deeper into the Bible to find answers to the questions that were arising within me. So I concentrated on the first Christians and the effects of the Holy Spirit's presence and power in their lives. That research—and meditation upon it—left a lasting impression on me.

226

Shortly before Christmas, I was approached by a student who asked me if I would like to go to the Boston Pops Christmas concert in his place. He had to work that night, he said, but his parents would be glad to pick me up and take me, if I'd be their guest and use his ticket. Of course, I jumped at the chance.

Not only was it a great concert performed locally, but I discovered that the conductor, Arthur Fiedler, was celebrating his eightieth birthday that day. During the intermission someone wheeled in a giant birthday cake shaped like a baby grand piano. Then and there, I joined the audience in singing "happy birthday" to the renowned maestro—an unforgettable moment that would seal itself in my memory.

I had spent a wonderful evening being entertained with music of fantastic quality, while being present for the world-famous conductor's spectacular birthday celebration. The day that Arthur Fiedler was born really did matter. The world would not have been the same without his musical genius. His life with its contributions did make a difference.

One day in the new year I received a strange long-distance call from Sister Lourdes. My Superior from afar said she had good news— "that my name was drawn."

"I don't understand, Sister," I replied.

"You must remember the letter Sister Clara Mae sent out. In it, she informed the Sisters of the Province that names would be drawn to see which Sisters would attend Mother Seton's canonization in Rome next September. Anyone interested was asked to submit her name."

"This is the first I heard about it, Sister."

"Then someone else must have put your name in. It doesn't matter. You are on the pilgrimage list now. So, be grateful to God."

"I AM grateful, Sister, to God and the Sister who put my name in the pot."

As the realization sank in, my excitement grew. Although I had always been an explorer at heart, I hadn't traveled much—above all, not outside the United States. It was supposed to be a pilgrimage, a holy trip, but it would be much more.

I anticipated my forthcoming journey as an adventure. I had something pleasurable to look forward to after my intensive studies, and I was glad. I needed this to boost my spirits. Thank you, God, I must have repeated over and over again.

For now, I had some serious studying to do. My brain already felt like it was going to explode, and Easter would soon be here. My comprehensive exams were scheduled forty days later on Ascension Thursday and Friday in May. The task was beginning to look over-whelming. Getting nervous about all the cramming I still had to do, I kept my nose to the grind.

The Sisters with whom I lived were going to spend the Easter holidays at their Central House in Portsmouth, Rhode Island, and I received an invitation to join them.

When I arrived, I was led upstairs to a large guest room with two windows overlooking Narragansett Bay. I was thrilled to discover I would have the most fabulous view I could imagine, while sitting at my desk studying.

What a surprise! God was giving me what I loved best—water. And when I needed to take a break, I could walk along the rock-laden beach where I could be myself, be inspired and where I could feel at one with nature and with God.

God was comforting me, providing me with what I needed most—a miracle that would help me face the future with fortitude and calm.

My countdown had begun, and my head could not have held any more knowledge, I believed. The theological themes I was expected to be able to explain filled a large box. Just seeing the box on the floor near me triggered feelings of nausea.

Why was I doing this? What good would all of this theology do me? A Master's Degree in Religious Studies would seal my fate—label me forever as a theology teacher in my Religious Order.

Yet, all I really wanted to do was live a simple life—being me, not somebody else's version of what I should be. It was hard to believe my life had come to this. Was this really God's Will? That recurring question continued to haunt me.

What I didn't realize at the time was that my whole Providence College experience was going to be my ticket to freedom. It was an essential step along the way.

I had spent four summers followed by a school year in Rhode Island, and I was letting myself feel free inside, thanks mainly to Sister Julie. Two other factors that enhanced my journey to freedom were my involvement at the time in the charismatic movement and the Religious Studies program at the college.

The realization that God is Love and He sent His Holy Spirit to set us free sank in on a deeper, more profound level.

On the eve of the Feast of the Annunciation, I made a private retreat at the North Providence convent—spending most of the day in the Sisters' chapel. Feeling very close to God, I was moved to write down my reflections and prayers.

The next morning at Mass I renewed my vows of poverty, chastity, obedience, and service of the poor for another year. The Faithful Companions of Jesus joined me that day in my spirit of celebration and conveyed their best wishes. Afterwards, I had to change my mindset abruptly and get back to studying. I would have to take my comprehensive exams one month later.

On Ascension Thursday morning, I took the long written test, and the next day I stood before three theologians who fired questions at me for an hour. Then I waited for the next long, drawn-out days with abated breath for the verdict.

Finally, the answer came—I had passed! I now had a Master's Degree—a fact that would look good on paper and help a high school get accredited.

Was it an achievement for me? I suppose so. But humility had been drilled into me so deeply that I couldn't really feel any excitement over the milestone I had reached. It was hard to ignore the teaching of my Seminary Directress that humility meant believing I could do nothing right.

I felt so stressed out—like I was on the verge of a nervous breakdown. I wanted to go off and collapse somewhere, anywhere. I felt traumatized by the experience. But that kind of distress was still not acceptable in a Sister. Instead of having the opportunity to regroup and allow my body, mind, and spirit to heal, I had to go right back to my Provincial House with no detours. Once again, blind obedience was supposed to suffice.

My years at Providence College were over, and I felt sad. I had been set free, while I was there. Now I was being faced with the biggest fear of all. I would have to give up what I found in Rhode Island and begin anew in western Maryland where my behavior would be under constant scrutiny.

"Stay for graduation," some of my college friends insisted. But attending graduations—even my own—was still forbidden. No celebration for my achievement could take place. I would have to return and not discuss my Providence College experience, not mention my new degree, which would only make my pride more visible.

My diploma would simply be mailed to me, and I would have to put it away—out of sight—until I needed it for certification purposes.

Before leaving Rhode Island, I was devastated when I received word that my cousin Sandy had died. I had prayed so hard for her recovery from cancer. Her two young sons, as well as her husband Tommy, and her parents, my Aunt Elsie and Uncle Ed, were going to be devastated. She was only twenty-eight. Too young to die. But I knew that death did not take age into consideration.

When I picked up my mail that very day, grieving, I was surprised to open a letter from an elderly man who had been a fellow student the previous semester. He had enclosed a holy card from Jerusalem where he had gone on a pilgrimage. Pieces of bark and leaves from an olive tree in the Garden of Gethsemane formed a cross. Words at the bottom said the card was touched to Jesus' tomb, the Holy Sepulchre it was called.

I couldn't believe it! On the day of Sandy's death I had received something from the Garden where Jesus had spent His last hours in prayer and agony the night before He died. It seemed like more than a coincidence. Was Louis an angel in disguise? What he sent was a real comfort to me, as I struggled to come to terms with the death of my dear cousin.

Not long ago, we had buried her younger sister Lois, just after her twenty-third birthday. She had died of cancer too—leukemia—and left a baby behind with her husband Elmer. All three girls in that family had passed away in their youth. Only Billy, their brother, survived to carry on for that generation in his family.

This was just one more mystery of life that I had to take on faith, believing they would spend eternity in Heaven and one day be reunited with their family members in that world without time or space. I tried hard to believe, although I did not understand.

Sister Lourdes gave me permission to fly home and attend Sandy's funeral and share my family's grief.

Weeks later, I boarded another plane bound for the Baltimore area. As the plane took off and flew over the New England waters, my heart was heavy. I had to sever ties. I would miss Sister Julie and my other new friends.

I wanted desperately to hold on to the feeling of my newfound freedom—and not regress to that frightened Sister afraid to think for herself or make a move without permission.

But I was in a dilemma. How would I accomplish this? Why had my Rhode Island experience been so very powerful? Was it because my thoughts, words, and actions were not chained up? Was it because I slowly learned that what I thought and what I had to say might actually matter?

It had been so long a time—so many years of silence and controlled behavior—that I felt like a toddler taking baby steps, gleeful over the mobility in my life I suddenly recognized.

Soon after arriving in Emmitsburg, mission changes were announced. I was listed as going to Petersburg, Virginia. I would not be returning to Lynchburg. In a way, it was a relief to be sent elsewhere.

Reminiscing, I opened a gift my students in Lynchburg had presented to me, before I departed from the school. It was a silver medallion with an engraved image of Jonathan Livingston Seagull on the front. On the back these words were engraved:

"You have the freedom to be yourself here and now."

Was it a message from God? The thought briefly crossed my mind, before I dismissed it.

I was thirty-eight years old, standing at a crossroads.

7,284 days had passed since I left home. I missed my brown-shingled house and all its memories. Above all, I missed my loved ones.

11.

Clutching the Cliff's Edge

A few weeks before the start of a new school year, I arrived at Gibbons High School. Coed with twelve grades, Gibbons—like Holy Cross—was adapting to a modified "Trump" program in a continuous progress setting. Sister Joan Annette—despite her frail appearance—bubbled over with an exuberance and energy that produced dynamic leadership in her role as high school principal.

The elementary principal, Sister Clarisse, served as Superior for the Sisters of both schools who shared the same convent. Two years behind me in my Baltimore high school, she too was in the orchestra—the girl who never smiled. She was a quiet young lady, serious in her demeanor and in her approach to music.

Now in her thirties she was appointed a Superior—Sister Servant—for the first time in her life. And I found that her new role and her perceived sense of responsibility for the cooperation and obedience of all the Sisters under her care intensified the rigidity of her temperament, making her even more uptight.

I was glad that, just two weeks into the school year, I would be leaving for Europe to attend Mother Seton's canonization ceremony. I could get away from the atmosphere that was already becoming oppressive and stifling.

Before our departure, our major Superiors permitted us to visit our families to say "goodbye." They also gave us money to exchange for travelers' checks and foreign currency to pay for transportation, meals, and even souvenirs—a welcomed surprise.

On September 1, 1975, a bus took its load of Sisters—about sixty of us—to Dulles Airport, where we boarded the 8 p.m. TWA Flight #890. As the plane took off in the darkness, my excitement mounted, and I was more than ready to enjoy my first trans-Atlantic flight.

Enroute to Paris, I savored the delicious chicken dinner that was served, followed four hours later by a mouth-watering continental breakfast. The meals were so great that I kept the menu among my souvenirs.

Our flight was smooth, and we arrived at our destination—Charles deGaulle Airport—at 8:30 a.m., Paris time. According to my watch, it was just 3:30 a.m.

My first glimpse of Paris from the bus that took us to rue du Bac thrilled me. Beginning our visit with Mass at the Motherhouse, I felt dazed, as I prayed for the first time in the chapel where Saint Catherine Laboure had had her visions of Blessed Mother in 1830. I glanced over to see Saint Catherine's body encased behind glass under a side altar.

I remembered well the story of Sister Catherine's exhumation and the discovery that her body remained intact—even after having been buried in a damp underground vault for a hundred years. Looking at her, I felt chills.

My eyes searched for the other side altar that was sacred to the Sisters for its reliquary exposing the actual heart of Saint Vincent dePaul—to remind us of our holy founder's exceptional love of God and the poor, and of the kind of love we should be emulating.

After Mass, I excitedly joined two other Sisters on their trek to the River Seine for a boat ride. Floating under bridge after bridge, taking in the scenery along the banks of the river, I was the adventurer of twenty years earlier. Here I was, exploring the sights of Paris—ready to drink in all the marvels of Europe my religious community would allow me. And I found myself bursting with happiness!

The history reflected in the many bridges we saw amazed me, and I found the statue of Saint Genevieve, patroness of Paris, towering over the water at the end of one of the bridges, to be another awesome sight.

Stopping to buy a French ice cream cone on that hot first day, I was startled when we sat down and found ourselves yelled at, "No! No! Go!" We got the message and left. Later, we learned that you have to pay extra to sit down inside, and it costs even more to eat outside on the terrace.

I slept soundly that first night in my French bed, which was soft and comfortable. Since the Motherhouse bathtubs were narrow and made me feel wedged in, I decided to try the shower the next night. That was worse. I could only get a trickle of water out of a showerhead located directly over my head. I guessed the water pressure on an upper floor was a factor. For the rest of my stay, I used the bathtub.

The following days were delightful, as I enjoyed bus tours of the city and some of its outlying areas. The artist in me thrilled at seeing the treasures of the Louvre Museum, reminding me of my teenage dream now relegated to the "attic of my soul." Those emotions intensified, when we went to the Basilica of Montmartre, then sauntered outside to watch the artists at work painting the city below.

I could have been one of them, but I made another choice.

By now I had learned that we have to live with the consequences of our choices. I still didn't realize I had the power to redirect my life and make changes. That wisdom would come later.

One day, when we were allowed free time to sightsee, I went with Sister Mary Thomas to the Eiffel Tower, where we were treated to a fabulous view of Paris from three hundred feet up. There I snapped slide pictures with my camera.

On the way to Notre Dame Cathedral, I desperately needed a restroom. When I finally succeeded in conveying my message to a French storekeeper, she beckoned us to follow her next door. We entered a five- or six-story building that appeared to be centuries old.

Once inside, we found ourselves in a dark lobby and followed her to a doorway that led to a mini-courtyard enclosed by the building itself. Opposite the doorway I could see massive stone steps leading down to what looked like an old dungeon. The woman pointed to our right, and then departed.

Walking through the portal, I found myself in what appeared to be a medieval outhouse. There was nothing to sit on, just two indentations for feet in the stone floor that sloped down to a hole in the center. It was a kind of "squatter's toilet" with only a semblance of privacy.

I had to gather my clothing around me before squatting to do my business in the semi-darkness. Noticing a ray of light, I looked up and was shocked to find that the walls of the small courtyard rose as high as the building with an opening at the top.

Returning to the creepy-looking lobby, I found myself alone. My Sister-companion had abandoned me. I found her waiting outside.

We arrived at Notre Dame Cathedral at dusk, as planned, and prepared to eat in Pope John XXIII Square behind the church. We had planned supper, before leaving the Motherhouse that morning—taking from a table a bottle of the Sisters' watered-down wine, a loaf of French bread, and some wrapped triangles of cheese. We had noted beforehand that those staples were always on the refectory table. So we figured they wouldn't mind if we took our meal out to eat overlooking the River Seine in the shadow of the gargoyles. Fortunately, Sister Mary Thomas had a black cloth bag in which to carry the food.

Sitting beside the famed cathedral, I found the setting extraordinarily peaceful, and I thanked the good Lord for giving us the opportunity to dine in such a unique place that we had all to ourselves. Eating our meal and innocently drinking our wine with the sun setting over the water, it was as if the saintly Pope of Vatican II were saying: "See! You ARE free!" It was a rare, unforgettable experience.

Paris was all that I expected—and more! Ever since I studied the French language and culture in high school, I had yearned to feel and smell and absorb Paris, and here I was! I thoroughly enjoyed my adventures!

Early one morning we got up for Mass and breakfast with groggy eyes, then headed to the airport for the flight to the Shrine of Our Lady of Lourdes in the Pyrenees Mountains. At the airport we sat for hours—only to discover that our seats had been inadvertently given to a pilgrimage group from Buffalo, New York. Airline employees eventually found room for our oldest Sisters on that plane, while the rest of us had to wait for another flight.

Finally, after waiting for much of the morning, I was put on a plane bound for Toulouse with the remaining Sisters. After landing, we were hustled to a bus heading for Lourdes. It was a comfortable ride; and, for three hours, we were treated to magnificent scenery in southwestern France—first, the rural countryside; then, the mountains. But we had not eaten since 5 a.m. and not expected to reach our destination before 3 p.m., so I was too famished to really enjoy the bus ride.

The Lourdes Shrine was world famous. Saint Bernadette had her visions of Mary there in the 1800's. A spring had started flowing at the sight where Mary told the child to dig. And, from that time on, the waters flowed, and the site became a place of healing dedicated to the glory of God through the memory of His Blessed Mother's apparitions there.

I watched throngs of people—a silent crowd—flock to the water, praying for miracles. It was awe-inspiring to see wheelchairs, casts, and crutches left behind by persons who walked away healed, according to reports. I got in line and waited my turn to enter the "baths." Then, I heard someone tell her companion that my line was for sick people. Healthy people, she said, went to the other lines: one for women and one for men.

Realizing I was in the wrong line, I didn't know what to do. I had already waited for a very long time, and it was almost my turn to enter a cubicle. As I pondered my options, I made an act of faith. I came here to ask for miracles, I told myself, so going into the spring water used by the sick shouldn't really matter.

An attendant beckoned me to come forward behind a curtain. Once inside, she told me to disrobe and cover myself with what looked like a white sheet. Her assistant pointed to the few steps that descended into a large stone tub filled with water that had been used all day long. As soon as I reached the water, I felt a hand on each of my shoulders shove me down suddenly.

I sat for a moment—speechless—as I felt the water inundate me. Closing my eyes, I whispered a prayer. Just as quickly, I was lifted out of the cold water. I was told to dress without drying myself, then I was ushered out. Back in the sunshine, I noticed something unexplainable—I was dry. How could this be? I felt a sense of awe and wonder, and my faith was deepened.

I had looked forward to the Candlelight Procession but discovered the afternoon Procession of the Sick to be even more touching. Ill people from around the world had been flown there in jets—some with IVs attached. I felt a Presence I could not explain, as priests, sisters, and lay people offered prayers for healing, while pleading for miracles.

Afterwards, when a group of Sisters said they were going to take a cable car to a peak in the Pyrenees Mountains, I tagged along. Reaching the top, I was speechless, as I gazed at the magnificent panorama that lay before me. I felt overwhelmed by the indescribable beauty, and when the others said they were going back down, I could not tear myself away.

"Go on without me. I'll catch up later," I replied. Sitting on a ridge surrounded by wildflowers, I was enthralled—feeling like I could reach out and touch the clouds. I hated to go back down. My heart and soul wanted to stay there forever.

That night I lay awake in my hotel room, struggling to hold onto the feelings of the day, while revelers outside danced and sang and played their bagpipes.

Returning to Paris for our parting farewells, I made one more visit to our Motherhouse chapel. I had come to love its "out-of-this-world" atmosphere. I walked up to the "chair" Blessed Mother had sat upon during one of her apparitions to our Saint Catherine Labouré, and I reverently placed there the note I had written to the mother of Jesus. As it mingled with the notes left by others, I knew that later the Sister-Sacristan would burn all of the bits of paper, as she made them burnt-offerings to God, reinforcing each of our prayers, I believed.

Reluctantly, I left to board a bus and join the Sisters who were waiting to head back to the airport and take a plane for Rome. Once seated, I made entries in the diary of my trip I had been keeping. I especially wanted to write down my experiences in Paris, so that I wouldn't lose those precious memories. But suddenly, I became aware of my Provincial Superior hovering tall above me.

"What are you writing, Sister?" she asked.

"I've been keeping a diary to remember the trip," I replied.

"That's not necessary, Sister. You don't need to do that," she said and walked away.

Her words left me confused. I wasn't sure what Sister Clara Mae meant, but I did stop writing for a while. Then, I thought about my diary and why it was so important that I write down my experiences and my feelings. I would need them back in the United States to give me hope. Finally, I picked up my pen and continued where I left off. After all, I rationalized, I didn't receive a direct command.

Our suitcases were color-coded with strips of tape to enable us to divide up more easily when in Rome. Being among the youngest, I was in the third group that would stay at our Roman orphanage beside the Tiber River. The children who used the dormitories were still away for summer vacation, so hospitality was offered to about twenty of us, as well as some Sisters coming in for the canonization from other countries.

The ceremony proclaiming Mother Seton's sainthood took place during a Mass celebrated by Pope Paul VI on the front steps of Saint Peter's Basilica in Vatican City. Sitting only rows away from the altar, I was overjoyed to be present in Saint Peter's Square amid the throngs of pilgrims and other spectators that day.

Earlier that morning, I was nervous when the bus that was supposed to take us to the basilica did not show up on time. With another Sister I hopped a public bus. Noticing that the people ahead of me aggressively made their way onto the bus, I did likewise. I could not risk being late for the canonization ceremony.

The sight of the Pope celebrating Mass in his ornate vestments just yards away from me was spectacular. Behind him a giant banner depicting Mother Seton, who was about to be canonized, hung down the facade of the basilica. To his right, I noticed familiar faces in the places of honor. Henry Cabot Lodge, the American ambassador to Italy, was seated among leaders of the Catholic and Episcopal Churches and our own Superior General and Superioress General from Paris. Officials of Mother Seton's other branches of Sisters in the United States also sat in prominent seats.

Between the Pope and the grandstand stood a Swiss Guard in his colorful medieval uniform. He would have to stand at rigid attention for two and a-half hours, a phenomenon that amazed me, as I periodically glanced his way. At Communion time I noticed that only designated people with special tickets could receive the Holy Eucharist from the hand of the Pope.

After Mass I mingled with the pilgrims in the square, awaiting the Pope's noon blessing from the balcony of his living quarters. Seeing the immense crowd impressed me; after all, 400,000 persons were expected to attend. It was thrilling to meet so many of our Sisters from other countries. They came from as far as Mexico, Brazil, Japan, the Philippines, Mozambique, and Sardinia; as well as, various European countries.

I was amazed to find a Sister there from Jerusalem, too. She was the first person I spoke to after Mass. When I told her of my desire to visit that city someday, she told me to ask Mother Seton. That was my first request to the saint after her canonization.

I spotted Ann O'Neill. I had seen her go up to the Pope at Communion time. That was as it should be, since she had been miraculously healed of leukemia as a toddler. But I was surprised to see sadness on her face now. She recounted what had happened at Communion time, when she and her family members stood in line to receive Holy Communion from the Pope. Some of her relatives were turned away for not having the right tickets. I could understand her frustration and felt sad that what should have been a joyous occasion for this woman was marred by an oversight. After all, without her miracle, this day might not have come.

I spent my afternoon praying at the Roman Forum, where I marveled at my opportunity to walk where a civilization had thrived 2,000 years ago. An unexpected surprise came when I found myself in front the prison where both Saint Peter and Saint Paul had been imprisoned at different times. I followed the crowd down to the dungeon and gazed upon the remains of a pillar said to be the spot where Peter in chains converted his guard. Deeply moved, I knelt down and prayed.

The next day I went back to Vatican City with two Sisters. Upon our arrival, we were reminded that money and stamps were not interchangeable between Vatican City and the city of Rome that surrounded it. Vatican City was a city-state apart from the country of Italy. In the afternoon we toured some major churches in Rome, ending up at the Catacombs where a Filipino seminarian gave us a tour.

My walk through this burial place of the early Christian martyrs moved me deeply. It was one of those unique places on our itinerary where a Sacred Presence could be felt. Needless to say, the experience was awe-inspiring.

Outside the Catacombs the North American College presented a special tribute to Mother Seton. This was a big event; and, in the audience, dignitaries included the American ambassador to Italy, all of the American cardinals and bishops who were in Rome for the event, and Mother Seton's biographer, Father Dirvin.

Music was provided by the United States Navy Brass quartet and the Capitol Quartet Strings. Maryland's own Emmitsburg Chorus sang, and, to my surprise, the event was climaxed with an amazing rendition of "America the Beautiful," sung by Joe Feeney of the Lawrence Welk Show.

I thought all the assembled participants left with hearts swelled with patriotism and American pride. Elizabeth Seton, after all, was the first canonized saint to be born in the United States.

On the way back to San Clemente Children's Home where some of us were staying, the bus followed the Appian Way—the ancient road that leads to and from the Catacombs. I felt humbled and honored to actually ride that "via." Would that it could recount the stories it kept buried within the rocks. But, on the other hand, many of those stories—so tragic—could not be adequately expressed in human words. Yet, perhaps, those very unspoken words carried a more powerful message for those with hearts that could listen.

Later that week we returned to Saint Peter's Square for a public "audience" with Pope Paul VI. It was a momentous occasion celebrating the Jubilee Year of 1975. Still, I would have appreciated it more, had the 5 p.m. heat not topped 100° and had the message not been prolonged by its translation into six languages.

The next day I took a leisurely stroll through the basilica, awed by the architecture and art treasures. surrounding me. Then I prayed at the underground crypts where Saint Peter, Pope Pius XII, and Pope John XXIII were buried. I felt flooded with peace, as I knelt at Pope John's tomb.

That pontiff had appeared to one of our dying Sisters in Naples a short time after his death and healed her instantly. That miracle would probably lead to his canonization in the future, since it was well-documented. I hoped so, as I admired the courage it took for him to call for the Second Vatican Council—despite the opposition of some of his contemporaries. In my estimation he was a "holy hero."

Upstairs again, I looked for Michelangelo's PIETA. Finding that spectacular sculpture standing in place majestically, I yearned to reach out and touch it. But I made myself be satisfied to gaze in awe. I knew that I was looking at one of the world's greatest masterpieces and its magnificence took my breath away.

I felt so close to the sculptor in whose footsteps I had wanted to walk, when I was still in art school. His earth-shaking achievement mirrored the dream I believed I had to stamp out—the dream my religious community snatched away from me.

Before turning away, I left my unfulfilled yearnings there with my friend Michelangelo. Were they gone forever? Only God knew that answer.

I was anticipating our side trip to Assisi for many reasons. I had always loved animals and felt a bond with Saint Francis who always, according to legends, cared for them. And I admired the saint who embodied simplicity, and contentment with a life devoid of material things. He had his priorities right, I had concluded, even before I became a Sister.

Periodically, after I entered the convent, I wondered if I should have joined the Franciscans, the Religious Order he founded.

But the day of the bus trip brought an unsettling realization—I had diarrhea out of control. And no medicine given by the Sister-nurse who accompanied us could make it stop. Finally, I told my tale of woe to an older Sister:

"I can't bear the thought of missing out on that tour. I've waited all my life to go to Assisi and imbibe its atmosphere."

"When in Rome, do as the Romans do. The same goes for Assisi," she said. "Drink a beer with your lunch at the restaurant and that will cure you." Probably reading my thoughts, the Sister added: "Trust me. It's acceptable over here, since we can't drink the water."

Not only was I going to eat in a public restaurant, but I was also going to drink beer with my meal. What a mind-boggling thought! So, beating down the shouts of guilt my inner self tried to make me hear, I forced myself to drink my first beer ever—in Assisi, of all places. It tasted terrible, but the Sister was right. I had no more diarrhea, and I could enjoy the rest of my day.

I learned something else on that trip. The public restrooms were for both sexes. As I entered one, I noticed a man sitting in the center, pointing men in one direction and women in the other. When I started to leave, I heard that man yelling furious expletives in Italian. Looking back to see what was going on, I discovered he was shouting at me. I did not know I was expected to leave him a tip. Embarrassed, I kept going—glad to get away from the man and his obscenities.

Walking the cobblestone streets, I went back in time with the saint to the thirteenth century, enjoying similar scenery and letting it enthrall me. I sauntered through the Franciscan Basilica for the purpose of praying at the burial place of Saint Francis in the lower crypt.

Kneeling down, I could see people throwing notes they had written inside a grate above the tomb. So I sat down and proceeded to write my own note to this "bigger-than-life" saint. After slipping it through an opening and letting it drop down on his tomb, I knelt and prayed:

"Now, it's your turn to talk to me, Saint Francis," I whispered. Sitting down in the pew, I shut my eyes and listened to the message that came through. I hastily jotted it down on a piece of paper, then placed it in the small New Testament and Psalm Book I carried in my pocket—not wanting to lose it ever.

Did I understand it? No. But it didn't matter. Maybe in the future it would take on meaning. For now, I had it safely tucked away.

Upstairs in the basilica, I gazed in awe at the frescoes that Giotto and others like him created, art work that depicted the life of Saint Francis. I allowed the artist in me to go back in time and feel at one with those painters, before leaving with the other Sisters.

Once outside, I bent down and picked up a stone, which probably had broken off the building as it aged. I saved it with the other little rocks I had kept as souvenirs of the special places I visited, labeling them with masking tape.

Years later, I would feel urged to pass my "basilica treasure" on to a young American Franciscan nun who had just taken her first vows. It was hard to give it up, but she should have it, I thought.

Before leaving Assisi, we visited the Basilica of Saint Clare. Saint Francis had been the female saint's spiritual advisor, as she started the cloistered Religious Order that came to be called the "Poor Clares."

Entering the shrine, we saw a Poor Clare Sister standing with a veil over her face. She handed us holy cards through a grate that separated the nun from us. Looking at my holy card, I had a picture of the famous crucifix with the prayer Saint Francis used to say as he knelt before it.

A grated gate in the back of this small chapel prevented anyone from getting too close to the actual crucifix the Poor Clares had venerated and watched over for centuries, proclaiming that it was the original crucifix through which Francis received so many graces.

As our bus drove down the hill through miles of olive orchards on our ride back to Rome, I thanked God for the unforgettable experience. It was truly profound.

Back in Rome, water like a magnet drew me. But I felt the Tiber River was not enough, especially after watching a woman walk to the middle of a bridge near our Sisters' orphanage and dump her load of trash over the side. I had been an avid map-reader all my life, and I knew that the Mediterranean Sea could not be far away. So I searched until I found a Sister who would be my willing companion for an unscheduled side trip.

Sister Alexis and I hopped a subway underground, then overground, getting off at Lido—only to discover that there were two Lidos, the ancient city and the resort town. Standing among the ruins at the wrong stop, we waited for another train. When we finally approached the seacoast, I was excited. But we arrived at our destination only to find still another obstacle. Walls separated the beach and its water from our view everywhere.

Refusing to be frustrated, I went from door to door using sign language to say all we wanted to do was see the water. Most people— not understanding English—looked at us like we were crazy. Had they never seen Sisters in religious Habits at the water? What I wanted so badly to see—the water—seemed so innocent.

Finally, my perseverance paid off. A kind woman opened a door and ushered us in. Pointing to an isolated part of the beach away from the other people, she left us alone. The sand was very dark, unlike any beach I had ever seen. We walked to a spot where we could sit on a rock by the sea. Finally, unable to control the urge, I took off my shoes, lifted my Habit a few inches, and walked in the water—feeling my black stockings get soaked. I literally loved the sensations that surged through me!

How can the others not experience my yearning for the sea—not be out here too? I was ecstatic, as I stood in the water that was all mine for that moment. Then, I sat back down on the rock savoring the emotions I felt.

"Thank you, God, for bringing me back to the sea!" I whispered. I thanked the proprietor profusely before tearing myself away and returning to Rome with my companion.

That week I found out that one of our Italian Sisters, a housekeeper for the Pope, had taken some of the other Sisters on a tour of the Vatican Gardens—an area usually off limits to tourists. Sister Mary Thomas and I had missed that opportunity, so I convinced her to accompany me to Santa Marta's Convent where I told that Sister how disappointed we were that we didn't know about the tour.

"I'm too busy now to take you, but I'll do this: I'll let the two of you in the Gardens, and you can walk by yourselves."

We couldn't believe our ears! Following the Sister, we thanked her, then off we went to explore the grounds that popes had walked on, meditated on, since the time the Vatican Gardens came into being during the Renaissance. It proved to be an experience almost impossible to put into words.

We walked through a magnificently-landscaped paradise replete with fountains and some of the most exquisite flowers and shrubbery I had ever seen. Many centuries had left their mark on the sculptures and other unique creations, and their very antiquity added to their appeal, in my estimation. Somehow, spirits of the past still lingered. I felt their presence. In this instance, it paid to speak up and express our desires.

Our visit to Rome and Vatican City was winding down, as we traveled back to Da Vinci Airport and prepared to leave. I noticed once again the airport's high security. As we trudged along the walkway with our suitcases, soldiers dressed in camouflage uniforms carrying machine guns stood only twenty feet apart, lining the way. A woman at customs hand-searched our luggage, while a soldier next to her aimed his weapon in our direction. A strange sight to behold in 1975, I thought. I was glad to board the plane.

As we flew over northern Italy, a Sister looking down called out: "I see the Alps!" Immediately, those of us seated on the other side of the plane arose, crossed the aisle, and leaned over to see what we could see. Although we were high above the Alps, the sight was still awesome.

Back in my seat, I visualized what had just transpired, and I chuckled. What a picture we had presented to the lay people aboard that plane—thirty nuns dressed alike crossing the aisle to look out the window with the other nuns sitting in those seats—just to get a glimpse of the Alps. For most of us, it was our first and only chance ever. Did we make the airplane wings tilt, I wondered—wearing a smile on my face.

Following a weekend crossing and touring Ireland by bus, we found ourselves flying over the Atlantic Ocean heading back to the United States, and I felt a renewed sense of patriotism. In Paris and Rome I was shocked to see Communist posters on display. Also, I could feel the anti-clericalism that some people openly expressed, when we walked by dressed in religious garb. I was happy to be returning to my free country.

I wanted to continue soaking up my wonderful experiences and their meaning before switching gears. But, once back in Petersburg, there was no time to dwell on my trip or even get over jet lag. The next morning I was in my classroom teaching religion to teenagers. Still, I wanted to hold onto my experiences for a long time—keep that feeling of floating on clouds. I would try desperately to hang onto them.

Life now brought with it super challenges. The students, their parents, and the high school principal were fine. But my Sister Servant seemed bent on making my life a hell. Approaching her use of authority scrupulously, she always appeared rigid like a statue, radiating lightning bolts of censure in the atmosphere around her.

Too often she was ready to find fault with what I was doing, as if she were looking for a reason to admonish me for wrong-doing. I came to feel like nothing I could do would be right in her eyes, and the stress kept me as uptight as she was.

Our convent, connected to the school, shared one of its problems—its infestation with roaches. I dreaded the periodic visits of the exterminator who would leave the Sisters' quarters reeking of roach bombs—making it almost impossible to breathe and giving me terrible headaches. I needed to leave the convent at such times, inhale the outdoor air—go off for twenty-four hours. But our Sister

Servant's body language communicated a single message: Don't complain. Don't say anything. Just offer it up!

While I put up with the ordeal the best I could, I understood why the pesticide killed the roaches. It was a miracle that it didn't kill the Sisters, too. Inhaling roach bombs was one of the worst experiences of the kind I ever had to endure as a Sister.

Petersburg was home to a large military installation known as Fort Lee, the city's principal employer. Second to the Army post in providing work for citizens was a cigarette factory located across the street from the parish church.

On most mornings we'd walk a few blocks to the church for Mass. Now normally, I would have appreciated the opportunity for exercise and fresh air, but not in Petersburg. Often the air reeked of tobacco, practically gagging us. It was a subject no one brought up, since the factory gave needed employment to so many people.

Many of my students came from families that worked for the Army—a fact that would lead to my next crisis. One of my students, the son of a Fort Lee soldier, was having problems. As with any troubled student, I tried to work with him and finally called his home. I discovered that Bobby lived with a single parent, his divorced father, who came in for a parent-teacher conference.

As the boy's problems continued, I ended up contacting the man regularly to give a progress report. But then, something happened. I found myself drawn to this man, and soon I was completely infatuated with him. I found so much about him attractive, and I liked the feeling I got when he was near—even when we discussed his son on the telephone. It sent shivers down my spine.

For a while, I battled those feelings and struggled to fight them off—but I discovered that years of putting up with those inner battles was wearing me down. I was sick and tired of fighting my natural female drives. And my unhappiness with convent life there made matters worse.

Meanwhile, I had secured the reluctant permission of Sister Clarisse to start a charismatic prayer group in a classroom just outside the convent wing. I found solace from my miserable religious life once a week, as I prayed with the group that included lay people. I liked the charismatic movement's philosophy of loving one another and expressing it with a hug.

Starving for affection, those hugs—as innocent as they were—had come to mean a lot to me, when I discovered that form of prayer in Rhode Island. Now I took up where I left off and could count on a weekly hug at my prayer meetings. I needed hugs to keep me from shriveling up like a prune.

I needed desperately to feel some affection. I was going through the motions of living as a Sister—following the rules—but it wasn't working anymore for me. Living without love was impossible, I had discovered.

Were Superiors burying their heads in the sand by enforcing policies aimed at killing the Sisters' humanness? Did they not realize that killing their spirit was just a step away from that?

Bobby's father could benefit from participating in our prayer group, I rationalized, as I began inviting this man to join us. A man raising two boys alone certainly had great need of faith and hope.

I was excited to see Ray come to pray with us. And I found myself becoming more and more eager for each prayer meeting night. As the group embraced one another to say "hello" and "goodbye", I found myself looking forward to hugging Ray and being hugged back. Although I justified the hugs as being innocent, my anticipation of them became disproportionate. I knew that, deep down, they made my heart skip a beat, and I couldn't deny that I liked it. I felt like a woman when Ray was around. And it felt good. What was wrong with that?

At night in bed, alone with my thoughts, I couldn't get Ray out of my mind. Just thinking of him made me tingle inside, and I started experiencing sensations in my body that I didn't understand. I fought what seemed to be a losing battle.

Nevertheless, I took every opportunity to call Ray under the pretext of apprising him of his son's progress. I denied the truth that I cared for this man, that I needed and wanted to hear his voice—that maybe, just maybe, I was falling in love with him.

Struggling to keep the padlock on my heart, I was having a desperate, inner "tug-of-war". I felt backed up against the wall of a dam that was ready to crumble. My fights within myself at night escalated. I wanted to scream out: Why, God, why can't I love and be loved? Is there no end to the anguish of my soul that has become torture? Help me, Lord, please! I'm losing my grip!"

In a weak moment, I decided to visit Ray's home. After all, we were encouraged to visit the homes of our students, I rationalized. There's no reason why I shouldn't go to Bobby's house, too. So, off I went to make that visit, anticipating it like a child who can't wait to open her Christmas presents.

Standing at Ray's door dressed in my religious Habit, I smoothed it out and rang the doorbell. I was so excited! I could hardly control my emotions! But suddenly, a door opened, and a woman stood before me—an attractive woman.

"I must have the wrong house," I blurted out.

"Come in. Ray's expecting you," the voice spoke up.

Confused, I reluctantly walked in.

"I see you've met Helen," Ray said, as he walked in the living room. "I'm glad the two of you have finally met. You've both been such a big help to the boys and me. Tell us how Bobby is doing, Sister."

As I sat there feeling terribly uncomfortable, I stuttered my report, finding the right words with great difficulty—struggling to hide my bitter disappointment. I just wanted to get out of the house and run away from the situation that made me feel like a fool, that made me realize the awful truth: I was in love and I was jealous—jealous of the woman who shared Ray's home and his hugs and his children.

I was devastated, as I opened the convent door and let it shut behind me—locking me in once more. I wanted to cry—no, scream—as the awful realization sank in. The truth stared at me like the face of a hangman about to put to death his victim. I wanted to crawl in a hole someplace and die.

With Christmas not far off, the holiday nostalgia made things worse. I felt dangerously close to panicking. I needed to go off somewhere, let out my frustration, and cry my eyes out. But all doors seemed closed to me.

Who could I talk to? Certainly not my Sister Servant, who was as cold as a block of ice. She wouldn't understand my attraction to a man. Even my higher Superiors were inaccessible emotionally. My kind of problem would certainly not be acceptable.

A loyal Sister, even in the 1970's, managed to keep her feelings under lock and key, buried them like she was supposed to. She was a Sister for God's Sake, up on a pedestal the world and earthlings could not reach.

What, then, had happened to me? Why couldn't I be like most religious women?

Another Sister in the convent seemed to be going through personal struggles, too. A teacher in the elementary school, Sister Faith started disappearing, presumably to work on art projects at the home of a lay volunteer. Our Sister Servant would certainly not have allowed it. Some of the Sisters raised their eyebrows whenever others asked: Where's Sister Faith?" But, deep down, I understood.

Unfortunately, we could not share our troubles or even let off a little bit of steam together. So we remained silent about our struggles—agonizing over solutions, while we strained to "save" our vocation.

Finally, one day, I picked up a pen and wrote to my Provincial Superior. Without giving her a reason, I made a plea: "I cannot remain here. Please allow me to leave Petersburg and return to my Provincial House NOW!"

The promptness of her affirmative reply surprised me. She said I could leave at the end of the first semester in January. Although I had mixed emotions, I was relieved.

Once back in Saint Joseph's Valley, I was sent for. My Superior, Sister Clara Mae, gave me a double command: "You are being assigned to Tour Duty at Mother Seton's Shrine. While you live with us, I want you to start seeing a psychiatrist."

When the names of possible doctors came up, I chose the Jesuit priest. He would understand me better than a layman, I thought.

When the priest declined to take me, I was disappointed. He gave me two other names of men and told me to choose between them.

Had he been contacted by my Superior, before I could contact him? Did he already know he'd have a conflict of interests—that Superiors who were paying the bill had their own agendas? I selected the psychiatrist in a Maryland suburb outside Washington, D.C., because his office was closer to Emmitsburg. And soon, I began weekly visits. Once having met the man, I approached him with mixed feelings. Appearing to be totally emotion-free, he had an uninviting look about him and a personality that was dull and distant. He did not inspire my confidence!

Each week when I arrived at his empty waiting room, I would open an inner door—according to his instructions—enter, and sit in a semi-dark cubicle, while waiting for a third door to open. Then, I would be invited to enter his inner office. I couldn't understand why all the secrecy.

The doctor spoke little, and we did not have any real conversations. Somehow, he got me to open up about my childhood. But he never allowed me to discuss the convent. I got the impression he was always aware of the fact that my Superiors were the ones paying him, and he wasn't going to bite the hand that was feeding him.

It seemed to me that my goal given by Superiors was to get what was out of control in my life back in control. They wanted me to function as the Sister they trained me to be, the Sister I was supposed to be. I needed to curb my inmost desires and live my life without letting my feelings take over—without letting myself "feel".

My Superiors wanted me to stamp out that woman who wanted to burst out of me, and they wanted to annihilate any individuality that remained a part of me. That's what their unspoken words seemed to communicate.

Even now, I believed that leaving the convent was not an option open to me. My Superiors had made it very clear over the years that God called me to live the life of a Sister, blessed me with a religious vocation not given to many. And they said I owed it to God and myself to be faithful to death—not to be a coward in the face of difficulties. They said Divine Grace would always be there to help me persevere. But where was it hiding, when I needed it now more than ever?

After months of therapy, I sensed that those same Superiors expected an explanation. At this point, I was in denial of my romantic feelings for Ray. And I tried to convince myself that, if I could finally get out of teaching and into social work, I would find happiness at long last. So I relied on the excuse that I was in a career that had always been repugnant to me.

My visits to the psychiatrist had not begun to scratch the surface of my problems. And I was deceiving myself by thinking that a change of career would solve anything. There were no easy solutions. Nevertheless, I was eager to start over—far from the soldier in Petersburg—as if distance and a new focus could blot out memories, even feelings for that man in the military.

That summer I was sent with three other Sisters to teach Vacation Bible School in South Carolina. It was terribly hot and humid, even wearing the white summer Habit, now permitted. Still, I loved teaching those poor children of the rural South about the God who loved them. And I was happy to throw myself into my work and try to erase my troubles.

While there, our paths crossed that of a Sister from another Religious Order who ran a health clinic some evenings for migrant workers. She invited us to help out by coming and talking to the people as they waited.

I was appalled, as I listened to one tragic story after another. A young woman just seventeen said she had buried her baby a few days before our arrival.

"What happened?" I asked.

"One hospital after another sent me away with my sick baby. Nobody wanted to treat my child, because I was a migrant worker and had no medical insurance."

When the baby died, the Sister who ran the clinic had led a prayer service at the spot where the grief-stricken mother had to part with her baby—the child who never had a chance at life.

It seemed so unfair. The young lady didn't even have time to grieve. She had to go right back to the fields and suppress her grief.

As I conversed with the farm workers who were struggling to eek out an existence the best way they knew how, my heart ached for those persons born in conditions they had not chosen for themselves.

I went up to an old man and asked why he was there.

"What's wrong?

"I have a bad toothache," he replied.

"How long have your had it?"

"For four years."

His answer astounded me. I thought the world outside the convent was supposed to be a "land of plenty." Yet, the people around me were shut out from that world. Once again I was confronted with the reality that, even in America, the gap between the "haves" and the "have-nots" was very large. Was anyone seeking a permanent way out of poverty for the disadvantaged and the downtrodden?

In a world where so many claimed to be Christians and so many non-Christians, too, claimed to care about the down-trodden, why were the rich getting richer and the poor getting poorer? How I wished I could rid the world of greed and selfishness and hypocrisy— and show the "haves" how much more meaningful their lives could be, if they stopped hoarding their wealth in banks or spending it so profusely on non-essential luxuries. I wanted to show the wealthy what happiness they would experience, if only they would share generously with the "have-nots."

The people I mingled with touched me deeply. There was so much that I took for granted in my life, while they could not get their most basic needs alleviated. I wanted to do more, but my hands were tied. I would have to leave South Carolina at the end of the week. The best I could do was offer a bit of love during those brief moments and thank God for the Sister who was running that clinic.

7,787 days had passed since I left home. I missed my brown-shingled house and all its memories. Above all, I missed my loved ones.

12.

The Shock

It was the beginning of the end, but I didn't know it as I headed for Greensboro, North Carolina—where the Sisters ministered to poor people in a predominantly-Black parish.

The previous spring the school had closed because of dwindling funds and low enrollment. Sister Vincent, the social worker, remained, and I was sent to assist her. Finally getting the opportunity to serve the really poor, I arrived motivated and dedicated. After all, in the final analysis, that's why I became a Sister.

Now, forty years old, I was doing what I had always wanted to do. I hoped it wasn't too late.

"Dear God," I prayed, "bless my work here, please. Renew me and revive me."

My Sister-companion, fairly short and stocky, exuded determination like that of a longshoreman intent on getting things done. She was frank to the point of being blunt, appearing totally intent on alleviating poverty and helping poor people become independent—a great role model, I thought.

Following Sister Vincent's lead, I threw myself into my assigned duties from the start—focusing entirely on giving all I had to give to the work of the parish.

The people around me were easy to work with and showed it by their friendliness and appreciation for all the help they received. Obviously, our Sisters—who had served the neighborhood for generations—had paved the way for us by developing a reputation for dedicated service.

We tried to walk in their footsteps, while focusing on the goal of showing people the way to become self-sufficient. Saint Vincent's writings were imbued with Christ's teachings—reflecting the Chinese proverb that showing a person how to fish was far better than feeding them a fish.

While helping Sister Vincent to run the emergency center for the poor, I was assigned to teach religious education to high school and college students. Since my heart was still very much into guiding and motivating young people, I liked this aspect of my work.

In fact, I was very happy to be immersed, finally, in helping the poor rise out of poverty and deepen their faith in God—through the teachings of Jesus—so that they would find the tools they needed to make it in the secular world and survive.

Since visiting the sick and the elderly was always an important priority for our Sisters, I started keeping a list and making my rounds in the neighborhood.

Beulah, a woman in her eighties who lived alone, was one of the first shut-ins I adopted for visits. Well-educated, she had been on the faculty of the nearby Black college in her younger days. Standing tall and straight in a proud sort of way, her beautiful face carried its share of ruts that told a story of struggles for racial equality and her rightful place in American society. Her bravery and bold determination still radiated from her fading countenance, and I came to value the knowledge and wisdom she shared with me.

Another woman in the parish had fallen in love with a Black soldier in her native Spain, then came to the United States and settled in North Carolina. Finding it difficult to understand attitudes of hostility she encountered in her racially-mixed marriage, she poured out her frustrations. I offered her encouragement and moral support, while I watched out for her daughter and the other children in my Sunday school class.

When the parish adopted a Vietnamese family with eight children and one on the way, I was given charge of them. As I guided them and referred them to supportive services, I could see how determined they were to learn the English language as fast as they could. They wanted to be totally self-sufficient and assimilate as Americans.

Having a child every year would certainly not help them, and I discussed this with Sister Vincent. The family was Catholic and afraid to practice birth control.

Sister Vincent approached a compassionate priest and asked him to advise the parents on that issue. Above all, she insisted that he tell them it would be no sin on their part if the woman got her tubes tied. And so I dropped the subject. The woman had her surgery, and the family continued adjusting and becoming part of American society.

I admired the courage of my Sister partner and her willingness to follow her convictions. After all, in teaching my students in previous schools about the Pope's birth control encyclical, I had emphasized their need to read carefully the final pages which—when paraphrased—acknowledged that everything in life was not "black-and-white." In the final analysis, each Catholic couple had to follow their own consciences.

I still remembered my trip to Indian Gap, Pennsylvania, two years earlier, after my comprehensive exams were over and I returned to my province in Maryland. Our Provincial Councilor for Social Services had approached me, asking that I accompany her to the old Army barracks that now housed the Vietnamese people recently flown out of their country, when the Americans pulled out and withdrew from the conflict. Her job was to assess their plight; and, I thought, assist in developing a plan to assimilate them into American culture and life in the United States.

Upon our arrival, I was shocked to find them in an abandoned Army compound, fenced in an area that looked like a concentration camp. I wished I could personally and actively help resolve their problem and find them a home, but my job that day was to keep my mouth shut and merely accompany the Sister who had authority to figure out a solution and advise those in charge.

My heart ached for those people—more of God's children—who had suffered the ravages of war, had fled to a democracy, and now found themselves refugees in America—awaiting someone's decision about their fate.

So I was happy to assist the Vietnamese family that was shipped to our parish to begin anew. Obviously stunned and suffering from culture shock, the whole family was determined to find a way to fit in and overcome their repugnances and their pain.

Accountable to the principal of a school in a middle-class neighborhood in the city, Sister Vincent and I ate, slept, and prayed—just the two of us—in a convent built to house six or seven Sisters. Still, it came as a surprise, when our Sister Servant at the school informed us that our Provincial Superior wanted us to pack up and prepare to move.

We learned that our pastor, a Vincentian priest, had requested that the rectory and our convent be switched. The Sisters didn't need all that room, while the priests could use the extra space for fellow priests who needed a place to rest—even retire.

Obediently, we went right to work, opening closets and pulling out bed linens, towels and washcloths, nightgowns and other wearing apparel kept in the common stockpile. We emptied kitchen cabinets and the pantry until countless cartons lined corridors. Removing spiritual books from the reading shelves constituted still another challenge, and it seemed ironic—maybe symbolic—that the books on holiness were so heavy.

Obviously, inventory had not been taken before the school closed and the teaching Sisters left. So, Sister Vincent and I had loads of merchandise to take to the "new" convent.

Although the pastor said men of the parish would move the heavy furniture, we were expected to lug the cartons across the field that separated the convent from the rectory.

Sister Vincent, unwilling to be daunted by any assignment, was more than equal to the task. Sometimes appearing to be a human bulldozer, she carried box after box to its destination. I marveled at her endless energy and strength. After all, she must be fifteen years older than me, I thought.

Having no other option, I tried to follow her example—ignoring the physical repercussions as I felt my body react. But soon I developed chronic numbness in both wrists and hands, alternating with severe pain.

Once settled in our new convent, I tried to imitate my companion and continue throwing myself full force into my work. I tried to be "all things to all people" without complaining about the pain that persisted. I did my best to do as I was trained—ignore what I was feeling and work hard in spite of it.

All the while, I acted like a guard over a pit of snakes—continuing to beat down my body's other cries for the satisfaction of its needs and drives—its yearning for love in my life. This task became more formidable, more crushing, than the move into a different convent. I felt terribly wounded from battling so many storms—scarred even.

I continued counseling our parish college students, helping them articulate their long-range and short-range goals. I taught children how to pray and how to live like good Christians. I visited the elderly, shepherded "my" Vietnamese family, and assisted families having emergency situations—all the while struggling to ignore my own needs and put up with whatever pain I had to endure.

Sister Vincent was always gracious, but her smiling face resembled a mask she had adopted through years of suppressing her true feelings. We never really communicated, even at "scheduled" recreation times. Only her work and her prayer consumed her mental energy. As a result, she lacked personal warmth and creativity. And I found it more and more difficult to balance work with prayer in my own life.

Although North Carolina's map showed immense beauty from the mountains of the West to the ocean in the East, I felt deprived aesthetically. I needed to go off on a hike in the mountains or to a concert or a ballet or a movie—anything to clear my mind and uplift my soul—but I had to keep on starving myself.

There were no outlets here—except to walk the grounds around the convent where the soles of my shoes had already worn trails to the extent that I lost count of my myriads of footprints.

One of those times as I walked, I was approached by some neighborhood boys who struck up a conversation. We chatted for a while, before I noticed they had something they wanted to say. Finally, one of their number spoke up:

"Whatever happened to the Catholic dog, Sister?"

"The Catholic dog?" I asked.

"Yeah, the Sisters used to have a big dog. We liked to pet him when a Sister walked him outside. We haven't seen him in a long time. Where is he?"

Suppressing a chuckle at the idea of a "Catholic dog," I continued the conversation:

"That's right. The Sisters used to have a big dog here—the one you called a Catholic dog. I really don't know where he lives now. I think the Sisters gave him to somebody else. I'm sure he has a happy home somewhere. I never met that dog."

"That Catholic dog was really nice and so playful."

"You miss him?"

"Yeah, Sister—we don't have any dogs at home."

I went on. "I used to have a dog I loved when I was growing up." I said. "She was a Chesapeake Bay retriever we called Lassie. She was like part of the family. When I was sad, I would sit on the top step of our back porch and tell Lassie my troubles. Sitting next to me, she would look up at me with her big brown eyes and I knew she understood and cared. She gave me unconditional love."

"Where is Lassie now?" one of the boys asked.

"When I was fourteen, Lassie got sick. All night long she moaned. So the next morning my Dad took her to a vet, and I never saw her again. She was so sick that the vet put her to sleep, I suppose. I cried for a long time after that, because I loved her. To answer your question, Lassie's probably in 'dog heaven.' She was a very good dog."

"We can get you a dog," the second boy said.

"Thank you, but Sister Vincent and I are too busy to give a dog all the love and attention it deserves. I do thank you for your kind thoughts, though." I didn't want to add that we weren't usually allowed to have pets.

As they turned to leave, I added: "Animals are amazing. Always be kind to them. They are wonderful creatures God gave us. Pets give people lots of love."

One day Sister Vincent invited me to accompany her on a visit to the local prison. I went with her and was glad to have another opportunity to bring hope to inmates who were considered the dregs of society—many of whom were considered by society not worth rehabilitating.

Later, I received a letter from an incarcerated man there—not anyone I had actually visited. Rather, it was from a Jewish inmate who had gotten my name and address from someone else. In it he poured out his soul about his anguish and a plea agreement not honored. Would I intercede for him? he asked.

We started a regular correspondence, and I kept encouraging him to believe and pray, although I never got there to meet him. The man, in turn, revealed his spiritual journey and his hopes for his future.

My responding to him was an innocent gesture, and my motives were pure. But somehow, my feelings got in the way again. My emotions, which I thought were under "lock and key," kept resurfacing, like streams of water seeping through cracks.

At first, this seemed insignificant. But before long, I felt out of control again. In this case, I found myself enjoying the inmate's letters. This man whom I had never met, needed me to give him hope, I rationalized. But I could not keep a lid on my emotions. I was in deep pain over this latest tug-of-war, yet I kept on writing to him and encouraging him.

Finally, one day, I discovered in our convent library a book destined to show me new pathways. Should Anyone Say Forever? was written by a Jesuit priest, presumably for persons considering divorce and their counselors. I devoured that book—pondering deeply its message that, whenever a person finds herself dying inside, she owes it to herself to "choose life."

The message got to me, and I began to admit that I was dying inside, that I wanted and needed to choose life. Barbra Streisand's lyrics haunted me once again, as did Neil Diamond's.

Bombarded by the same truth from so many directions, why could I not follow it to its logical conclusion? Why did I continue to smile "with a dagger in my heart?"

Was it because I never truly lost my idealism? Was the side of me that wanted to love and serve God as a kind of "earth angel" so strong it could battle any hurricane?

I liked being God's instrument of love and healing— programmed to make the world a better place—to be there when anyone reached out for someone to care. I had to admit that.

On the other hand, a big part of me yearned for fulfillment as a woman—a female earthling wanting to really celebrate life. I craved to be my unique self: exploring like a Captain Cook, communing with nature like a Thoreau, creating Art like a Michelangelo, playing the piano like a Van Cliburn, even loving passionately like a Cleopatra. I still had bottled up inside me an "adventurer-artist-musician-philosopher-lover" yearning to burst free and blossom.

What a predicament I found myself in!

Still, I struggled to remain faithful to my Calling in the manner in which my Religious Order had taught me. I fought like a tiger to hold on, but I was losing my grip. For years I had held together the heavy chains I had wrapped around my heart—the chains that were supposed to keep my body in check. Now, nothing worked anymore.

Meanwhile, the pain in my hands and wrists worsened, until I could bear it no longer. The doctor's diagnosis was carpal tunnel syndrome. Unable to concentrate on my work or prayer, I requested surgery.

"Get it over with all at once," I pleaded, without discussing the matter with my Superiors.

So it was that I landed in the operating room with a surgeon on each side of me, making incisions from my wrists to the middle of the palms of my hands. I left the hospital looking like a boxer with both hands wrapped up, with just my fingers sticking out.

Back at the convent, I felt more helpless than ever. I was no help at all to Sister Vincent who must have taken matters into her own hands.

I wasn't surprised to receive word early in the new year that I was ordered to return to my Provincial House. Another Sister would replace me—temporarily, I thought. It certainly would help Sister Vincent to have an able-bodied Sister fill in for me and keep the parish work going.

That way, nothing would slow down because of me. Before I left, the doctor expressed his concern about my blood pressure.

"You have a mild case of hypertension that needs to be followed up. Have you had problems before with your blood pressure?" How should I know, I wanted to answer. I live in a Religious Order that says I'm not supposed to get sick or be concerned about health problems. I've lived in denial about those issues for over twenty-two years.

"I don't know," I finally said, speaking up. "No doctor has ever mentioned it to me, and we don't have the equipment in the convent to check our blood pressure."

"It's important to keep track of your blood pressure. So, be sure to follow it up," he said.

As my plane flew north to Baltimore, and a Sister drove me from the airport to the mountains of western Maryland, I reflected on the day it was—the Feast of the Epiphany, the Feast of Light. Was today ushering in a new period of light for me? Was my darkness turning into light? I wondered, as I prayed.

I had returned to the Provincial House to recuperate, I thought. And the next day I was sent for. My Provincial Superior must want to wish me a speedy recovery, no doubt. I felt grateful for Sister Clara Mae's consideration, even before I entered her office. I was learning to lose my fear of crossing that awesome threshold, I noted.

I did not anticipate what was about to happen! I could not have imagined the bomb she was about to drop. My life as I knew it was going to be shattered to pieces.

"Sister Patricia Anne," she said without asking about my surgery, "I want you to use this time to see if the Lord is calling you to another lifestyle."

Shocked, I felt as if she were yanking the rug out from beneath my feet. What was she saying? What was she directing me to do? Had I heard correctly?

I left her hallowed office and fell apart. Going off alone, I cried my eyes out. I did know what she was suggesting. And it was a way out, wasn't it?

But I had never asked for a way out. I had lived this life since I was eighteen, and I was about to turn forty-one. I couldn't just start over—like a person changing jobs. This was the only life I had known as an adult.

Was I now being discarded like a rag doll? No longer useful, was I being tossed aside—thrown away? Was my religious community not taking any responsibility for what my Superiors and our rules had turned me into? For what they had taken away from me?

I had lived a safe life all these years—a life that provided peace, in the chapel, at least. A life that promised Heaven in the hereafter. Although my life had become as confining as a fish bowl, I couldn't live without the water of that fish bowl—the "convent" water that had become my life-support for twenty-two years.

I felt utterly lost.

Here and now I was being offered my freedom. And I didn't know how to handle that offer. I no longer knew how to make major decisions or even how to think critically. What would I do on my own?

I was scared—really scared.

8,156 days had passed since I left home. I missed my brown-shingled house and all its memories. Above all, I missed my loved ones.

Still, faced with the prospect of leaving the convent, I froze.

266

13.

Uncovering the Truth

It was a grand chapel as big as a church, dedicated to the glory of God and the memory of Mary and our religious community's saints. More recently it had become the National Shrine of our saintly foundress, Mother Seton.

I gazed up at the crucifix, that giant carved image of Christ Crucified suspended over the solid marble altar. Together they made up the chapel's centerpiece. Behind it, I could see the larger-than-life mosaic depicting Saint Catherine's apparitions of Blessed Mother at our Motherhouse in Paris.

I lost count of the endless hours I had spent here in those early weeks of 1978—pondering, agonizing, fighting my internal war. Nobody ever said that living an angelic life in a human body was easy. But the constant struggle had become too much for me.

I had tried to put my whole heart into each preparatory retreat before renewing my annual vows. I had laid down my life in my fight to persevere in my holy vocation. Yet the tug-of-war between my spiritual and human aspirations was tearing me apart. As hard as I tried, I could not get beyond that phase of my life that had become torture for me. I wanted to blink my eyes and make the pain go away, make the decision disappear.

There was so much peace that pervaded the atmosphere of this chapel. Something "other-worldly" reigned here. I knew God was present. Whether I was praying alone or with the assembled Sisters, my soul was flooded with tranquility within these walls. Why, then, could I not carry that feeling outside and keep it?

267

Deep down, I knew the answer. In the chapel I felt very close to God, loved by Him and totally accepted for who I was. Outside the chapel I was surrounded by intolerance, judgments, pressure to conform. Constantly squashing my true self, I nevertheless lived in a state of denial.

I headed back to the office where Sister Clara Mae had put me in a state of shock. The hallway seemed longer than before, and the doorway to her office had regained some of its awesome aura. My feet wanted to hesitate, but I pushed them forward anyway.

"I've been praying, Sister, and this I know. Whenever I'm in the chapel, I feel close to God. I know I'm in the right place."

"Have you made your decision, Sister?"

"I feel so much peace in the chapel when I pray."

"But you can't live your life in the chapel, Sister. Do you hear me? You can't live your life in the chapel!"

Like the shock of an earthquake, her response shook me back to reality.

Still, I wanted to ask questions: How in the world could I even consider leaving, if that's what she was implying? I knew nothing about life outside convent walls.

She must have read my mind, since she added:

"I'm not telling you to leave the Community, Sister. Whatever decision you make has to be your own. Take your time and pray some more."

I walked the grounds of the valley and looked up at the mountain. Unlike the gracious hills I used to love, that mountain now left me with a sinking feeling. It had come to symbolize all the grief that had accumulated inside me over the years. And it didn't seem right that a mountain reflecting nature's magnificence should turn into a reminder of all that was negative in my life.

My Superior left me confused. I had always believed she spoke to me in God's Name. At least, I tried to believe it. I wanted to be a good Sister and that meant practicing blind obedience. As difficult as that became, I never considered turning my back on my vocation. I never entertained the thought of leaving.

And now I felt traumatized. Were the opinions I offered in the practice we called "dialogue" misconstrued? Was I a threat to my Provincial Superior's authority? Did she believe I acted in disobedience in Paris, when I continued writing in my diary after she suggested I stop? Was I being misjudged about anything at all? Had I been spied on?

Or did she really notice my unhappiness? Was she genuinely concerned about my welfare?

She never asked why I had to have surgery for carpal tunnel syndrome. She probably never stopped to realize the impact that switching the convent for the rectory would have on Sister Vincent and me. Sisters were always expected to do, and be able to do, whatever task was assigned them. Obedience supposedly gave us super-human strength to push and shove and lift and carry. Not having a man around made that mandatory. So, Superiors buried their heads in the sand, assuming we could do whatever they asked of us.

At any rate, she made one thing clear. I had her permission to think seriously about leaving my convent home. Reflection on these considerations and the options I now had, seared through me like a sharp knife.

Recently, I had visited one of my former teachers in Villa Saint Michael—the Sisters' retirement wing of the Provincial House. I knew that Sister Aurelia had suffered a lot as a Sister. She had shared some of her life-experiences, baring her soul to me. Implying she had fallen in love while doing graduate work in college, she let me know that she had to put up a big fight to overcome the feelings that had threatened to overwhelm her over the years.

As we spoke that day, I listened and came to realize that her pain went far deeper than I could have imagined. She confided that, not long ago, she had begged to be permitted to leave the Community. She revealed that, while she had no immediate family members still alive, she had a distant cousin somewhere out west. Surely, he and his wife would take her in and give her a home—take her away from the anguish her life had become.

She added that the Provincial Superior would not listen, that Sister Clara Mae refused to consider her request—much less, grant it. I could feel her pain, and I wanted so badly to take it away. If only she had been younger, at least at an age when she might have had a good chance to start over and make it. Maybe, then, she would have had a second chance at life.

I reflected on the dwindling years left for that Sister and the others who shared the retirement wing with her. As I looked around, I could see that those Sisters fit into one of two categories. Either they were sweet saintly souls who had devoted their lives to the Lord and were now waiting to reap their heavenly reward. Or they were like bitter old maids, abrupt and irritable, who probably would not find a willing roommate in the hereafter.

As I tried to decide my future, I asked myself which one of these categories I would fall into someday if I remained a Sister. And I didn't like the answer that came back to me.

My own struggles were real. I had to admit that. So, how long was I going to keep up the charade—until I became a shriveled-up old maid living in a prison of my own making?

Why should I keep fighting pleasurable feelings? Why not tell myself it's all right to feel satisfaction—to feel good, to feel love? Why not divest myself of all the battle gear and choose life? Didn't Jesus tell His followers He had come that they might have life and have it to the full?

How my life contradicted those words. Years earlier, I had forfeited my freedom, along with my feelings of self-worth. I had allowed myself to become like a bird locked in a cage, and I yearned to fly free again—to be like my literary friend Jonathan.

There was only one way to do this.

I went back to where my Provincial Superior stood before me—tall and erect—holding her authority firmly in place. I considered Sister Clara Mae to be a just person and kind in a business-like sort of way.

As I headed to the chair she pointed to, I wished she had shown more leadership and discernment, that she had forged a way to greater openness and understanding of the basic needs Sisters had to struggle with. I wished she had encouraged the Sisters to honestly bare their souls, to admit their true feelings and inner battles without fear of repercussions.

Perhaps, had she allowed more outlets suited to individuals, while safeguarding our Religious Order's way of life. But all of this was irrelevant now.

I sat down, intent on concealing my nervousness. My mouth was dry, and I could feel the loud thump of my quickening heartbeat. My eyes followed my Superior whose Habit looked spotless—lint-free. She sat down in front of me and paused.

Looking at her, I spoke up: "I want to leave."

Looking me in the eye, she repeated words she had said before:

"Sister Patricia Anne, I'm not asking you to leave. That decision is up to you."

I couldn't believe what I said next:

"I have made up my mind. I want to leave the Community."

Even as I spoke, a surge of relief rushed through me. Pain accompanied my words, but it was pain followed by a sense of release. It was as if an invisible angel had lifted a heavy burden from my shoulders. I felt like a prisoner about to go free—a bird that could fly away.

In the subsequent days I followed the required protocol in the manner Sister Clara Mae advised me to do. In our papal Religious Order we were directly accountable to the Pope through our highest Superior in Paris—the priest who ruled over the Vincentian priests, brothers, and Sisters. I sat down and wrote to our Superior General, as he was called, asking his permission to leave what had been my religious family for the last twenty- two years.

A few weeks later, he replied through a letter that my request had been granted. I would be free to leave on the next Feast of the Annunciation, at which time my annual vows would expire. It meant a wait of ten weeks to plan my life all over again.

I tried to let the Sisters around me think I had an extended recuperation period. But as time went on, they figured out what was going on. Some Sisters raised questions, while others raised their eyebrows.

Since great secrecy still surrounded a Sister's departure from the Community, I confided in just a few of the Sisters. In those days, Sisters who left our Order were treated like defectors by some, so I took great pains to avoid any conversation about my status as a Sister.

I was surprised, however, when one of the higher Superiors approached me and suggested I inform Sister Andrew that I was leaving the convent. Now, I had hardly seen that Sister after she persuaded me to follow in her footsteps so many years earlier. Why would I tell her that I had decided to leave and possibly have humiliation be heaped upon me? Had she been credited for adding me to the Community's statistics, maybe even rewarded? Needless to say, I did not follow up that advice.

My sister Carole took me on a shopping trip to get me clothing to wear home, and I decided to wait until it was closer to my day of leaving, before notifying my parents of my decision—and for good reason.

My Dad had been against my entering the convent, and I felt certain he would oppose my leaving. Over the years he had started to carry around a photograph of me dressed as a Sister. My mother had revealed he was proud to show me off to his friends and acquaintances. Imagine that!

On the day I announced I was going to leave the convent, he did as I suspected. Shocked, he spent the whole afternoon trying to convince me I could change my mind. He couldn't believe I would give up the benefits my Religious Order gave me—reminding me that, in the convent, I always had a roof over my head, meals on the table, a bedroom to sleep in, and medical care when necessary.

As hard as I tried to explain, he could not understand what I was saying—that I was not happy and that was the bottom line. After all, I always had a smile on my face when he came to visit and snapped my picture. He had no idea I was suffering from emotional abuse, because I was not allowed to reveal my anguish to anyone—above all, my parents. Besides, I did not want them to suffer—to know I was in torment—so I consciously concealed what I truly felt.

Dad, finally, stopped arguing. Reluctantly, he accepted the fact that my decision was final.

My Superiors informed me they would give me $1,000 to start over, since I had been a member of the order for twenty plus years. Never having received a paycheck, that seemed like a million dollars at first. But when I began to divide the money up mentally, I realized how far I would have to stretch it. I would need a car to drive, clothing for this season and the next, a place to live—and, of course, a job that would support me.

Imagine that—I had given my all—living by unreasonable rules that had stamped out my personal dreams—my individuality, even— denied me needed outlets and vacations, and tore me away from my family. I had lived my life without love, without choices—working much like a slave.

I had never received a paycheck for my work. So I would have no social security for all those years. And the Catholic Church—through my Religious Order—was offering me no retirement monies and no health benefits. My work through the best years of my life was worth a mere $1,000. Where was justice now?

As the reality of my situation began to sink in, part of me wanted to panic. I felt like I was jumping out of an airplane in the dark. I knew what I was leaving, but I had no idea what I would find in the darkness. Yet, I believed I had made the right decision. There could be no turning back. I would think of the path before me as an adventure. I would look to the future with optimism and confidence.

8,241 days had passed since I entered the convent. I truly missed my brown-shingled house and all its memories. Above all, I missed my loved ones.

Now, finally, I was going home.

And so, on my first day out of the convent, I stood on that hill overlooking Bird River. Refusing to yield to fear, I delighted in my new-found freedom. Eager to fly with the seagulls, I was ready to soar. I had no regrets.

At long last, I was back where I belonged.

IV
The Aftermath

A Final Thought

EPILOGUE

"The book is closed. Now go in peace." These words my Mother spoke to me after I revisited my convent roots for the first time since leaving there in 1978. She and my sister Carole had persuaded me to overcome the dread that had kept me from returning to my former home base until 1995. I finally concluded it was therapy I needed.

While in Emmitsburg, a Sister escorted us through the previously-sacrosanct convent quarters. The changes startled me. Colorful curtains replaced the drab white of my era. Small vases of flowers punctuated each square table in the refectory. A refreshing openness saturated the air as we walked the corridors and visited the retired Sisters who sat in comfortable couches watching a television talk show.

Mixed emotions churned inside me, while a voice wanted to shout out, why not sooner? I went home to my husband and animals in New Mexico, still not in peace.

The following year, while visiting my family in Maryland, I went back to the valley at the foot of the Blue Ridge Mountains. Too many questions gnawed at me. I needed answers.

Instead of going to the Provincial House erected in the 1960's, I went right to the grounds of the old Provincial House and college to retrace my beginning steps as a Sister.

The buildings and land, now owned by the federal government, had not lost the aroma and atmosphere left there by thousands of Sisters who had trained there, lived there—and worked and prayed, and fought inner battles there.

I walked the worn paths to sites of former shrines. I meditated along the banks of Tom's Creek where the ripples spoke silently to me of decades past. I sat in the chapel where the now-hollow walls stood in stark contrast to the immovable marble altars and the pews well-worn from praying hands that remained in voiceless testimony to the past. I sat there and cried.

I dragged my feet through two cemeteries and cried my heart out some more. I was shocked to see tombstone after tombstone bearing the names of Sisters I had lived with. So many were saints, in my opinion. They had persevered to the end, while I had not been able to bear the rigors imposed upon me.

The next year, I poured out my pain in a letter I sent to the Provincial Superior of my former religious order. Essentially, I was saying they erased who I was and abused me—and that I, and others like me—had needed a halfway house that wasn't there for us when we left.

In a letter dated September 5, 1997, she responded, as follows:

"I received your letter of August 24, and was pleased that you felt free to tell me about your feelings regarding your departure from the Community in 1978 and since that time. I am sorry that things happened the way they did.

"Many of the things you mentioned in your letter hopefully are of a time past. I am not aware of any such practices that take place today. Those entering postulancy and seminary go through a careful discernment period before and during their formation and are encouraged to look carefully at the life they are choosing. If someone decides that she does not have a vocation, she is encouraged to follow another path.

"It would please me very much if you and I could sit down sometime and talk…"

Living far away in New Mexico, I did not return to Maryland for further discussion. Rather, after being persuaded to write my autobiography, I started my own therapy by plowing up memories of the past and writing my life story in seven drafts over seven years. Revealing the truth began the healing process. Now, at last, I can heed my Mother's prophetic words: "The book is closed. Now go in peace."

A Final Thought

My significance does matter:
    I am a human person
        with a mind, memory and imagination;
            feelings, drives and yearnings.

No one else is just like me;
    I am unique and worthy of respect:
    I am God's Handiwork.

I am a whole person,
    the sum of many parts—not isolated fragments
    but an interconnected network;

A rainbow of diversity
    that meets in my heart and soul
        where my "pot of gold" lies hidden.
Don't destroy
    that which
        makes me
            what I am.

PHOTO GALLERY

Pat ... First professional portrait after leaving the order.

Last picture taken before leaving the order. Pat on the dock built by her parents over frozen Bird River, in White Marsh, MD, next to a crab trap ...
"That's how I felt ... frozen and trapped."

Mel, Jr. and Pat

Pat, Mel, Carole

Pat with baby Anne

Pat in orchestra, Spring Concert at Seton High School, 1954. Mr. James Hipp, beloved Conductor, lived to be 100 years [...] furthest to the right, her sister Carole, a sophomore, on violin behind first violinist [...] and the student next to her.

283

Pat's Junior Prom, 1953.

Pat canoeing with Dad, at Loch Raven, 1952.

Pat's going away party, September 6, 1955. She entered the convent the next day.

Mother, Postulant Pat

Anne, Postulant Pat, Carole

Postulant Pat

Postulant Pat with Mel Jr.

Dad, Postulant Pat, (white) visit, January 1956.

Seminary Sisters, (commonly called novices by other orders) not allowed to talk with externs, but allowed to talk with toddler (Pat's niece, Teresa), during Summer Visitation Day.

Seminary Sisters ... shrine in background, one of many on the Sisters' grounds at Emmitsburg, MD.

Mother & Pat, Main Street, Endicott, NY; spring 1962

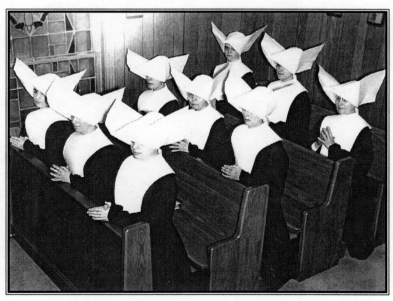

Sisters at prayer ... Pat, middle, front pew, St. Ambrose Convent Chapel in Endicott, NY, 1960.

Pat with nieces and nephew, 1965 following the lifting of ban on home visits ...first visit home since 1955.

Mother and Dad visiting Pat (wearing her new habit) at St. Charles Convent, 1965..

Picture taken by Dad on first family visit after Pat entered the convent...
(far left, behind) Best friend, Theresa (Luzzi) Myers, Harry Marsiglia,
(Middle row) Mother, Pat Carole, Anne, Mel Jr.; Audrey kneeling, 1955.

Dad, first visit, leaning on the statue of St. Vincent de Paul, trying to
interject humor into the situation of a tour of the Sisters' Cemetery ...
"There were so few places to take visitors." 1955.

Pat in Vatican Gardens, Vatican City ... For centuries the private gardens for the Pope ... The Daughters of Charity serve as housekeepers for the Pope ... these gardens were off limits to tourists ... the Santa Marta Sisters allowed our Sisters who were visiting during the canonization of Mother Elizabeth Ann Seton, foundress of Sisters of Charity in America, to stroll through the gardens. 1975.

Pat, Bird River with Amtrak train in background, 1970's. A train taking people places, living their lives ... Pat, oblivious of the train, felt her life was a closed box.

Pat by Mediterranean (that portion called the Tyrrhenian Sea) on trip to Vatican City, (Rome) Italy, September 1975.

Portrait of Pat ... taken Christmas 1987, in Winston-Salem. First photo given to Karl Beasley the year before they married. Karl was a retired law enforcement officer from El Paso, TX. They eventually settled in Magdalena, NM.

First photo of Karl given to Pat the year before they married. 1987.

Karl & Pat on their wedding day, Baltimore, Maryland, August 6, 1988

ABOUT THE AUTHOR

*Pat with her 92-year old mother, Anna Grueninger, at Manor Care
Nursing Home in Towson, MD, 2006*

Following her years as a Sister, Pat Grueninger-Beasley settled in North Carolina, where she took a temporary position with the North Carolina Job Service, before the late Louise Wilson hired her as Counselor/Coordinator of the Experiment in Self-Reliance's high school drop-out program for low-income young people.

Eventually, she became a Human Relations Specialist for the City of Winston-Salem and was elected vice-president, then president, of the North Carolina chapter of NAHRW (National Association of Human Rights Workers).

In 1988, Pat married Karl Beasley and settled in the magnificent Southwest. She returned to teaching and commuted between Magdalena and the Alamo Navajo Indian Reservation School, followed by a teaching stint at the local public school.

After retiring from teaching, Pat became a freelance writer for a county newspaper and an author.

Pat lives with her husband in Magdalena, New Mexico, where she delights in nature's beauty and cares for animals. She treasures her bonds with the Navajo and Apache Indians of the nearby reservation.

Breinigsville, PA USA
19 January 2010
231037BV00002B/43/P